(Un)knowing Diversity

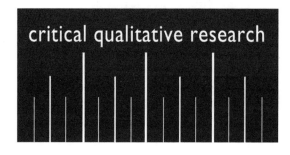

critical qualitative research

CRITICAL ISSUES FOR LEARNING AND TEACHING

Shirley R. Steinberg and Gaile S. Cannella
Series Editors

Vol. 5

The Critical Qualitative Research series is part of the Peter Lang Education list.
Every volume is peer reviewed and meets
the highest quality standards for content and production.

PETER LANG
New York • Washington, D.C./Baltimore • Bern
Frankfurt • Berlin • Brussels • Vienna • Oxford

TRICIA GALLAGHER-GEURTSEN

(Un)knowing Diversity

Researching Narratives of Neocolonial Classrooms through Youth's Testimonios

PETER LANG
New York • Washington, D.C./Baltimore • Bern
Frankfurt • Berlin • Brussels • Vienna • Oxford

Library of Congress Cataloging-in-Publication Data

Gallagher-Geurtsen, Tricia.
(Un)knowing diversity: researching narratives of neocolonial
classrooms through youth's testimonios / Tricia Gallagher-Geurtsen.
p. cm. — (Critical qualitative research; v. 5)
Includes bibliographical references and index.
1. Children of minorities—Education—United States—Case studies.
2. Minority students—United States—Identification—Case studies.
3. Multicultural education—United States—Case studies.
4. Postcolonialism—United States. 5. Qualitative research—United States.
I. Title. II. Title: Knowing diversity.
LC3731.G345   371.829'00973—dc23   2011033071
ISBN 978-1-4331-1007-8 (hardcover)
ISBN 978-1-4331-1006-1 (paperback)
ISBN 978-1-4539-0213-4 (e-book)
ISSN 1058-1634

Bibliographic information published by **Die Deutsche Nationalbibliothek**
Die Deutsche Nationalbibliothek lists this publication in the "Deutsche
Nationalbibliografie"; detailed bibliographic data is available
on the Internet at http://dnb.d-nb.de/.

The paper in this book meets the guidelines for permanence and durability
of the Committee on Production Guidelines for Book Longevity
of the Council of Library Resources.

Contents

Preface

How often do educators hear directly from multicultural or *minoritized* students about their school experiences? I intend this book to help preservice and inservice educators and administrators become better equipped to listen to and understand multicultural students. Through interviews constructed as *testimonios,* or the urgently told first-person narratives of youth's profound life experiences, and analysis that makes visible the deep and complex resources that youth with hybrid identities possess, educators have the opportunity to make curriculum and teaching more meaningful, thereby working fissures into the structures that hold a normalizing, narrowing, and neocolonial pedagogy firmly in place.

Through youths' testimonios, the complexity of students' identities, or *hybridity*, will be described. In order to make hybridity come alive for the reader, I will operationalize it as postcolonial flows. Postcolonial flows are unique combinations of discourses that diverse youth bring to school and negotiate, such as a Chicana identity or a family ethic of care. Taking up hybridity as a tool for understanding youths' lives answers calls in the literature for a more complex understanding of student identity around race and culture. Additionally, when positioning identities as made up of and as creating postcolonial flows, educators are inclined to see the grand and complex resources and negotiations of youths' postcolonial flows—thus inspiring us to respectfully listen to youth and make our pedagogy more *meaningful*. In essence, as students apprehend flows, braid them, reject them, (re)construct them, they rage against a curriculum created to normalize students' actions, knowledge, beliefs, and lives (Bhabha, 1994; Dimitriadis & McCarthy, 2001; Dutro, Kazemi, Balf, & Lin, 2008).

The ocean of youths' flows calls into question an aconflictual Western curriculum and teaching, rendering them incomplete, fair game for scrutiny, and diminished as merely narrow and narrow*ing* flows of Western-centric imperialism. Youths' performance of postcolonial flows shows that their lives inside and outside of schools are complex, conflictual, and hold promise that youth will usurp power in order to govern their own lives—broadening their possibilities and life futures (Spring, 2008; Willinsky, 1998).

This book is the culmination of 10 years of work. First, I attempted to make sense of postcolonial theory based on my experiences teaching and learning in diverse urban schools. Then, I endeavored to apply postcolonial theory to the schools, classrooms, and students that I have worked with and continue to serve. Drawing upon analyses of theoretical works, documents, and interview data with preservice and inservice teachers; formal and informal observations in dozens of urban schools in a major city in the Northeast and in the Mountain West; and in-depth interviews with youth from three different regions of the United States, I have attempted to construct a collage of sorts of how young people from diverse backgrounds encounter and are encountered by neocolonial classrooms and schools. I intend the resulting work to be a decolonizing project; one that the reader can clearly recognize as pointing a finger at destructive neocolonial acts in schools, in classrooms, and in the lives of students. The collage is uneven and complex—meaning that although there are discernible patterns and practices, the testimonio of each youth is unique. I have two main goals for this book: (a) to decolonize, and (b) to show postcolonial theory in practice. Methodologically, I attempt to unmap as I map postcolonial concepts onto youths and their lives. Denying the anthropological tradition of defining the other, we hear from youth directly through their testimonios.

That said, this book is a particular reading and writing of the world, one that embraces the concept of transnationalism, wherein youths' ties to locales across the globe both "accentuate and flatten difference" concurrently (Khagram & Levitt, 2007, p. 216). The overlapping and contradictory processes of postcolonialism open possibilities for listening and responding in new ways to minoritized youth in schools. Ultimately, my hope is that this book will offer opportunities for educators to make curriculum and teaching for youth more meaningful, reflecting the complex experiences and negotiations of youth in neocolonial school settings.

Acknowledgments

It is a pleasure to be able to thank the many people who have made this, my first book, possible. Perhaps it is not often admitted, but writing a book is a scary pursuit. As a woman, I became friends with the "imposter syndrome" (Clance & Imes, 1978), which frequently visited while I sat at my desk trying to convince myself that I was someone who could write a book that a few people might find worthwhile reading. What allowed fear to sit curled up on my lap as I wrote was the thought of the following people who reside in my heart, reminding me to listen to them and write for and because of them.

Heartfelt thanks go to the great teachers in my life: the brave, inspiring, and forthcoming youth that I interviewed across the United States for this book; my students and their families in California, New York, and Utah; my friends; my mentors at Teachers College-Columbia University, Utah State University, and University of California, San Diego; and my loving family. Thanks to Dr. Nicki Newton for reminding me to be clear about where I was going with my writing and for her encouragement. I am grateful for Dr. Djanna Hill, who is a continual support in my academic and personal life. To "Soni" Vatsala Krishna, whose reading of chapters and support of my work mean so very much to me. Thanks to Dr. Grace Huerta, Dr. Leslie Flemmer, Dr. Marilee Coles-Ritchie, and Christie Hansen for their support in my research for this book. Thanks to Dr. Shirley Steinberg for giving me the opportunity to write this book, as well as to Sophie Appel for her guidance and support through the process, and the incredibly helpful, hardworking, and kind staff at Peter Lang. Finally, I thank my immediate family: Scott, who always supports me in recognizing and living out my passion for social justice in education; Sam for loving me; Addie for forgiving me for the hours I spent not playing with you but typing at my computer; and Greg, for the sweet joy you bring all of us.

Thank you to Taylor and Francis for permission to reprint portions of an earlier work: *Inspiring Hybridity: A Call to Engage With(in) Global Flows of the Multicultural Classroom*, by Tricia Gallagher-Guertsen, *Multicultural Perspectives 11*(4), 200–203, Dec. 14, 2009, reprinted by permission of the publisher (Taylor & Francis Ltd, http://www.tandf.co.uk/journals).

Introduction

What Makes A Real American?
Diversity in the Neocolonial Classroom

> Our solid American citizen awakens in a bed built on a pattern which originated in the Near East but which was modified in Northern Europe before it was transmitted to America. He throws back covers made from cotton, domesticated in India, or linen, domesticated in the Near East, or wool from sheep, also domesticated in the Near East…. He slips into his moccasins, invented by the Indians of the Eastern woodlands, and goes to the bathroom, whose fixtures are a mixture of European and American inventions, both of recent date. He takes off his pajamas, a garment invented in India, and washes with soap invented by the ancient Gauls. He then shaves, a masochistic rite which seems to have been derived from either Sumer or ancient Egypt. (Linton, 1936, p. 326)

Ask yourself the difficult question, *What makes a real American*[1]?, and your answer may be a simple "A citizen of the United States," or, if you think about it long enough, the answer can become complex and even contradictory. What might it mean to be part American or 100% American? How do different South Americans, Southern Americans, Native Americans, and immigrants define an American? The point is that the answer is not something that most educators consciously think about. However, we may act upon our subconscious definition of a real or legitimate American more often than we recognize, to the benefit of "the West" and to the detriment of "the Rest"—minoritized[2] youth in United States schools (Hall, 1992). In this book, I will show how educators' ideologies and school practices related to what constitutes a legitimate American often harken back to a time when people were explicitly rank-ordered by the color of their skin through pseudoscience, and to an era when biological determinism ruled the day (Gould, 1996). When I asked this question of minoritized youth, their answers were decidedly complex:

> I have searing debates with one friend who INSISTS that I am American, though I resentfully deny it. Personally, I feel a very strong connection to my Gypsy-Cuban heritage and relate much more to that than i do to hot dogs and the statue of liberty. Though I've spent all but 8 months of my life in this Country and though I have a passport that says clearly that I am American, at heart I don't feel connected enough to America to call myself an American. I feel much more exotic that that. (Nadya*, Gypsy-Cuban high school student, email, 2008)

---

* Pseudonyms have been used for all participants.

Given Nadya's answer, educators may be compelled to call upon tenets of multicultural education to understand her dynamic and conflictual identity as an American in school. But what kind of multicultural education might be culturally relevant and socially just for Nadya? How can educators respond to her Gypsy-Cubanness, (non)Americanness, Femaleness, her self-described exoticness, and the many other intersections of her identity that are in constant motion? Current maps of multicultural education and cultural relevance may not be able to easily comprehend Nadya and determine what would make schooling meaningful to her. She does not, for example, fit our formula for biculturalism wherein we might thoughtfully promote both her heritage as a Gypsy-Cuban and as an American. It would not be a simple procedure to draw meaningfully upon Nadya's cultures and languages, not to mention her sense of exoticism that is important to her identity construction. Further complicating our desire to be culturally responsive, Nadya denies her Americanness but, at the same time, her contention that she is *not* American is an overt exercise of her freedom as an American (Au & Jordan, 1981; Ladson-Billings, 1995; Ovando, Collier, & Combs, 2003; Sleeter & Grant, 2007).

Some may feel Nadya is a marked example of a minoritized student with a particularly complex identity, but if we ask the right questions and listen ever so carefully to minoritized youth, we witness identities that evade our predictions and theories again and again. For example, Wanda is a Black second grader who explained to her teacher that she feels "more American" at her grandmother's house and "more Black" at her mom's house. Similar, but decidedly more complex, is when Myrna, a bilingual Puerto Rican American second grader explained that she feels "more Latino than English at her Grandma's" and feels "really different" around her cousin who is light-skinned (Gallagher-Geurtsen, 2003). Or, consider Samuel, who is Puerto Rican, Cuban, and an American citizen; speaks English, Spanish, and Spanglish; and listens to country music with his White friends and to reggaeton with his Cuban American grandfather. Finally, take note of Claudine Chiawei O'Hearn's (1998) description of the shifting and conflictual aspects of negotiating Chinese, American, White, and popular media cultural identities or flows:

> It's easier to be White. To be Chinese, to be half Chinese, is work. I often find myself cataloguing my emotions, manners, and philosophies into Chinese and American, wary if the latter starts to outweigh the former. Three points Asia. How can I be Chinese if I prefer David Bowie to Chinese pop, if I can more easily pass as an American.... And yet I play the part of a foreigner here all the time. (p. xii)

Who are our American youth telling us they are? How are youth already educating us multiculturally? Are we listening to them? Are we asking the right questions?

If we could cobble together answers to these questions, what should multicultural education in the United States look like? As postmulticulturalists, or educators who engage in the complexity of multiculturalism as our world rapidly globalizes, our focus on defining multicultural education, compiling evidence, and formulating our arguments for transformative multicultural education is essential to growing the legitimacy, effectiveness, and impact of our work but perhaps has distracted us from pushing to do exactly what we have been calling for from the beginnings of multicultural education: making schooling *meaningful* in the short and long terms for minoritized youth (Banks & McGee Banks, 2004). By *meaningful*, I am describing pedagogy and policy that *truly* respond to the lived realities of minoritized youth including, but not limited to: youth's complex identities as described above and the inequitable treatment of youth (i.e., classism, racism, heterosexism, etc.) This book is an attempt to ask new questions and listen differently to minoritized youth than we may have in the past, utilizing the powerful lens of postcolonial theory.

Why Postcolonial Theory?

Postcolonial theory[4] is a complex lens applied in many scholarly fields. It has different camps, perspectives, and even conflicting ideas. However, most postcolonial theorists base their thinking on the history of colonialism:

> Postcolonial—or tricontinental—critique is united by a common political and moral consensus towards the history and legacy of western colonialism. It presupposes that the history of European expansion and the occupation of most of the global land-mass between 1492 and 1945, mark a process that was both specific and problematic. (Young, 2001, p. 5)

The criticisms postcolonial theory offers are particularly useful and often overlooked in thinking about a neocolonial power such as the United States and its institutions of schooling. However, there is a danger in utilizing postcolonial theory to look at education "because postcolonial studies threaten to undo education, to unravel the passionately held-onto thought and knowledge of the modern Western-educated student and scholar" (Mishra Tarc, 2009, p. 195). I ask you to face that danger, given that it can be useful in beginning to unravel many complexities related to the success of minoritized youth in schools. Postcolonial theory unveils the past and present of colonialism and colonial ideology in the United States that I will show seems to be part of orchestrating the failure of too many minoritized youth.

Although many may think of European nations such as England, France, and Spain when they hear the words "colonial powers," the United States continues to engage in the control of distant lands that are not its own and in the dominance of native peoples—both colonial practices underpinned by false ideologies that reify a hierarchy of races, cultures, and languages. This domination is carried out in the name of freedom and benevolent care for those we designate as the "other." The United States' common belief in its natural greatness and inherently innocent assistance to people deemed powerless and perhaps perceived to be a bit inferior further blinds Americans to the presumption and violence of our colonial and imperialist actions nationally and internationally (El-Haj, 2010; Said, 1994).

Postcolonial theory draws into high relief the United States' history and present as a colonizing force both at "home" and abroad. From the 1500s early explorers' literal and figurative capture of the native and the 1800s remaking of the Indian in the White man's image, to the 1920s Americanization programs and the 1980s English-only legislation, I argue that our schools have been and remain a phenomenally powerful tool of colonization—a neocolonial power (Spring, 2004).

How does a nation become an imperial power? When one nation wants to colonize another, taking control of its land and people, what are the most powerful tools that can be utilized to achieve these goals? There are overt strategies such as military might and, later, the mere presence of a soldier or government officials can be enough to keep native people subdued and reliant on the colonizer. The corollary in schools might be security guards or teachers standing in the halls during passing period and at lunch reminding students of the civilizing mission of the school through their visibility. Less obvious is how the colonial discourse—the statements and practices that are used to define the colonizer and the colonized—can become a seemingly natural part of thinking and believing in a colonized mind. The colonial discourse asserts that the colonizer's culture, history, language, art, political, and social structures are superior to those of the colonized. In terms of schools, for example, think of the focus on English and American literature in high school and the lack of literature of minoritized groups in the United States. A pervasive focus on Western literature makes it clear that the authority—the school—does not deem non-Western literatures significant enough for sustained study. One of the covert means by which the colonial discourse is inculcated is through the financial support of practices in the native cultures that are similar to European or Western ones, such as privileging writing over oral language in school and in the arts, thus elevating its visibility and status over expressive and communicative forms deemed of lesser value. Another tool of colonization is exclusively permitting the colonizer's language in the schools and government. For example, in the United States, English is the de facto official language of schools and government. In order to colonize a people and attempt to make them see the world through the colonizer's eyes, it is not enough to impose religion, language, dress, social rules, and knowledge systems—the colonizer has to (re)write the colonized's histories. Fanon (1965) explained:

> Colonialism is not satisfied merely with holding a people in its grip and emptying the native's brain of all form and content. By a kind of perverted logic, it turns to the past of the oppressed people, and distorts, disfigures, and destroys it. (p. 210)

By changing the history of a people to imply the inferiority of their cultures, beliefs, knowledge, and practices—if done with a benevolent smile and through the power of books—the colonized often come to believe in their own inferiority and look to the colonizer for guidance towards the colonizer's more acceptable and superior history and way of living (Ashcroft, Griffiths, & Tiffin, 2000).

The strategies of colonization described above are only a few of the overt and covert ways of assuring that colonized people become and remain dependent on the colonial power through belief in their own deficiencies and in the colonizer's superiority. Postcolonial theory analyzes and critiques what happens in postcolonial and neocolonial societies. In the following section I will describe a few postcolonial concepts as I apply them directly to schools today—in essence, showing what can be called neocolonial practices or flows[5] in American schools.

Schools' Neocolonial Flows

How do we define youth in schools? What defines them? How do these definitions then determine their relative success or failure in the educational sphere? Many education scholars, notably Gaile Canella & Radhika Viruru, John Willinsky, Merry Merryfield, Greg Dimitriadis, and Cameron McCarthy, have shown how schools and schooling in the United States reinstate and reify colonial ideas. Neocolonial[6] manifestations of colonial ideas in schools include practices and structures that maintain the status quo of schooling and have resulted in inexcusable achievement gaps between White students and students of color, native English speakers and English learners, rich and poor students. Mainstream educators often subscribe to a vision of the school that denies the multiplicity of identities and complexity of the real world and lives of students outside of school. They "insist on a project of homogeneity, normalization, and the production of a socially functional citizen" (McCarthy, Giardina, Harewood, & Park, 2005, p. 156), echoing colonialism's desire to suppress the power of the colonized (minoritized students, in this case) and remake them into the colonizer's own image while punishing any critique of the colonizer or their system (for example, critiques of school leaders and the school system). Schools in the United States are normalizing and standardizing places, wielding neocolonial power in order to keep the current system intact. I will briefly introduce some of the neocolonial flows that govern schools and classrooms to orient you to themes I later use to analyze the testimonios of youth.

The entire power structure of neocolonialism is based on ensuring that people know their place and act accordingly. To communicate where one's place is, neocolonial institutions, such as schools, consistently and repetitively utilize *hierarchies* and *binaries* to classify people, knowledge, and ideas. Most important to the mission of colonialism is that a hierarchy of races be communicated and accepted as true. Unfortunately, a legacy of colonialism is that a rank-ordered list of races has been passed down to youth today. For example, Regina, a White mother of biracial children, recounts when her daughter told her about "the list":

> The next day we were driving home and my sixteen year old said, "Mom, we had this really interesting conversation during the *Star Wars* movie last night." And I said, "What?" She said, "I said the African American fighter, whoever he was, I don't know, was the best. And my cousin said he can't be the best because he is not that high up on the list. That list." Immediately, they have my attention. "Okay, tell me more about this list." So, she tells me, "I said the same thing—what list? And he said, 'Well, you know, the list…where White is first, either Japanese or Chinese is second because they are smart, third are…." She probably used the word Mexicans…because that is the most dominant Hispanic culture that he is familiar with "and African Americans are fourth…." I was so angry. I guess people do make lists ….Well I am thinking, there must be a lot of people out there with a list. I knew in the past, especially with race, there was a list. I understand with religion and with certain religions there is also a list. And I understood that. But I did not think it was so prevalent and so dominant to have it come out of the mouth of a child. (Gallagher-Geurtsen, 2005, p. 22)

Together with the posting of top spelling test results on the bulletin board, the maintenance of different academic "tracks" for different students, the conscious or subconscious use of *binaries* such as White/Black or smart/stupid, hierarchies of races assist in the inflexible categorization of people, knowledge, and ideas.

The power of binaries to pack things into boxes is in their mutual exclusivity. One side of the binary is always considered to be superior to or more legitimate than the other side. For example, the following binaries raise the status of "the West" and diminish that of "the Rest" and/or reify the power of the school to define the student: teacher/student; knower/known; native/other; us/them, White/non-White, civilized/uncivilized, etc. Binaries such as these are used to solidify the structure of schools that favor the needs of the majority White European educators and students who benefit from the school system as it is. However, if you reflect on the above binaries, it is easy to recognize there are shades of gray between the two sides as well as combinations of each.

In order to keep the hierarchical and binary classification systems intact, each entry on the ranked list needs to be a clearly accepted entity. For example, if Mexican Americans were not seen as a homogeneous group with identifiable traits, then we would not be able to insert them in their rightful place on "the list." Therefore, neocolonization requires that there are *authentic* and *essentialized* races and cultures. For example, "Taco Day" to celebrate Mexico and textbooks that essentialize all Native Americans as having similar characteristics—both continue a legacy of colonialism in the school and curriculum.

Cementing the superiority of the West and the inferiority of specific others is the neocolonial tool *hegemony* or "the power of the ruling class to convince other classes that their interests are in the interests of all" (Ashcroft et al., 2000, p. 116). For example, teachers make many decisions that are accepted as carried out in the interest of their students. Also, it is acknowledged that teachers generally have the status of benevolent leaders in the service of their students. This ideology is consistently communicated in various ways in the school, for example, the teacher as the source of all knowledge, teachers punishing students for infractions because it is for their own good, teacher appreciation days, etc. The sense that the teacher *always* has the students' best interests in mind is an example of hegemony.

Other aspects of neocolonialism are: Western-centric social studies and history texts (e.g., the Westward Movement as the natural and inevitable march of progress across Native American lands); a logo-scientific curriculum (e.g., narrow, objective-driven lessons); exoticizing the other (e.g., displays of foods, fashion, folklore in the curriculum); nationalism (e.g., all Americans share the same values); universalism (e.g., the same standards and curriculum are appropriate for all groups of people); and mimicry (e.g., copying information, formats, standard Eurocentric styles in the classroom and school). Still, given these many neocolonial flows, schools must assure that this multinodal system remains intact—through observation.

Observation or *surveillance* is among the most potent tools of colonization and, indeed, schooling. Constantly observing students with the expectation that they "do school" appropriately and act the "good student" results in each student *assuming* that they are being observed, taking away their power to define and develop their own identity as a student separate from the school's often narrow determination of what makes someone successful in school. Students then experience the insidious process of "conversion" whereby they act the part of "good student" even when they are not being watched. Conversion can be promoted by school staff with forms of coercion and disapproval when youth stray from the accepted norms and actions that constitute the official "good student." When students begin to surveil one another based on the school's mold of "good student," the surveillance becomes autonomous. But the question must be asked: Who should watch whom? Typically, students accept that they will be surveilled and monitored by their teachers and other school officials—being judged according to the written and unwritten rules of doing school. Seldom is a student allowed to challenge that gaze, reverse it, and monitor their teachers or principals, questioning their judgment, monitoring them for adherence to their charge of effectively teaching them with care. As we will see later in youths' testimonios, a reversal of surveillance allows young people to usurp power and begin to critique not just the rules of the game, but the neocolonial structures themselves (Ashcroft et al., 2000).

There are too many flows of neocolonialism to introduce them all, but that is exactly what makes the legacy of colonialism in schools so insidious and difficult to recognize. Neocolonial power is rhizomatous—like bamboo root systems, it spreads out laterally and grows through and from several locations. It is invisible and travels in underground networks. Precisely because many of these schooling practices are accepted as the norm, they exist and thrive unchecked. In the following chapters I identify neocolonial practices as described by youth so that we can begin to recognize them more often and decide what to do about them—especially when we note their often deleterious effect on the lives of students. But more importantly, furthering the decolonizing goal of this project, I will now briefly introduce the postcolonial flows that upend and challenge neocolonial flows—representing hope for decolonizing schools (Ashcroft et al., 2000).

Diverse Youths' Postcolonial Flows

In the United States, minoritized youth negotiate and create "global flows of ideas, practices, institutions, and people" (Spring, 2008, p. 333), making their experiences quite complex and difficult to predict. Not only do schools tend to de-emphasize the richness of what I will call *postcolonial flows* brought by diverse youth, more attention needs to be paid to the growing complexity within the 42% of minoritized youth enrolled in schools. Of the 20% of elementary and secondary students who spoke a language other than English at home, 44.9% were identified as Mexican, 5.7% were White, 5.6% were Black, and the remaining 43% were from one of *16* other ethnic subgroups. However, the diverse flows of our students are made up of more than just the crisscrossing of languages and nations of origin (KewalRamani, Gilbertson, Fox, & Provasnik, 2007).

If we visualize the "stuff" of diverse young people's lives, the image of flows is useful. Flows of particular colors, depending on how youth define them, move, shape-shift, and represent, for example, cultural, narrative, familial, linguistic, gendered, political, sexual, and media trajectories—to name only a few. The infinite processes that youth experience daily could be, for example, cultural interactions between the local and the global, macro- and micro-transactions between majority and minority ideas and practices—with assimilation, resistance, and something between the two occurring simultaneously.

Like Gee's (1996) "Discourses," flows are the unique combinations of

> ways of behaving, interacting, valuing, thinking, believing, speaking...that are accepted as instantiations of particular roles (or "types of people") by specific *groups of people* [emphasis added], whether families of a certain sort, women or men of a certain sort, church members of a certain sort, and so on through a very [infinitely] long list. (p. viii)

Gee reminded us that "each of us is a member of many Discourses, and each new Discourse represents one of our ever-multiple identities" (p. ix). What makes flows distinct from Discourses is that the flows may come together to represent, say, a "Chicana" identity, but the different flows braided together that represent Chicana for one young woman will be decidedly different for another Chicana—however, they both share a Chicana group identity. By utilizing flows as a metaphor for the ideas, practices, institutions, and people that individuals create and negotiate, I am attempting to disallow hegemonic and essentialized combinations of traits while still acknowledging the existence of both collective and individual identities.

Similarly, in a world with increasingly diverse interactions we must also engage with what youth believe. Gen Nexters (youth born between 1981 and 1988) are the most likely of any generation yet to believe that the growing number of newcomers from other countries strengthens American society (67%). They also lead the way in their support for gay marriage and acceptance of interracial dating. Further, majorities of Gen Nexters believe they are more able to bring about social change, compared with youth 20 years ago (Pew Research Center, 2007). The aforementioned flows of immigration, interraciality, and self-efficacy can all contribute to the collective and individual identities of diverse youth. Youths' flows crisscross, carry power, shift, and clash with the neocolonial flows in schools described above. In order to think about the performance of flows in the classroom, I will show how young people can deny neocolonial flows as they forge their own way with practices and conditions associated with postcolonialism.

Given the legacy of colonialism in the form of neocolonialism in schooling, minoritized youth have discovered ways to survive within a largely demeaning and narrow system. These survival strategies can be described as postcolonial flows, given the fact that they arise out of a neocolonial system. Indeed, postcolonial flows are a method of decolonization because their existence, or mindful performance, questions neocolonial flows and systems. One of the more robust postcolonial flows capable of upending neocolonial power structures is *hybridity*. Hybridity has to do with multiple, shifting, and dynamic identities. Consider that American identity is not unitary or homogeneous, and "all cultures are involved in one another; none is single and pure, all are hybrid, heterogeneous, extraordinarily differentiated, and un-monolithic" (Said, 1994, p. xxv). This fluidity of identity is reflected in the stories youth shared in their testimonios. Due to the common practice of stripping youth of their home languages and cultures in schools, youth develop new cultures, languages, knowledges, and forms that allow them to survive—hybrid forms. For example, the creole language is a kind of linguistic hybridization. An example of hybridity in action in a classroom would be a student utilizing Spanglish with her peers while planning a group project in an AP History class—disrupting a school hierarchy of languages that places Standard English at the top of the list.

Hybridity, as I conceive of it in this book, critiques the status quo of schooling in the United States because as students perform hybridity through the creation of and negotiation of multiple and complex flows, they reimagine and restructure schools and society. Hybridity is not a simple mixing of two or more cultures; rather hybridity critiques the oppressive and violent imposition of neocolonialism in schooling and society. Hybrid youth experience neocolonialism described above and negotiate and create postcolonial flows that disrupt and apprehend neocolonial power with the opportunity for students to name and make the world in their own complex image. The processes of hybridization are multiple and multidimensional. For example, in her study of multiethnic teens in New York City and London, Warikoo (2007) found hybrid consumption practices of youth:

> Bhangra music's presence on mainstream hip-hop radio was especially important in New York, where there are no major South Asian–focused radio stations like there are in London. For Indian teenagers, this was an aspect of hip-hop radio that they could claim as authentically their own to non-Indian peers, just as hip-hop was claimed by African American and Afro-Caribbean students. The South Asian youth engaged with the popular culture of their general peer culture, but they also gained authenticity by hybridizing it with something with which they had more legitimacy in the eyes of peers, traditional bhangra. Their solution to peers' sanctioning for boundary crossing was to participate in a consumption culture that blurred ethnic and racial boundaries (pp. 402–403).

Power is implicated when apprehending and coupling the flows of both hip-hop and bhangra. Indianness and Afro-Caribbeanness, when combined, gain more power and status for Indian teens in this study. This study is just one example of how youth and their classrooms are made up of and negotiate postcolonial flows stemming from their hybridity that, in turn, marginalize the "Western" musical canon.

Beyond postcolonial flows of hybridization, young people struggle against fixed neocolonial conceptions of race, class, and gender and often display *multiple national affiliations*. For example, students may display loyalty to both the United States and their home countries at a school assembly by holding up flags of the various home nations. The public performance of affiliations to multiple nations is a postcolonial flow of youth that educators may not readily recognize as a disruption of nationalistic neocolonial school structures (Dimitriadis & McCarthy, 2001; Gallagher-Geurtsen, 2003; Young, 2003).

Another interesting way that youth are able to reverse the flow of power emanating from neocolonial brokers to students is through *mimicry* and *mockery*. As discussed above, students are required to mimic many Western-centric school structures in order to be successful in school, for example, writing a linear, formal essay. However, mimicry is never far from mockery, and a student could, for example, mock (through the practice of mimicry) neocolonial powers through writing an essay test in formal English about racism in the school. This performance would denounce the neocolonial practice of maintaining a hierarchy of races—all of this done, ironically, through appropriation of the school-sanctioned formal use of the written language in school. Compare this more legitimate form of mockery to writing "RACISTS!" on the school walls with spray paint or painting scenes of school racism in an art class—examples of non- or less-legitimate forms of school communication that surely would receive a different response than that received from a well-written essay.

I will close my brief review of postcolonial concepts with a flow of post-colonialism that offers great hope to decolonizing efforts. Homi Bhabha (1994) described an aspect of colonialism that he believed would sow the seed of its own destruction: *postcolonial ambivalence.* Translated into the schooling context, it looks something like this: Because the school wants to recreate minoritized students in its own Eurocentric White image, but doesn't want them to be *exactly* like them because this would allow minoritized students to compete with White students for power, there is a disjuncture that students can come to recognize, shaking the foundation of the school's authority. For example, schools tell students they are on equal ground if they Americanize and learn English, but they are often tracked into pull-out English as a Second Language classes so that they miss important school content that would give them tools for academic and social success. This can cause students to question the legitimacy of outward benevolence and the unquestioned power of school leaders and the policies utilized to define them. This recognition of the ambivalence of the neocolonizer, in essence, undresses the neocolonizer. The postcolonial flows described above are a few of the strategies that youth utilize in the neocolonial schooling context. You will learn about more of them in the next chapters as they are performed by students in their testimonios.

Classrooms: The Boardrooms of Postcolonial Flows

How do postcolonial flows work in the neocolonial classroom? Students are ambassadors of their own, their family members', and their ancestors' home(s) and along with their peers and teachers determine what happens to the rich global resources that they bring to classrooms. It is often the case that youth are expected to check their flows at the classroom door in order to "fit" into the classroom's increasingly standardized curriculum and teaching. Imagine being told by your teacher (as many of us as educators have done or have implied based on our grading systems and curriculum) that students are free and equal so they should strive to the best of their ability, and then to find out that you are not free nor are you treated equally. This creates a disquiet, anger, self-doubt, and power—if harnessed. How can youth become aware of this double bind or contradiction and harness it to decolonize their schooling experiences (Du Bois, 1903/1996; Hargreaves & Shirley, 2008; Valenzuela, 1999)?

Consider that students, despite policies and practices intended to subdue or erase them, bring their postcolonial flows into the classroom. The entrance of postcolonial flows into the purifying classroom creates complex hybridization. For example, English-only language policy and practices in the K–12 classroom colonize the native languages of students but, at the same time, creates powerfully meaningful languages like Spanglish that represent the survival of multilingual students' experiences as they (re)create their identities.

As board members of postcolonial flows, students examine the robust and valuable, the inequitable and purifying flows that govern their lives inside and outside schools. For example, my former fifth- and sixth-grade students would tell me about my colleagues who did not like Mexican Americans, and about how the police followed them and questioned them as they walked home late from an after-school advanced math program. With a critical and skilled teacher, able to help students identify the flows that students create and use to govern their lives, students can critically look at the rules of the game and institute change that is meaningful to them (i.e., how their families immigrate; how they are building the future of media economies; how their languages are taught/not taught in school; how their physical health is implicated in practice and policy; the fairness of testing that determines their life futures; how their social circles are expanded and limited; and how they gain and lose power in the cafeteria, school offices, and hallways).

Engaging with(in) the Postcolonial Flows of the Classroom

As you will see in the stories that youth tell, our students live extraordinarily complex lives due to the postcolonial flows that they emit, control, and divert. These flows are somewhat invisible to many educators because we need not negotiate with(in) them to survive and thrive as teachers—but our students do. When we refuse to engage or even allow the flows of our students into the classroom, we reduce our ability to be culturally relevant. If educators are out of touch with the vast technological and sociopolitical knowledge that diverse students bring to the classroom, we risk being left behind—and, in turn, we hazard leaving our students behind.

Recall Nadya from the beginning of the chapter. How could we engage with(in) Nadya's postcolonial flows? Perhaps teachers could engage Nadya with the history of Gypsy-Cubans; facilitate discussions about racism, sexism, and classism; ask her to choose inquiry projects about United States immigration policy from different perspectives, and legislation around Americanization and elections; study the social construction of exoticism in art and music from multiple international and postcolonial perspectives; and carry out a survey and create a committee on leadership equity for high schools in her city.

Given postcolonial flows of Nadya and multicultural youth in schools and the neocolonial flows governing schools and classrooms in the United States, we must rethink how we conceptualize the academic and social lives of our students. We can no longer consider an American to be someone loyal to just one nation-state with one identity based on nationally shared values. As we will see in youths' stories, written as testimonios, we must imagine the social and academic spaces of youth to be much wider and deeper— extending beyond the prescribed borders of the United States and a narrow view of what it means to be an American student (Basch, Glick Schiller, & Szanton Blanc, 2008).

Why Testimonios?

Because I want you, the reader, to take a fresh look at multiculturalism in schooling, I use narrative analysis. Unlike traditional research that is intent on identifying the admittedly slippery, verifiable truth, narrative analysis relies on stories as a way of knowing. The stories or testimonios that youth tell can facilitate your meaning-making, allowing you to draw multiple interpretations of the text without the interference of my direct analysis interwoven throughout the presentation of each youth's story. Reading each full-length testimonio with both lived experience and emotions intact at the opening of each chapter may seem an unexpected way to reflect on multiculturalism in a scholarly work. It will, therefore, hopefully find you feeling off-balance and more likely to critique and question your own and my assumptions (Barone, 2001a; Barone, 2001b; Coulter & Smith, 2009; Denzin, 1992).

Each testimonio began as an interview transcript that was minimally edited into a first-person account of the youth's important experiences in schools and society. Jara and Vidal (1986) called testimonios a "narración de urgencia" or a story that urgently needs telling. Indeed, the often not-told stories of what it is like to grow up and go to school as a minoritized youth need to be heard by educators—especially given minoritized students' well-documented struggles to find academic success in American schools. The utility of testimonio as a device for telling educators about the experiences of students in school is particularly pressing in the case of immigrant youth:

> We urge that *testimonios* be used as pedagogy, especially to educate future teachers and to raise the consciousness of people who do not have sympathy for immigrants, especially immigrant children, as they encounter an unfriendly and often hostile educational system. (González, Plata, Garcia, Torres, & Urrieta, 2003, p. 233)

Because the youth interviewed are not professional writers and many are English learners, I was able to put their words into a dominant form, a formal English register, making their urgent stories accessible to future and current educational leaders and decision-makers. This is one of the main functions of testimonio—to give the subaltern (minoritized youth in this book) a powerful audience for their urgent stories.

My construction of each testimonio is a somewhat analytic process whereby I organized and minimally edited each youth's words in a way that made their story clearer. Because each testimonio is derived from interview transcripts, the questions I asked and the postcolonial concepts I introduced during the course of the interview might be mentioned—for example, the concept of homelessness. I added a few transitions and introductory phrases so that the reader could follow the participant's thinking based upon my questions.

The formal analysis that follows each testimonio is mine, presented separately so that you can compare and contrast your own interpretation that you developed as you read. My analysis is just one way of reading the meaning of each youth's testimonio and presents a single-minded focus on postcolonial theoretical constructs.

> *Testimonio* gives voice to a previously anonymous and voiceless popular-democratic subject, but in such a way that the intellectual or professional is interpellated, in his or her function as interlocutor/reader of the testimonial account, as being in alliance with (and to some extent dependent on) this subject, without at the same time losing his or her identity as an intellectual. (Beverley, 2005, p. 554)

Therefore, I acknowledge that my account of youths' stories is a specific and focused one—intentionally so, in order to ask and answer questions of youth from a postcolonial viewpoint.

Guide to the Chapters

The remainder of the book includes one chapter on testimonio work, five chapters of testimonios, each one followed by analysis, and finally, a closing chapter that attempts to find meaning across the testimonios and suggests actions that honor the testimonios of the students I interviewed. In chapter one, "Praxis: Testimonio Work," I describe both the work necessary to construct testimonios but also the work involved in interpreting them in order to safeguard their role as a form of praxis with minoritized youth. In chapter two, "Ana's Testimonio: 'I'm not just one or the other, I'm all of it,'" I show how Ana struggles to find a solid identity, having experienced cultural and linguistic loss due to neocolonial binary flows and pressures in schools and society. Ana is able to disrupt binaries and hierarchies as she plans reclamation of her identities. Chapter three introduces Cynthia's testimonio, "They think, 'A White person is tutoring me. I'm brown. I must be dumb,' so, if I could tan, yes, I would definitely tan." Cynthia describes a self-reflective anticolonial stance wherein she consistently and consciously disciplines the neocolonial flows that pervade her life inside and outside of schools. In chapter four, Nadya analyzes her identities in relation to how her teachers and peers have interacted with her over the years as she strives to find her place among powerful neocolonial messages. She addresses the question, "I'm sitting right on the cusp, and I think, do I belong here or do I belong there, you know what I mean?" Amelia challenges traditional concepts of what it means to be American in chapter five, "I always feel Filipina first. …It's okay to be both Filipina and American." Amelia's testimonio introduces the reader to the complexities of hybridity within a transnational identity. Finally, we hear from Dung Tran in his testimonio, "I have more knowledge than people who live here. I learn everything I see" in chapter six. Dung unapologetically disqualifies neocolonial schooling structures and admonishes teachers to make the margin the center of their teaching through care and responsibility for immigrant students. In chapter seven I attempt to bring together the lessons from youths' testimonios and outline concepts and actions that may help to decolonize schooling for all youth. At the end of the book there is also a study guide with questions and projects to help deepen understanding of concepts as well as apply them to real life.

Given that one of the goals of this book is to operationalize postcolonial theory in classrooms and schools, it may be helpful from time to time to return to the introductory chapter to review the purposes, concepts, and strategies of postcolonial theory, neocolonialism, and decolonization. I admit that postcolonial analysis can be quite dense and often laden with enigmatic terminology, but I believe the effort to understand and apply these concepts to schooling is well worth the trouble—possibly offering new ways to approach some of the most vexing and troubling problems that exist in schools today through (un)knowing students.

Notes

1. The term "American" is rightly contested and often thoughtlessly applied. Here, I purposely do not define the term "American," so that the reader can debate the multiple and conflictual meanings of the term.

2. I define minoritized youth as young people whose ethnic, cultural, and/or linguistic backgrounds are treated as deficits to overcome, and whose school success is relegated to the margins of concern of those in power, typically White European Americans.

3. Although we may be living in a time when few nations are colonizing other nations—a *post*-colonial era—this term should not be confused with what I will call postcolonial theory. Postcolonial theory recognizes that even after nations have begun the process of decolonization, the legacy and practices of colonialism remain in both the colonizers and the colonized. I will use the term *post-colonial* when referring to the time period after major European colonization ended.

4. Flows are a useful image to conceptualize the hard-to-detect messages and practices of neocolonialism. The concept of flows will be described in more detail in the next section when I introduce post-colonial flows.

5. I will be addressing the problematic effects of what Young (2001) calls *cultural neocolonialism,* which emphasizes the continuing effects of cultural, linguistic, sociological, and psychological imperialist dominance in education and educational policy in the United States

Chapter One

Praxis

Testimonio Work

Testimonio work breaks rules. It is the private made public; it is critical of those in power; it is research and advocacy. All of this rule breaking requires careful work on the part of the researcher and participating youth. This chapter is an attempt to describe how I carried out testimonio work while considering important tensions such as: How can I negotiate the private nature of minoritized youths' stories about who they are before, during, and after the interview? How can I construct testimonios that reveal minoritized youths' urgent messages in their own right in a way that might be meaningful to educators reading them? How can testimonio work critique schooling while providing educators routes to reflection and action? Finally, how can testimonio work be constructed so that it is legitimized as research but also be deeply involved in advocating for the futures that minoritized youth envision for themselves?

Testimonio work is meant to be an empowering process that begins with the student experience of minoritized youth. Telling young people's urgent stories of their time in school is one way that researchers and educators can work *with* youth to assure their stories are heard by an audience that has the power to change their futures. Because the subaltern's testimonio seeks to make their stories visible and heard, it is a good example of Freire's (1970) praxis: a cycle of reflection and action through words that is meant to transform the world. The purpose of this book is to inspire change that transforms educational structures, making them more equitable. So, as I engage in praxis through the research and writing of this book, I hope the reader will also reflect and act in solidarity with the youth who tell their stories here and, for example, act on the advice that the youth give to teachers at the end of each testimonio. I encourage readers to choose to take responsibility for the inequitable practices and conditions in schools that necessitate the urgent telling of minoritized youths' stories. I want the reader to position youth as their teachers—learning about young people's strengths and struggles, and understanding how the reader is implicated in taking, giving, and sharing power with students in schools.

Before I begin describing the process of praxis I undertook to carry out testimonio work, a brief description of testimonio may be useful. More detailed explanations of my process will follow in the body of the chapter. Testimonio's roots are in Latin American Studies and are stories told by people who have been oppressed about their experiences and survival in unjust structures. Testimonio is now utilized in a range of scholarly areas such as women's studies, literature, psychology, and education (for a review of testimonio research, see Pérez Huber, 2009). Most testimonios have the following in common:

1. They are based on traumatic historical and/or social episode(s).
2. They are told from an individual perspective.
3. The individual experience serves as an allegory for the communal experience as a whole.
4. The author has been oppressed or silenced in some capacity, and the work contains political statement against the perceived oppressor or suffering caused by that oppression (http://digitalunion.osu.edu/r2/summer 06/herbert/testimoniosubaltern/ testimonioroots.html).

Typically, a writer, journalist, or researcher audiorecords an interview, transcribes the interview, and edits the account into a testimonio. The testimonios found in this book are lightly edited interview transcripts wherein all of my words as the interviewer are removed. The testimonios are written in the first person, for example, *"As for my family's culture, I really don't have one at all—none."* I have followed each youth's first-person testimonio with analysis of the testimonio from a postcolonial perspective.

Testimonio Work

I am calling this chapter Testimonio Work because the term *work* describes both the process and the product of creating testimonios. Not only do the steps in the process require the exertion of the physical, cognitive, and emotional energies of both researcher and participating youth, but the resulting testimonios and analyses are a structure of sorts that reflect the careful skill, creativity, and fashioning by the people who created it—a work. I forefront the two meanings of work (i.e., process and product) when describing this form of praxis because recognizing one without the other would be dangerous. A testimonio cannot simply be constructed by getting hold of an interview transcript and editing it—the construction requires work in the form of action *with* reflection. Likewise, a testimonio does not stand on its own as a neutral account—it is a reflection of the work (i.e., reflection and action) put into it.

Care must be taken in the work or process of constructing testimonios, given that they are made up of the deeply personal and private stories of youths' often painful experiences of survival and success. The work is physical, for example, and it may include lengthy travel to the interview site for both the researcher and the youth. The cognitive work required of the researcher to prepare for the interview involves creating an interview protocol that attends to myriad issues, for example, the power differences between a White female adult academic and a minoritized student youth, the complexity of postcolonial concepts, and the need to advocate for youths' equitable experiences in schools. Likewise, many of the youth I interviewed told me that they had thought about what they were going to say prior to the interview based on my description of the study in their informed consent documents. For example, Dung told me, "*I'm thinking a lot of what to say with you today.*" Testimonio work is also emotionally charged for many reasons. Because youth shared their urgent stories of racism, critiques of their schooling, and feelings about their identities, they exhibited strong emotions during interviews. For me, as an educator who began working for social justice in education as a bilingual teacher in California, I have seen firsthand how minoritized youth are treated inequitably at the classroom, school, neighborhood, and institutional levels. Because of my experiences, I am passionate about critiquing inequitable schooling practices and structures, and thus, I am emotionally involved in my work with minoritized youth. Therefore, the physical, cognitive, and emotional work necessary to create testimonios must be taken on with an embodied responsibility, for all we do during this process will affect minoritized youth forevermore. As educational researchers, I believe we owe it to youth to carry this load.

Not only do we need to navigate the tensions and responsibilities of the process of testimonio work, but the product itself, in this case, a book containing testimonios and analyses of those testimonios, should rightly be called a *work*. Each testimonio is a construction, an iteration, an edited version of what the youth said that does not include the Kleenex passed, checking of the digital recorder, facial expressions, perceived approval and disapproval, and more that went on during the interview. In the work itself, I omit my voice during the testimonio, but speak loudly after it, utilizing big words and the sometimes distancing postcolonial theory in my analyses. Throughout the process of testimonio work, from member checks and follow-up communication with youth, the academic should be careful to keep the final product's growing form in mind. Also, the reader should take care to consider the final work as one might critique a work of art, driving to reveal the multiple layers of construction and meaning. The reader of the work might ask critical questions from multiple perspectives, such as: How was the work constructed? What might the work mean to different people? Who had power and who did not before, during, and after the work was made? Whose interests are served and whose are not by the work? What are the social and historical contexts that shape the work? Why do I respond the way that I do to the work (Bailin, 2009)? Both kinds of work need to be carefully attended to and considered when doing testimonio work.

There are many ways in which I could describe my praxis with testimonio. I have divided the chapter into five somewhat arbitrary but hopefully cohesive categories of work: working with youth, working with trust, working with the interview, working with words, and working with meaning. These categories were not necessarily practiced in the order I have addressed them in the chapter. Moreover, each kind of work was going on while at least one (or more) of the other kinds of work was taking place concurrently. For example, during the interview, I had to maintain trust, draw upon my experiences with youth, and interpret meaning in order to choose what question it made sense to ask next. Or, when writing an analysis of a testimonio, I might go back in time to the experience of the interview to consider how the youth was portraying an event while concurrently considering if I could maintain the trust and care the youth and I developed by writing about a particular event. However, although there is significant overlap in the processes of work described below, each section should give the reader a sense of how they might draw upon my experience, for example, to write a testimonio from an interview that they conducted. I will begin with how I approached working with youth through testimonio.

Working with Youth

There are ways that I endeavored to responsibly engage youth from the first contact in writing or over the phone to introduce them to the research, to the face-to-face interview, and finally to the latest and possibly last contact for member checks and follow-up conversations. The following considerations for working with youth are also closely tied to the next section—working with trust. When working with youth, especially minoritized youth, we are working with a vulnerable population that historically has been objectified, excluded, divided, and dominated by neocolonial schooling. Therefore working with youth requires that the researcher recognize that youth may rightly distrust adults in the school setting. Also, the researcher who chooses to work with minoritized youth should agree to take responsibility for acknowledging, protecting, and empowering youth as well as taking action alongside youth to disrupt harmful practices. Each element of working with youth described below includes an effort to develop trust with them: protecting youth, being authentic, confronting racism, offering support, and actively utilizing experience.

Young people are vulnerable in many ways, and when working with youth it is our responsibility to protect their interests. At a very basic level of protecting youth, I underwent a criminal background check and made the cleared documentation available to schools. I kept my responsibility to protect youths' interests at the fore of my thinking when writing the informed consent documents. For example, I positioned youth as the teacher and teachers as their students: "The book intends to improve teachers' understanding of the experience of multicultural youth in schools and how to better meet the needs of multicultural youth in schools." In the same vein, the final interview question explicitly asked: "What advice do you have for teachers?" I also structured the interview to be an educational experience whereby youth would be introduced to a postcolonial critique of schooling and have the opportunity to question postcolonial ideas. For example, the interview protocol reads: "There are some new ideas out there about multicultural education, and I want to see what you think of these ideas—if you can relate to them or not."

During the interview, I elaborated on the idea that I was inviting youth to disagree with the postcolonial ideas that I would present, giving them power. The following is one example: "So I'm going to share lots of ideas with you, but I'm hoping you'll push back at me and be like, 'You know what, that's totally off.'" I also tried to protect youths' interests by giving them examples that they might more readily relate to. During the interview I shared examples of other minoritized youths' performances of postcolonialism in action, such as a poem or a self-portrait authored by students, and then invited youth to respond to the piece (see Appendix for the full interview protocol). In addition to looking out for the interests of young people's safety, relative position of power, and education in testimonio work, we need to protect them from a common blind spot: the dishonesty of adults.

As adults we are skilled in ways to cloak aspects of ourselves, sometimes to gain power and be perceived in a particular way and sometimes to survive. Youth are aware of adult cloaking and tend to disrespect this inauthenticity. When working with youth, I remind myself to be real—to peel back the layers that I have built up over time. Youth seem to be particularly cognizant of dishonesty. I think that educators, in classrooms and in administrative offices, oftentimes treat youth as if they are immune to our performances as adults. From kindergarteners to high schoolers, I have often seen classroom teachers dysconsciously and sarcastically rebuke, coldly correct, or even inauthentically praise a young person. I have seen numerous overt and covert instances of racism in classrooms (King, 1991). By dysconscious, I draw upon King's (1991) description: "an uncritical habit of mind (including perceptions, attitudes, assumptions, and beliefs) that justifies inequity and exploitation by accepting the existing order of things as given" (p. 135). Older youth seem to be better at hiding their reactions and their ensuing distrust of the adult, while younger students show their confusion, act out, or physically turn away. Knowing that these instances of insensitivity and blatant racism are common in school settings, I strived to be authentic with youth. A key piece of authenticity that must be addressed when working with minoritized youth is to be able to talk about racism.

I have a Black colleague who told me, "I like you, Trish. I can say Black to you. I can say White to you. We can talk about race." This is the degree of comfort I work towards with minoritized youth. Beyond a youth- and parent-friendly informed consent document, working with minoritized youth to support them in telling their urgent stories necessitates acknowledgement of a history of mistreatment. Because this study focused on the experiences of minoritized youth, as a White person, I needed to take responsibility for the institutional and individual racism, achievement gaps, and educational malpractice that young people I was going to interview, given statistics, were likely to have experienced. I talk about my condemnation of all-too-common racism at the outset of my interactions with youth as part of the mini educational autobiography I present before I ask them to talk about themselves (see Appendix for interview protocol). The mini biography came out in different ways during the interviews, depending on the young person's response to me. If I felt they might need more convincing that I believe racism is endemic to United States schools, I would add more detail to my story and show that I take responsibility. For example, in one interview, I explained how I was confronted with my own racism as a teacher:

> I had one Black student in my class. Most of my students were Mexican American. I had a few Vietnamese American students and a few White students, but mostly it was Mexican American. I had like 36 kids. And parent-teacher conferences come and my one Black student and her mom, who is Black as well, came in, and said, "Okay, Chanel, ask Ms. Geurtsen," you know, "tell Ms. Geurtsen what happened." And she said, "You never call on me." And I was completely horrified. I thought of all the excuses in the world I could think of: Oh, she's out of my line of sight, you know, but I was like, wow. It was the first time I was really confronted in my face with my own racism. And then, you know, I kind of was going on this journey as a White person to get to know my own racism.

Not only do I need to acknowledge a history of racism, but as a White person, I also needed to bring with me into the interview space, the understanding that the minoritized youth sitting with me is an othered Other that I cannot fully understand no matter how much I want to think I know them. I had to allow the space to be big and empty enough for the youth to fill it with their stories as I remained largely silent and even silenced. At other times I was strategically condemning mistreatment: for example, when Ana talked about her teacher telling her mother not to speak to Ana in Spanish, I said: "Yeah, I mean, you deserve your language. I think it's a human right, a basic human right, you should be able to speak the language that you are born speaking; that's your mother language." The condemnation of linguicism, in this case, can become a supportive structure for the youth to reclaim power and act against injustice in schools.

Clearly, testimonio is work for youth, therefore they need support throughout the process. Youth and their parents have to expend energy reading and understanding informed consent documents, thinking about and choosing what to share, engaging in member checks of the transcript and testimonio itself, and engaging in follow-up communications with the researcher. It must be acknowledged that testimonio work can be emotionally taxing. Youth exhibited both anger and sadness as they told stories of their experiences in school. Frustration was evident as youth talked about teachers who ignored them or structures of schooling that left them without tools to succeed. I felt it was my responsibility to reflect back the strengths and successes I noticed about the individual youth I was interviewing. For example, at the close of Dung's interview I wore my educator's hat and offered specific praise that responded to Dung having apologized numerous times for his English and having made the comment that maybe he was not so smart:

Trish: *Thank you, Dung. It was so nice to meet you. Your English is very good.*

Dung: *Thank you.*

Trish: *You should be confident.*

Dung: *Yeah, you know.*

Trish: *You should be confident. You're very smart. I know you're gonna get what you want.*

Dung: *Yeah, I do.*

Just as teachers should not ignore it when a student does not understand the lesson they have just presented, it is the responsibility of the interviewer to intervene when youth need support.

Lastly, reflecting upon my work with youth for this project, I want to make the point that it is important to come to testimonio praxis with your experiences intact rather than assume the position of the unbiased recorder of information. Having interacted with minoritized youth in schools and classrooms for 15 years, I have developed a sense of when youth are comfortable with my presence and how they feel about interacting with me. Always trying to engage youth to express themselves and learn and grow from their current understanding and experiences, I know there are times to back off and others when a question or comment might help them deepen their understanding. I actively brought this experience with me when I interviewed youth and interacted with them over the phone or in writing. By actively engaging this experience, I mean that I suppressed the impulse to walk into the interview session with a blank slate as the objective observer and recorder of words and themes, as many are trained to do in graduate school research methods courses. Leaving behind my less tangible experience of working with youth in schools and how I read youths' expressions and body language, for example, would be a denial of what I bring to the interview process and limit my ability to engage youth from where I perceive them to be at the moment. For example, in one of the interviews for this book, in the first few minutes of the interview I noticed that despite my initial impressions, the youth was very informal and used filler words like "things" and "stuff" to characterize her experiences. I later found myself mirroring her more informal language in an attempt to make her more comfortable with me: for example, I said, "your background and cultures and languages and that kind of stuff." By actively utilizing my experiences with young people in schools to engage in praxis with youth, I was able to draw out rich descriptions of minoritized youths' experiences, working *with* them instead of working *on* them as an objective and distant interviewer might. All of the aforementioned elements of working with youth require trust, which I will now address.

Working with Trust

Trust is a constantly present and pressing question in testimonio work. Because testimonios are primarily utilized with oppressed or silenced people, in this case minoritized youth, it is essential that researchers not only create a trusting relationship, but that they actually be trustworthy. Gaining and keeping trust with those you work with as a critical multiculturalist is a living, breathing process. It requires trust before, during, and after encountering youth. In this section I will discuss how I attempted to be trusting, trustworthy, and trusted throughout the research process.

I care about the youth with whom I worked and I cared about them before I worked with them. I am passionately involved in making the educational experiences of youth equitable in my work in schools, in my research, and in my own family with my children. I want minoritized youth to know that if they want me to be, I am their advocate in schools and in society. What follows are some examples of how I set out to make my sense of caring and sense of responsibility for social justice clear.

In my initial communications I positioned young people as the knowledge producers. For example, I wrote to one youth that "I would be delighted to learn from you about your experiences in school." As discussed in the previous section, I shared a mini autobiography of my schooling experiences that foregrounds my acknowledgement of racism in schooling so that students know that I will accept any stories of racism or other critiques that they want to share. I fully accept that as a White person I may be judged guilty until proven innocent. In this manner, I am showing that I am not cloaking myself and will be honest with them.

Similarly, during the face-to-face interviews I tried to remain open, and even brave, while bearing witness to youth's urgent stories. I knew that it was likely that I would hear disturbing accounts and that I must not recoil or show disgust about the abuses because it could be misinterpreted. I had to keep my heart open to the youth, accepting and believing all that they said. I needed to not just remember this internally, but also show this explicitly with my expressions and actions. For example, after Ana shared that her mother, on the advice of a teacher, stopped speaking Spanish with her when Ana was a young child, the following took place in the interview:

Ana: *See, I don't know why I'm crying. Uhm…*

Trish: *You've had a hard day, week and.…*[Looks in purse for Kleenex].

Ana: *Yeah. That's why she never spoke Spanish. And you're like, prepared for this.*

Trish: *No, actually it was…here you go.* [Passes Kleenex].

Ana: *Thank you.*

Trish: *You're welcome.*

Ana: *I'm a cry baby, actually.*

Trish: *That's okay.* [Wipes tears]. *I am too.* [Laughter].

Another example of how I worked to maintain trust was in my interview with Amelia. After she talked about how family was very important to her and then shared that her parents were separated, I said, "That's very hard. So family is very important. My parents separated, too, when I was young, so I understand. That's very hard. When did you see your mom last?"

Although I tried to remain caring, open, and trusting during interviews, unexpected things happen when doing research that relate to negotiating trust. When choosing interviews to include in this book, I reflected on one story that was too much for me to bear. As I was listening to a young woman's story during the interview, I had a very hard time holding back tears. She divulged too much to protect her identity. It was a story of survival and strength, but mostly it was a story of sadness and despair. I am thankful now (although at that time I was horrified) that for some reason, my digital recorder ended up not recording, so that I would not be able to consider her story for inclusion in the book. But had the story been recorded, I would not have been able to maintain the overwhelming trust she offered me in telling me so much, if I had published her story. First, it would have been almost impossible to protect her identity while telling her whole story; and second, it seemed to me that she left the interview with a great sense of relief, having told her story in such detail, and that seemed to be the most important part of the process for her.

Not only is developing and maintaining trust the responsibility of the researcher in order to not repeat the historical abuse of the minoritized "research subject" once again, engagement with trust presumably leads to a fuller account of the youths' urgent stories—which is what I wanted educators to hear in the final work. I imagine the stories I leave the interview site with are fragile pieces of art of all shapes and sizes that I must ever so carefully wrap in tissue paper and carry home and check on often so as to assure their safety. Young people have entrusted me with their most urgent messages, and I am charged with bringing them to the reader. That brings me to you, the educator, and how much you trust what I have done here.

Will the academic community determine that praxis-oriented testimonio research (i.e., the decolonization of minoritized youth) is trustworthy? Testimonio as a research praxis is new in educational research and continues a decade-old push to show that the complex experiences of youth in schools cannot be accurately studied with only positivist, often exclusively quantitative, research paradigms. The reader may ask if we can trust the stories told by minoritized youth contained in their testimonios. How different have their stories become through the passage of time? In defense of testimonio as a device, and in defense of youth, I will now address points intended to engender trust in the research praxis I have carried out with youth (Denzin & Lincoln, 2005).

First, I took care to utilize crystalization techniques in my work, including member checks where youth were sent the entire interview transcript and testimonio and asked to read and revise it accordingly. For example, after I received a transcript edited by one youth who posed a few questions to me, I wrote:

> Thanks so much for taking the time to "set the record straight" on a few items. I am working on amending what I have based on your requests. It is very common to read a transcript of an interview and be surprised by what was said or for there to be errors in the transcription, so I apologize for any mis-transcriptions. I will honor all of

> your requests. Also, I have changed any identifying names, locations, etc., to protect
> you and those you talked about. I am very careful about this.

I also solicited feedback about the school settings of the youth by talking to classroom teachers, administrators, and university faculty who are familiar with the schools and classes the students attended. As I analyzed interview transcripts, I made marginal notes of alternative explanations outside of a postcolonial framework. I also shared my analyses with academics and non-educators alike, asking for their reactions and thoughts. Finally, when comparing across all of the interviews I conducted with youth from four different states and five different countries, I found that inequitable treatment based on assumptions related to language, culture, ethnicity, class, gender, and academic standing was identifiable across all transcripts (Marshall & Rossman, 2011).

Second, as educators, we need to ask ourselves: For how long will we continue to "other" the recipients of our research? When will we trust youth enough to ask them how they experience school? When will we decide to believe even our youngest students when they tell us how they feel about who they are, what they are learning, and what they think of their teachers? Do we really believe that children should be seen and not heard? Finally, testimonio praxis does not seek to find out quantifiable truth "out there." Rather, the goal is to create a stage with a microphone and a full house in order that minoritized youth can tell their urgent stories as they experience them in their own terms.

Working with the Interview

I did not know that I would be transforming the interviews I had conducted into testimonios until I had completed all of the interviews for this project. Therefore, I did not know that when I determined my focus and research questions and created the interview protocol that I was engaging in what I am now calling testimonio work. Had I known that the youths' stories would be told in the form of testimonios, would I have asked different questions or structured the protocol differently? Would the testimonios be vastly different? Why was I able to create testimonios out of these interviews? These are the questions I will briefly address in this section as a way to think about the role of the interview in testimonio work.

To begin thinking about what I might have done in planning for and conducting the interviews if I had known they would eventually be testimonios, let us start with what I actually did. Before the semi-structured interview, I took care to create a protocol that was clear in its intent, drew upon multiple ways of knowing to reach different kinds of people, and offered many ways to engage with the postcolonial concepts I offered. For example, I planned to share a poem and ask for reactions or show a self-portrait that a child drew and ask how the youths would draw themselves. The youths that agreed to be interviewed were told that the final work, the book, would be about ways to help teachers do a better job of teaching diverse students. Six of the 20 interview questions ask youths to question and critique their teachers. Also, I explicitly asked the youths to give advice to teachers based upon their multicultural experiences. Therefore, the youths seemed to know that teachers were the audience for their answers to my questions, as evidenced by the ease with which they critiqued their teachers and offered them advice.

The questions I asked were meant to introduce youths to postcolonial concepts in an accessible way, ask what they thought of the ideas, and offer examples that they may have experienced in school. Because postcolonial theory is a critique of traumatizing neocolonial schooling practices that target minoritized groups for oppression, it makes sense that the stories that we elicited by my questions would be urgent stories—testimonios in the making. Without explicitly intending to do so, I designed praxis that would ask an oppressed population to formulate urgent messages for people in power about their inequitable schooling experiences—just what testimonio work is intended to be.

If I were to conduct interviews that I knowingly would edit into testimonios, I might tell youths very explicitly that this is an opportunity to tell any stories that they felt teachers needed to hear. I might ask them to tell teachers what they have wanted to say about who they are and their powerful schooling experiences but were afraid to tell for fear of retribution. The stories I would try to draw out would be those that they were bursting to tell, that would help other minoritized youth who would come after them in the schools they attended. I might even tell them that it was possible that teachers would be assigned to read their stories as homework to learn from them. Finally, I would assure them, especially the youths learning English, that I would create a draft in Standard English for them to review.

It is difficult to conjecture if the testimonios would be very different from those presented in this book if the topics of dialogue were still related to the injustices inflicted upon minoritized youth in schools. One can presume the experiences of youth in these areas would not have changed markedly. However, it is possible that the delivery may have been more focused, and that the stories may have been more urgently told, with a clear audience and purpose in mind. Alternately, it is also possible that the youths might have felt more pressure and possibly would have come up short when given such a power-laden task—to tell teachers stories they needed to hear to be more socially just. Perhaps utilizing a lesser known lens like postcolonial theory to frame the interview along with vignettes, poetry, and art to elicit stories made it easier for youths to tell their stories. I will now turn to how I went about transforming each interview into a testimonio.

Working with Words

Writing testimonios can surely happen in a variety of ways. My process was somewhat complex but retained a simple goal: edit the testimonio for clarity and organization but keep as much of the original language and wording as possible. In practice this felt a lot like combing tangles out of hair. Part of the process is about taking the interview and combing it until the main ideas are visible in all of the strands of speech. The transcript reveals tangles such as what I would call filler utterances such as "um" and "kind of" and short side conversations unrelated to the story being told. Many of the tangles I encountered were created by my encouraging voice and talking out loud about what I was thinking. I needed to remove myself from the stories so that they could flow, and to get out of the way to give the youth narrative authority. To illustrate this combing process, I will present an excerpt of an interview transcript and follow it with its corresponding testimonio excerpt:

> Ana: *Oh, for sure. Yeah. I don't know…it got better. I think my mom kind of like noticed the change in my second grade teacher, Mrs._____, which is the main reason why I'm becoming a teacher.*
>
> Trish: *Tell me.*
>
> Ana: *She was just like the most loving person. She was the one that touched my mom, take your children out. Travel with your children. Why have your children not gone to Colombia? And you need to take them to enrich them and enculture them. That's when my mom really started making us travel. And she kind of like a little bit tried speaking in Spanish, but I think at that point we were so like, my mom's speaking some Spanish, you know. We don't understand you. And then we kind of pushed off. She's the one that said…they're your kids and they're different and that's a good thing.*
>
> *I don't know…it got better. I think my mom noticed the change in my second grade teacher, Mrs. Tohsaku, which is the main reason why I'm becoming a teacher. She was the most loving person. She was the one that touched my mom, told her, "Take your children out. Travel with your children. Why have your children not gone to Colombia? You need to take them to enrich them and enculturate them." That's when my mom really*

started making us travel. She started to speak Spanish to us, but I think at that point my brother and I were so removed from it that we'd respond with, "Mom's speaking Spanish. We don't understand you." And then we kind of pushed off. But Mrs. Tohsaku was the one that said...they're your kids and they're different and that's a good thing.

In addition to combing out filler language, side conversations, and my voice, I also edited the language so that it was written in Standard English. For example, Amelia's description of a helpful teacher, "She teach us how to be responsible and to make our works and be respectful" became, "She teaches us how to be responsible, to do our work, and be respectful" in her testimonio.

Once I had removed all of my utterances, filler language, and off-topic conversations, I started combining sentences and creating cohesive paragraphs that represented one topic. At this point, I read the testimonio that was forming and tried to see an emerging organization. Because with a few exceptions the interviews generally followed the protocol, most of the testimonios had a logical and readable structure. The first topic discussed was the youth's familial, cultural, and linguistic history. This was followed by questions about identity, and then the testimonio finished with critiques of schooling and teachers. If I found a paragraph that addressed these topics in another place in the testimonio, I moved it to where it was first addressed and created a short transition if needed to integrate the paragraph.

Now the testimonio was shaping up. I was pleased as I read this version of the testimonio because it brought me back to the experience of witnessing youths' urgent stories during the interview. The wholeness of the stories and the emotion I experienced were found again after having been lost in the choppy and clunky interview transcript. I felt moved again. At this point, I edited this version for power. I wanted the youths' stories to have the power and urgency they deserved. I tried to start the testimonio with an engaging quote that showed the confidence and strength of each individual youth. In this run-through with the comb, I thought about making the language that was there more readable for an educator, with smoother transitions, clear topic headers for the different topics the students addressed, and starting paragraphs with a topic sentence that might be buried in the middle of the paragraph. These steps did not take long. I found myself reading the resulting testimonios over and over again, reexperiencing the interview and understanding the youths' stories in a new way, without having to think about what to ask next as I did during the interview and without my interruption constant in the interview transcripts. It was after these multiple readings that I proceeded to analyze the youths' testimonios, which I will address next.

Working with Meanings

Just as there are many ways to construct a testimonio from an interview transcript, there are even more ways in which to make meaning of the testimonios. Less interesting perhaps, but important to attend to, is how I constructed my analysis of the testimonios that appear in the final product. As discussed in the introduction, I purposively present the testimonio separate from and before my analysis so that the reader can interpret it from multiple perspectives without my interference. Given that my analysis utilizes the lens of postcolonial theory in order to decolonize the educations of youth, I used predetermined themes to consider each testimonio. I followed a highly structured five-step process to analyze testimonios from a postcolonial perspective.

First, for my initial analysis I used the reviewing comment tool in my word processing program to highlight quotes that showed major neocolonial and postcolonial themes such as hybridity and exoticism, and noted them in the margin comments in all caps. For example:

HYBRIDITY

> *But Filipinos can live with their family up into their 20's. Americans look different: their hair, eyes, etc. I am both Filipino and American, because of language. I speak English and Tagalog, so I'm both. Americans are friendly and nice.*

When possible, I identified analytic themes and placed them as headers in the body of the analysis section of my draft manuscript.

Second, I analyzed the testimonio, now with explanatory comments for quotes that showed major neocolonial themes, for example:

DISCIPLINE subaltern competes with one another to form a mega-panopticon to get to the colonizer's language as quickly as possible. A public display of English knowledge is highly prized among the subaltern. This also reflects the shift from the collective to individual competition that is a goal of the civilizing aspect of colonization—pitting students against each other.

> *There's a lot of competition in ESL class. When we are having a class discussion about something and the teacher asks a question, and a student raises their hand but they get the answer wrong, another student will raise their hand to feel like smart and to make you feel bad.*

After analyzing the entire testimonio in this manner, I had identified enough postcolonial themes and had thought through and written the evidence for them. I was now ready to determine the preliminary headers for the analysis section, for example, "Transnational in a Neocolonial Smog," or "Complex Hybrid Flows within Neocolonial Policy."

Third, I dragged and dropped quotes into the appropriate sections and added new headers for the analysis section as needed. Fourth, I considered all of the sections and quotes I was going to use and began writing an introduction to analysis of testimonio as a way to organize my thoughts and think about the meaning of the whole testimonio—how all of the analytic themes worked with and against one another to say something about both neocolonial, decolonial, and postcolonial flows in the youths' stories.

In step five, I fleshed out each header section with explanations of quotes and explanations of neocolonial and postcolonial themes, and added citations and quotes that support and/or build the argument encapsulated in the header. The last step of my analytic process involved editing the analysis for clarity, transitions, sufficient scholarly evidence, sufficient examples, and readability.

Final Thoughts

Describing praxis through testimonio work has helped me to see, once again, how much goes on behind a research project that is not often described. It is the recording of both the work related to the process and the product that more fully allows for an authentic dialogue for the reader of this book. For testimonio work to be transformational for researcher, youth, reader, and schooling, it needs to include the action and reflection described here. For action without reflection is inauthentic, and reflection without action is missing the commitment to transforming schooling (Freire, 1970).

Chapter Two

Ana's Testimonio

"I'm Not Just One or the Other, I'm All of It."

You should know that I'm comfortable telling you my story and more than happy to disagree with you. My name is Ana Smith.[1] I was born in the Mountain West but I was raised on the West Coast with my mom, dad, and younger brother. My mom is from Colombia and my dad is from the Midwest. My dad's heritage is Norwegian, German, and Irish.

Language and Culture

I grew up speaking only English. My mom spoke Spanish on the phone every day, but we never learned it. I can't speak it at all. My mom didn't teach me Spanish. Why? This is what she told me. In kindergarten, my grandmother in Colombia had a stroke, and so my mom was the only one who was able to go down and help my grandmother. In that process, my dad couldn't take care of me with his job, so I moved to another state when I was five to live with my aunt. So when I came back to the West Coast in, say, November, I hadn't seen my parents and so I was a little, like, shy. I hadn't seen them for such a long time. In kindergarten at my elementary school, as I recall, I was the only Latina girl in my all White class…so I never spoke. Ever. I was so shy. I could speak English but I didn't speak, because I didn't know anyone. I wasn't doing well academically in kindergarten, so my teacher, Mrs. May, told my mom, your daughter's not doing well and it's because you're speaking Spanish to her. My mom…she is a freaking firecracker—just blew up at her and screamed in her face, she told me. From that day on, she swore she'd never speak Spanish to me. That's the reason. I talked to my dad a couple weeks ago, and he says one of his biggest regrets is not forcing my mom to teach us Spanish. I don't know why I am crying now.

My family lives here in Green City. They're half Colombian, half Austrian, so they're completely two different cultures and they're Mormon. We don't speak German or Spanish because of the same ideology—two languages isn't a good idea. Spanish is definitely part of my culture but I don't speak to my grandparents in Colombia at all and it's because of the language barrier. When they call during Christmas, it's like, "Hola, Abuelo. Sí, sí, sí," and I desperately whisper, "Where's mom?" I tell my brother, "Go look for mom." Or when mom's in Colombia, I'm always asking, "Mom,

*what is grandpa saying?" It hurts her that we can't connect to her parents—
it hurts a lot. We're not mad at her but it hurts her and it hurts us. I'm an
English as a Second Language minor. I'm trying all this stuff—but not Spanish. Academically, I probably would have done better if I had the advantage
of learning Spanish. My mom is kicking herself right now.*

*I don't know...it got better. I think my mom noticed the change in my
second grade teacher, Mrs. Tohsaku, which is the main reason why I'm becoming a teacher. She was the most loving person. She was the one that
touched my mom, told her, "Take your children out. Travel with your children. Why have your children not gone to Colombia? You need to take them
to enrich them and enculturate them." That's when my mom really started
making us travel. She started to speak Spanish to us, but I think at that point
my brother and I were so removed from it that we'd respond with, "Mom's
speaking Spanish. We don't understand you." And then we kind of pushed it
off. But Mrs. Tohsaku was the one that said..."they're your kids and they're
different and that's a good thing."*

*Mrs. Tohsaku was the first teacher that saw me. I was never a problem,
but she was the first that didn't look at me like I was stupid, didn't look at me
like, "You're never gonna get caught up in school!" She looked straight at
me and said, "You know what, it takes years trying to learn, but you're going
to get there and you're going to do fine." I remember enjoying class with
her. It didn't feel like I had to be there. I wanted to be there. I thought, "I
want to learn. I want to do the art projects that you're doing." You know, she
actually made life more interesting.*

*Her husband was an artist and she was a great teacher of the arts. She
enriched us with arts and cultures. There was a Japanese kid in our class
and she made the parents come in with their culture, and they would cook for
us and give us some little things from their culture. And we had a Hawaiian
kid, so we learned about Japanese things. We had a mom who was from England, so she brought in the English culture.*

*With my second grade teacher I remember my mom read a story about
some native Colombian indigenous people and a myth of theirs. I remember
her doing that but that's about it. In sixth grade we had to report on the culture and history of a country where you're from, so I did Colombia. But my
mom...she made a juice cocktail. That's the only thing she's ever done Colombian in my school. I never ate Colombian food until I went to Colombia
my sophomore year in college.*

*As for my family's culture, I really don't have one at all—none. And
that's what White people think about themselves. It is. My mom never cooked
Colombian food. Now, there's a lot of Colombian stuff around my house, like
pictures and little cups. Other than that, culture-wise—I have no clue about*

Colombian culture. Whatever I know, it's what I've been reading now, within the last year and a half and going to Colombia—once.

Colombia

I went because my grandmother got really sick, and so my mom said "I want her to meet the kids and for them to see her before she dies in my country," so, finally, we went for a week. It was worth it.

When we went, even in taxis, we were not allowed to speak, my brother and I. My mom said, "Don't talk in public. Don't say anything. You stand right beside me." My brother and me look a lot alike, but he is a whiter version. We were in this little street market and some guy just pointed out my brother and said, "Come here, kid!" He doesn't really dress American—he's got like a good sense of style, but he stood out. We stood out for sure. I think it was more because of the way we were dressed. We definitely looked Colombian down there. I tan really easily, so I was a lot darker. I got really discouraged there. I feel like I'm kind of culture biased. From what I've heard, from the news, is that it's an unfit, unsafe place to be. That's why it took so long for us to go.

Now, all of my cousins—everyone—is finally starting to go back to Colombia. A cousin who is my age is in Columbia now for six months. She is half Mexican. Her parents both spoke Spanish, so she speaks Spanish. So, I don't know. It doesn't really make me feel…it makes me feel jealous. Oh, I'm jealous. But other than that, it's like, "Oh, I could probably go to Spain."

Spanish

Spanish is really hard for me. I have taken, between junior high and college, five or six Spanish classes. I've never done really well. The only one I did well in was a summer class at a community college, and that was because we only talked about Antonio Banderas. In my sophomore year of high school, I had a Spanish teacher who was half Colombian and half Brazilian. Because my mom was a real stickler for good grades, I had to come home every Friday with a piece of paper with my grade that was signed by my teachers…my weekend was dependent on that. I was trying to do well. For example, she tutored me. But I wasn't doing well and I got a D. I was crying and I told my teacher, "I can't have a D on my report card. My mother is going to be so pissed." I had already gone through a situation in junior high where I pretty much failed every single class in junior high. I was grounded for three months. She's strict. For example, in the Colombian culture, you can't date until you're 16. And she found out that I had a boyfriend and she didn't talk to me for three months. That was probably the lowest point. So, that scared me. I remember thinking, "I can't have it. You don't have any idea what she is capable of." And so, I was really grateful when my mom only said to me in Spanish, "How could you? You're Colombian. You should be able to speak Spanish. Why can't you speak it? This should seem natural to you." And I thought to myself, "Yeah. Okay. The only time you hear mom speaking Spanish is on the phone. Yeah, I totally know Spanish, right?" My parents went and told her to stop tutoring me. My mom came out and told me, "You're so stupid...but it doesn't make any difference. You should be able to speak it. You should be fluent." After that, I decided, "I'm not taking Spanish. I'm going to continuously fail Spanish and cry over everything. My parents will demean me." I decided, yeah, screw Spanish. I think if I travelled abroad and stayed in a country for six months and picked it up, instead of being forced to learn it in school, I'd have learned more.

Hair

Growing up, I was always angry about these things. Why is America like this? Why is it that my country is supposed to be one way, but then in high school, everyone makes decisions based on looks and what you're supposed to look like? I was always wanting to dye my hair a lighter brown. Eventually my mom said, well, let's go get it professionally done. And so we did. I came out blond. For two years my hair was blond, like platinum blond. And I hated it—so badly. The first six months I was like, "Okay, it looks cool. It's fun, it's different." But then it lightened to blond. It cost $200. So it grew out and it was half dark brown and half blond. I was done. I wanted to change the color of my hair back to brown. I wanted my natural hair color. My parents and I got into the biggest fight, and they were just like, "No! You have to go back...the blond looks so good on you. Why would you want to change it?" I said, "Are you serious? Like, I want my natural hair color. How many people are fighting for their kids to keep their natural hair color? I want my natural color back. I don't want to be blond anymore. I don't look good." Two days later, I was back in the salon getting my hair dyed blond.

I don't know. They thought it looked so good. They thought it looked so pretty on me. It seems like, it was that whitewashing thing. I'm not sure if it was that, but it was one of those frustrating things. It seems clear. Why would you put someone who is super tan to the point of black tan, why would you put someone in blond hair? I don't know. So, I never know where I'm supposed to be. I think that hits the spot, to be honest. Where do I fit? For example, on college applications, they ask what ethnicity are you? I was always told to put Hispanic, put Latina because you are a minority. It helps your chances because you're a minority. But, really, where do I fit? I remember a conversation with my dad, about President Obama. We are talking about the fact that Black people will want him to win because he's Black. My dad says, stupidly, "He's only half black." I just looked at him, and said, "Are you serious right now? Do you know who you're looking at? Like you're always telling me to put Hispanic on my application. Are you saying that I'm not Hispanic and I should just do it because I'm…I look Hispanic? So, like, what am I Dad?" He realized that he made a huge mistake and just shut up after that.

Identity

There's definitely that hole of where do I fit? It's kind of a joke between my friends. A lot of my friends here are White. They always say, "That's just Ana's crazy Colombian side coming out." Or when I don't do something that should be Latina…like, like dancing, cooking, or making really spicy foods…whatever people think Latinas should do, I'll be like, "Oops, I guess my White side is popping out!" I'm either A or B at the moment. Where do I fit? What do I call myself? I'm half Colombian or I'm just a regular American White person. A lot of people always ask me, "What ethnicity are you?" What do I say? I look Colombian but I feel like I act more White most of the time, but there are times where that crazy flirtatious Colombian person comes out. I can see my mom coming out. Homelessness is a good way to call it. I'm not just one or the other, I'm all of it. I always looked at it as negative, but it's a positive thing—a talent, that you're able to go in and out, a talent.

President Obama is a good example. He was an American living in Indonesia; he's experienced some cultural difference and he didn't grow up like most of us. He definitely can think outside of the box. If you live outside of the country, I think that's the most amazing thing. If you've lived somewhere else, I want to talk to you more and know more about you. My mom didn't pass any Colombian culture to me. I don't know what Colombian is. I don't. She moved to the States when she was 16 to play basketball and stayed. So she's kind of got this hybrid identity. I know when she goes to Colombia, her Spanish isn't as good as it used to be because the only people she talks Spanish to is her family here in the States. And so, when she goes down, she has to be careful because people might think she's not Colombian anymore—or they can tell she's not Colombian enough.

Being American is different. If you're born here, you're an American. You're not more American if you have White skin. If you're born on this soil and you're raised here since day one, even if your family is from Mexico or wherever else, you're American. My mom is American now. She has had her citizenship for the last five years, and that took 10 years for her to convince her to get her citizenship. She's American now, but I don't think she's Ameri-can—and it's okay. She's not American to me. She has citizenship because of my dad's marriage, but other than that, I don't think so. I don't see her as an American. I can see my Aunt Rena (my mom's oldest sister), who I'm really close to, who lives here—I could call her American...but not my mom. From what I've heard, it takes three generations of living somewhere in a country to be considered that ethnicity. So these two generations, to be born, it's a standing that you have to grow.

My mom took a lot of English classes. Her English has gotten better over the years. You can still hear the accent. Whereas, my aunt here, it's so much thicker than my mom's—it's so much thicker. When they're together and they'll be talking in English, every five minutes you'll hear my mom correct-ing her accent and trying to change it. And so, that's like when I hear this, I think of this, I'm just like, "You know, you can understand what she's saying. You don't need to get on her butt about it. You get the conversation, you get the point. She's 50 years old, she's not gonna change."

High School

My high school was racist. I feel like I was always put in the dumb classes. It is a huge school, a national honors school, a blue ribbon school—half White and half not. We had a large Mexican culture. I was always put in the dumb classes. I did well in them and the teachers liked me, but it was always full of Mexicans. Some of the students were White and usually those were the kids who were like, "I don't want to work hard. I don't want to do honors. I just want to cruise by." I was never really given the chance to be in honors. Part of me was okay with it because I didn't really want to do the extra work, but it was demeaning sometimes. I thought to myself, "Oh, I'm in this class with all these Mexicans." Sometimes I thought, "I feel like they don't want to try. They're just trouble." I feel like the community was saying that. I didn't have a problem with them. I had a lot of friends who were Mexican, acquaintan-ces, not the kind of friend I would hang out with. My best friends were all White except for one who was Filipino.

I was put in this program called STRIVE my junior year in high school. I was the only White kid in this class. I just felt really dumb to be in there. I was there for two years. My counselor suggested I be in there because it was a college track program. It sounded good, it looked good, right? But these teachers thought I was in there because I wanted to hang out and listen to funny stories but I wasn't a troublemaker—I was a good kid in high school. Sports took up my life. So, I just kept quiet the whole time. Senior year was the worst ever. It was this crazy White teacher. She wasn't racist, I don't think, but she definitely picked on a few students. Some of them were Mexi-cans who were really smart and who were obviously hardcore college tracked. I wasn't really into college at that point. But the teacher picked on them. If you said, "Hey, like, I'm having trouble with this paper. You gave me a C and I want to make it better." She would say, "I don't know. You need to go figure it out." I'd say to myself, "Are you serious? You're on the ground right now helping these two other girls and you're ignoring the rest of us." The other girls were more involved with the school, I think, and they both go to university now. They're really nice girls. Maybe she was racist, or maybe she just thought I was more…I can't think of the word…privileged. Maybe she thought, "You know what, you're just in here for an easy day"—I have no clue. No, it didn't feel fair, and I kind of gave up…I wish I would have dropped that class, to be honest, but I just gave up. I slept all the time in that class. I just didn't even care about her anymore.

More on Identity

My identities didn't matter much to the school except when it concerned placing me in class. They placed me in Latino classes, but other than that, it didn't matter. For some classes—my electives like photography or student government—it didn't matter. It was just the racist placement that was obvi-ous. There was another time I remember when my high school was raising money for a community pool and we had to raise money for it. We created this really nice brochure and my water polo coach asked me to be in it; she told me it's because you're the most ethnic person on the team, so you have to be in it. I thought, "Whatever, I get to be on the cover." But, looking back, it was totally a case of using me because I was a dark child on the team. There was no one else that was any different culture. We didn't have an Afri-can American. There wasn't a Mexican or a Hispanic. I was the only His-panic person on the whole entire team, including the guys' team. There was an Asian, but I don't think we put him in there because he was kind of big.

If asked where I am from, I usually say I am Californian, but if my mom asked what I am I would say half Colombian. If my dad or my family asked it's always, "I'm half Colombian." That's what I know people are asking for…because I'm darker. If I looked more White, they wouldn't be asking me that question at all. If it were a stranger it would depend. More than Ameri-can, I'd say I'm from California. But it depends on the person. If they are a creeper—I've had creepers before—I'll just say I'm from California. I know there are people who are generally just interested and curious. I'll let them know I'm half Colombian. I do think of myself as half Colombian. But I do definitely think of myself as White, American, and Californian, too. Half Co-

lombian because it sounds more eccentric, in a sense. I'm trying to take pride into my culture that I am different. You do find yourself to be different in such a White community such as Green City.

If I were to draw a portrait of myself with flags of my origin, this is how I'd think about it: I'm really close to my dad. His mother was Irish and I was named after her, which is the Irish. I connect to my father through the Irish side. So that's what I would do, because to me I really appreciate people's cultures and where people are from, and I feel like that's where my family has come from—Ireland and Colombia, so that's what I would have drawn— a Colombian flag and an Irish flag—not a U.S. flag.

I can go from A to B, and I take advantage. Where do I fit and how am I going to use my heritage? I unconsciously do this. I get teased by other people, for example, "Oh, you don't speak Spanish? Like, you're Colombian and you don't speak Spanish?" We'll be going out to the bars and I'll start dancing and I definitely do dance a little bit like "Hispanic" with a lot more booty than most people. They'll be like, "Oh, hey, like, that's your Colombian side." It's always, "Hey, you're Colombian, you should do this." Or, "Why can't you do this, you're Colombian?"

I definitely do feel like I'm part of two worlds, the American side and the Spanish side. On my mom's side there is definitely that Latino background. We're very close. We talk to each other all the time. I'm on the phone every day with my mom, every other day with my aunt. I pretty much call them every day. When I'm home, I'm cuddling and I'm kissing my mom, you know. She's always stroking my hair, taking care of me. She always wants to take care of me. Where, with my dad's side, we're not very close with my dad's side, but it's more like, "You do it." "Oh, I love you" once every other day. Or, "I'll talk to you" every four months, kind of deal. There's totally less touching. It's more like how I grew up is touching. My White family is not like that. For example, I was at my aunt's house on Sunday, and I was sick, so my aunt was taking care of me. My little cousin, who is 15...we were spooning and cuddling and spent the night and we shared the same bed. Now that I think of it, the Colombian family culture is there and it's about loving and coming over for Sunday dinner and talking to each other. But like my dad's side is like...I don't talk to them...every two years maybe.

I think it's just mostly the Spanish side where there are expectations. I think a lot of it is like, you should dance. You should be able to look like Shakira. You should be able to know how to move your hips. When I go out with my friends and we go dancing, my friends say, "Your hips don't stop moving." But I think it's like...It's an annoying situation. Some people are like, "Oh my God, you really know how to move." And some are like, "You're such a whore." So does that mean then that if you're Latina, you are somehow promiscuous? My roommates are always like, "Oh, you're Colombian so you're naturally totally sexy," because they don't have the curves. But there are Colombians who are not—like my cousin who is 25.

Teaching

When I am a teacher I would want my students' parents to come and talk about their country and their history. I really like history. And I would tie in civil wars from other countries. I would definitely have days where parents could come and teach students about certain things from their country. I would be so excited if there was a parent from a different country and who could talk about their experiences and about America and what they thought about America. For example, if some of them are getting their U.S. citizenship we could talk about how to get your U.S. citizenship—you have to know more than an actual American does. So, it's hard to pass that test. Americans can't pass the test. They were asking me questions from the citizenship test the other day, and I was like, "What the heck is that?" I would bring parents in and have them teach…because they're supposed to know. It would be great for them. As a child, to have your parent come in would be great. I would do anything possible to bring their culture into the classroom.

If I were to give advice to teachers, I'd say, don't block their culture. If their culture makes them somebody, don't shut it down. Invite it and make it part of their life, bring it into the classroom. I think that's what killed me because my kindergarten teacher, she shut my mom out in a sense and said, "Don't raise your daughter in that culture." And that probably hurt in the long term. It's like a washing machine for me. You're just all over the place. Let students' cultures be teachers' main focus. That's what America is about: letting cultures be what they want to be here. We're not a mixing pot, we're a cupcake…or a fruitcake. You want to bring everything in but still preserve more—not melt them down.

It killed me…it definitely…there were so many mistakes. I finished reading this case study book from a class, and that made me understand my mom so much more in the sense like, how she was…like I think I was able to understand where my mom was coming from. Looking back it's like, okay, so that's how you grew up. She never explained her culture to us. And so, I think that's why there's so much pain between my family. If she was able to bring her culture in we'd be able to understand more.

I think teachers could be more open to different identities. Teachers should be more open to different ideas. If they could see more outside the box sometimes, that would help.

White Identity

I think there is a White or Caucasian identity. I've talked to people in class that I'm really good friends with and they grew up in a White community where they never knew someone of a different race or color, nor would they talk to them. As a White person, you don't realize how much racism there is on other people. Whites never dealt with that. To be White is to be privileged, financially privileged. I benefited. My parents paid for my college. I don't have a job right now. School is a lot of work, but I get a monthly allowance and when I was growing up whatever I wanted, I could do. But it was never to the extreme, but definitely it was privileged.

There is something to be said for hard work...we had to work hard at home with my mom. I remember every Saturday we had to clean the house. The house had to be spotless. My jobs were the toilets. I would be on my back scrubbing with a toothbrush. I found out that's what she had to do in Colombia to the point that if you didn't see your face on their tile floors, you were whipped. Which isn't fair for any child, but that was her culture and so that's all she knew. That was hard. It was so different when I would see my White friends who were waiting for the maid to come in while I knew that we were doing better financially than them. Why am I cleaning, you know?

There are so many different things that were in opposition to that privilege. I remember my mom, she's really strict. You could not talk back to her or she would slap you, hard, hard. She's super skinny and tall. It hurt. It hurt bad. I saw my White friends screaming and yelling at their parents and telling them to shut up. I would be in the back of the car and saying, "Oh my God, you just told your mom to shut up—your mom." Their parents would shut up. How are you talking to your parents? Even my Dad said, "Don't talk back to me. Don't you dare talk back to me," and we never did. We knew when we had to just shut it.

I definitely saw the difference in the way we were raised. White parents would never touch their kids. I remember in kindergarten, I couldn't count. It was one of those little snowmen connect the dot, 1 through 20, and I couldn't even count that. I couldn't do it. I didn't know it. My mom was like, "What is this number?" She went and grabbed a belt and she whipped me. I mean seriously, I'm five years old.

Future

I really want to learn Spanish. I'm mad at myself that I didn't stick with it, and I'm mad that I didn't force my mom to speak Spanish to me. I want to learn it because it's my culture. It's who my family is. It's part of where I come from. I would learn Gaelic, too, if I could, but Spanish is a goal of mine, so we'll see. But I just couldn't speak Spanish with my mom at all. I'd have to be like in a country where I'm forced to learn it, like survival of the fittest. My ex-boyfriend speaks it better than I do. Learning to speak it doesn't make me nervous. It's the academics of it, where I have to be tested and if I have to do homework that makes me nervous. I would love to. But if I study, it's more like…it's just to learn Spanish, it's not to go and like learn it and get a grade for it. It's just to be cultured.

I love bilingual education. The more I learn about it, I want to teach in a bilingual school. When I have kids, I'm sending them to a bilingual school. They have no option. I want them to learn languages—people respect other people when they speak more than two languages. Spanish wasn't passed to me—my language…my mom's Spanish, so I feel sad. It's part of me and where the family comes from. My grandparents. I'm crying now. They're really old. I'm not close to my grandparents on either side. It sucks because I know my grandpa is a really good guy. I hear that he tells the funniest jokes, like dirty jokes, really dirty jokes, and you can't translate them. It hurts that I can't talk to him and hear those jokes. He's got Alzheimer's and my grandma, she's in a wheelchair. I've only seen them four times in my life. If I spoke Spanish I would know them better. I would call them—always at Christmas.

I'm still just trying to figure out about myself—there's so much. You don't think about identity until now. I think I want teachers to think, "You do what you can, not because of where you came from or where your family's from." I just want them to believe in kids like me. If I'm having trouble, it's not because I get my problems from my mom or dad, it's because of me. Look beyond my skin or my background. Just because my dad's a lawyer and because my mom didn't finish school and my dad's smart, but then here's my mom who is not as smart, doesn't mean I got my problems in school from my mom's side. If I were a teacher, you don't even look at where kids came from…look at who they are as a person at the moment. They don't look at their culture determining like how they're gonna do. Look at their culture and how that benefits them as a resource, but don't think, "You're Mexican; therefore, you're gonna flunk school." Kids shouldn't have to think, "I'm not gonna excel in anything," or, "I'm Asian; I'm book smart and socially awkward." That doesn't mean anything. Look at the history of the Chinese and how we discovered firecrackers. Look at Mexicans and how amazing the Mayans were. Use that, but don't use, "I'm Hispanic. I'm really dumb," or "I'm European. I'm smart." That's how I would be as a teacher—using culture as an advantage, not a disadvantage.

My cousin is the youngest; she's 15, half Austrian and half Colombian. She's being forced to learn German, so she's in honors and she's in a Ger-

*man class and a Spanish class right now. My aunt actually took her to Co-
lombia last summer, and she can now speak Spanish because she had gone to
Colombia and learned Spanish. She's going to Europe this summer to learn
German. So I think that she, out of anyone, is the most culturally diverse, in a
sense. She's always telling me about Colombian culture. I think, finally, my
uncle and aunt thought, "You know what, this is who we are, it's part of you.
And we want our family to grow from it." I think she's definitely benefited
from everyone else making mistakes. Now she's starting to learn both languages. She can speak Spanish now; at 15 she could speak it because she's
had the experiences.*

Authentically Ana

Who is Ana? Much of her testimonio works within and around who Ana is as
a person in the world. Like many in their early 20s, Ana is searching for her
identity but is struggling with the multiple and often binding images that are
placed upon her by her school, society, friends, teachers, and parents (Erikson, 1975). She shifts between identities that are incompletely clear to her: a
Colombian young woman *"without a culture"*[2] and a White upper middle
class American whose family she feels doesn't have a culture (*"I really don't
have one at all—none"*). Meanwhile she's surrounded by flows of the mate-
rial and social worlds that pervade her life at school. The wrestling match for
a single and solid identity is much written about in postcolonial literature as
fraught with confusing colonial flows of authenticity, hierarchies, binaries,
and marginality. Similarly, Willy Colón, a self-described Puerto Rican who
is an American citizen, wrote about the conflicts between how he sees himself and how he is seen:

> Now look at my case; I'm Puerto Rican and I consider myself Puerto Rican. But
> when I go to the island I'm something else to them. And in New York, when I had to
> get documents, I was always asked: "Where are you from?" "I'm American."
> "Yeah, but from where?" They led me to believe that I wasn't from America, even
> though I have an American birth certificate and citizenship…. I live between both
> worlds. (Márquez, 1982, as cited in Flores & Yúdice, 2008, p. 347)

Colón was not accepted as legitimately Puerto Rican nor American, given his
appearance and lives "between both worlds." Troublingly, authorities in New
York had the power to spur Colón to internally strip himself of his American
citizenship: "They led me to believe that I wasn't from America." Similarly,
in describing her struggle to find her identity, Ana feels as though she is be-

ing "*tossed*" around in a "*washing machine*" and recognizes there is a "*hole*" where her identity should be. However, during the course of her testimonio, Ana finds solid ground for a moment and states, "*I'm not just one or the other, I'm all of it. I always looked at it as negative, but it's a positive thing—a talent, that you're able to go in and out, a talent.*" The conflict and clashes of the different flows of American Whiteness and Colombianness that make up and constrain her identities are part and parcel of being a minoritized person in a neocolonial context.

The neocolonial flows that serve to define and capture Ana include cultural and linguistic essentializations, marginalizing structures of her schooling, authenticity, and mimicry, for example. That said, Ana's testimonio is not simply a story of neocolonial forces creating cultural and linguistic loss, it is also a story of talking back to neocolonial structures and the people who support them. As Ana struggles to understand and reclaim her identities, she has often been able to reverse the stare of the neocolonial powers from surveilling her towards aiming her gaze at neocolonial powers. This ability to look at and recognize the ambivalence of the neocolonizer's contradictory messages and hidden agendas seems to have allowed her access to recognition of wrongdoing, and to take action towards self-definition. In the process of facing the neocolonizer, Ana is able to disrupt hierarchies and binaries, recognize the advantages of her hybridity and homelessness, as well as begin to plan ways to reclaim her culture and language. Through her performance of postcolonial flows, Ana is able to engage in a process of decolonization:

> Decolonization is the process of revealing and dismantling colonialist power in all its forms. This includes dismantling the hidden aspects of those institutional and cultural forces that had maintained the colonialist power and that remain even after political independence is achieved. (Ashcroft, et al., 2000, p. 63)

Cultural and Linguistic Loss, Recognition, and Reclamation

The neocolonial structure relies on the assumption that Eurocentric knowledge and ways of being of those in power are superior to those of minoritized groups. Curricular decisions are made in the neocolonial school that target the exclusion—and indeed, loss—of the history, knowledge, and culture of illegitimate groups (McCarthy, Giardina, Harewood, & Park, 2005). One of the results of such a powerful institution as the school denying the rich postcolonial flows of diverse youth is assimilation and cultural and linguistic loss of a "lesser" identity. For example, the pervasive use of binaries in schooling helps make the distinction between desirable ways of knowing and being and those knowledges and ways of being we should consider expendable. Maxine

Greene (2001) stated that "educators have become accustomed to notions of multiculturalism and diversity that focus on binary relations or dualities: majority/minority; White/Black; center/periphery; developed/underdeveloped" (p. vii). When describing herself, throughout her testimonio, Ana seems to fall back on two clearly distinct identities, using a binary of Colombian/White. Each side of the binary can be described as an essentialized and pure characteristic. Both her school and family encourage the shedding of a Colombian identity. As a result of her early schooling experience (when her mother was told to stop speaking to her in Spanish), this separation between Colombian and White is maintained as somehow a true distinction. It was as if speaking both Spanish and English would blur the line between the two sides of the binary, Colombian/White, and perhaps elevate her Colombian identity to a higher status. Ana's parents further legitimize this sense of clear margins around each side of the binary and the inferiority of her Colombian culture with their disdain for learning more than one language. Somehow, being bilingual might taint her pure American identity, made up of one language, one culture: "*two languages isn't a good idea.*"

Loss of the Spanish language for Ana is a painful reminder of her lack of knowledge about her Colombian family, culture, and ancestry. She cries when she talks about the cultural loss of not being able to communicate with her grandparents in Colombia because she cannot speak Spanish. Ana talks a great deal about how Spanish was essentially taken from her and voices regret, casting a net of blame on her mother, herself, and her family: "*Academically, I probably would have done better if I had the advantage of learning Spanish. My mom is kicking herself right now.*" But the neocolonial classroom with its overwhelmingly monolingual focus is much to blame:

> Language is a fundamental site of struggle for post-colonial discourse because the colonial process itself begins in language. The control over language by the imperial centre—whether achieved by displacing native languages, by installing itself as a "standard" against other variants which are constituted as "impurities," or by planting the language of empire in a new place—remains the most potent instrument of cultural control.... A systematic education and indoctrination installed the language and thus the reality on which it was predicated as preeminent. (Ashcroft, Griffiths, & Tiffin, 1995, p. 283)

Through her teacher education program, Ana is recognizing that the linguistic colonization in schooling that she experienced hurt her chances of academic success. Research has shown that allowing students to use their primary language in the classroom actually helps rather than hinders long-term academic success (Thomas & Collier, 2002). This is an aspect of the ambivalent nature of colonialism that Ana has now pinpointed, allowing her to critique neocolonial structures of schools. As Ana enters the teaching force, there is the possibility she will be able to critique and perhaps reverse the damage done to her academically and socially through her schooling experiences, recognizing that blame also falls on the school. Indeed, it was Ana's kindergarten teacher who gave her mother the advice to not speak Spanish with her daughter. This is exactly what Homi Bhabha (1994) explained will be colonialism's own seeds of destruction. The unwillingness of the neocolonizer to allow the colonized to be exactly like the colonizer will eventually lead to the colonized recognizing that they are restricted to being not-quite-exact copies of the colonizer. Once minoritized students realize that even though they walk, talk, and even think like White European Americans they still won't be allowed into the clubhouse because they will never look exactly like the powerful, they can begin to critique the neocolonizer.

Edging towards another criticism of the neocolonizer, Ana recognizes her own stereotype of the Colombian side of the Colombian/White binary. Ana discusses her negative view of Colombia, her mother's homeland. She admits her negative associations with Colombia—both from her travel there and what the news media say about the place: "*I got really discouraged there. I feel like I'm kind of culture biased. From what I've heard, from the news, is that it's an unfit, unsafe place to be.*" Even when she explains that her cousins are now beginning to travel in Colombia and learn Spanish, she halfheartedly mentions Spain as a place appropriate for her to learn Spanish—excluding the possibility of the country, Colombia, that seems to be the most convenient place to go to reclaim a sense of her Colombian identity and learn Spanish.

Ana is much more sure about wanting to reclaim her Spanish language:

> *I really want to learn Spanish. I'm mad at myself that I didn't stick with it, and I'm mad that I didn't force my mom to speak Spanish to me. I want to learn it because it's my culture. It's who my family is. It's part of where I come from. I would learn Gaelic, too, if I could, but Spanish is a goal of mine, so we'll see.*

Ana wants to learn Spanish to reclaim her Colombian, Spanish-speaking identity and culture—not to please others or fit a mold. She also explains that her children will have no option but to go to a bilingual school.

Naming Marginalization in Schooling

Neocolonial discourse—or what those in power promote in actions and words—maintains that there is a center and a margin. At the center are those with power and knowledge, for example, educational policymakers and teachers. Those relegated to the margins are those who receive and submit to the center's power and knowledge, for example, students and minoritized groups like English learners and students with dis/Abilities. Neocolonial power "places particular groups of people in the margins, signifying them as 'others' who are less advanced in thinking, underdeveloped, unqualified to speak, and undeniably less human than those with power (e.g. physically colonized, people of color, women, poor, children)" (Cannella & Viruru, 2004, p. 60). Ana turns the tables on the center and, from the margin, explains how she was unfairly marginalized in her high school and clearly names her high school for what it was:

> *My high school was racist. I feel like I was always put in the dumb classes. It is a huge school, a national honors school, a blue ribbon school—half White and half not. We had a large Mexican culture. I was always put in the dumb classes. I did well in them and the teachers liked me, but it was always full of Mexicans.*

Ana was physically marginalized by being placed in the lower academic track classrooms. Indeed, neocolonial schools are a sorting system: "For immigrant communities of color, education often serves to prepare youth to take their place in the racial, class, and gender hierarchies of the nation" (El-Haj, 2010, p. 245). In the second half of high school Ana was placed in an all minority college-track program that looked and sounded good. But again, she was seen and categorized as a troublemaker in this new classroom because of the color of her skin. When she asked for help of her White teacher she was told to figure it out herself—meanwhile the teacher would expend great effort helping other students. This had a profound effect on Ana:

> *No, it didn't feel fair, and I kind of gave up...I wish I would have dropped that class, to be honest, but I just gave up. I slept all the time in that class. I just didn't even care about her anymore.*

This and other experiences allowed Ana to pronounce her high school structure and system as racist. The neocolonizer's unwillingness to support her in being an exact copy of a "good student" revealed the neocolonizer's ambivalence (Bhabha, 1994). This created an obvious fissure in the neocolonial school structure for Ana. Likewise, "people from racially or ethnically subordinated groups—those who are not viewed as true national insiders—often face barriers to full and equitable participation despite their legal status as citizens" (El-Haj, 2010, p. 245).

Ana is very aware that her school marginalized her according to her brown skin color: "My identities didn't matter much to the school except when it concerned placing me in class. They placed me in Latino classes, but other than that, it didn't matter... It was just the racist placement that was obvious." Ana recognizes that school officials only saw her skin color when it benefited them: (a) placing her in a lower-track course of study to keep her from gaining power in a mainstream or an honors course, and (b) displaying her face on a fundraising brochure to show that the school does not segregate on the water polo team. Ana's ability to name the neocolonial flow of marginalization through an imagined hierarchy of races cracks the façade of neocolonial neutrality.

Reversing Capture: Surveillance, Authenticity, Mimicry, and Colonial Desire

Ana is metaphorically captured by four powerful neocolonial flows: surveillance, authenticity, mimicry, and colonial desire. As neocolonial flows attempt to encapsulate and, indeed, permeate her body, she is able to reverse and dispel them as they flow around and even flow from her. As complicated as it may seem, as Ana experiences neocolonization, she also engages in decolonization of her experience:

> Processes and methodologies of decolonization do not take a linear, goal-oriented, rationalist form. Decolonial possibilities can offer knowledges from the margin, unthought-of perspectives/life experiences, hidden histories, and disqualified voices as positions from which to reconceptualize discourses, individual values, and actions. (Cannella & Viruru, 2004, pp. 123–124)

The processes of neocolonization and colonization affect one another and, as we will see, are concurrent (Bhabha, 1994).

Surveillance

Ana's testimonio is peppered with powerful observations or surveillance of the neocolonial structures in her life—most often brought about from recognition of neocolonial ambivalence—a contradiction between what the neocolonizer claims and lived reality. For example, Ana recognizes that the neocolonial flow of the primacy of American meritocracy is not reflected in her high school, where people are judged based on their appearance rather than on how hard they work (Foucault, 1977).

Furthermore, it is important to note that Ana is aware of the neocolonizers' judging gaze from a young age. The perceptions that teachers exhibit can be "picked up" by youth and internalized:

> *Mrs. Tohsaku was the first teacher that saw me. I was never a problem, but she was the first that didn't look at me like I was stupid, didn't look at me like, "You're never gonna get caught up in school!*

Although Mrs. Tohsaku, her second grade teacher, surveilled Ana with an encouraging gaze, throughout her schooling Ana was observed and labeled as not measuring up to a Eurocentric ideal. The neocolonial tool of surveillance through the grades was doubly powerful because in Ana's case, she knew that she would not only suffer punishment from the school based on her performance, she would also be punished by her parents (in this case, ironically, for her lack of Spanish prowess): "*I had to come home every Friday with a piece of paper with my grade that was signed by my teachers…my weekend was dependent on that.*" Here, grades were used as an instrument of surveillance wherein the neocolonial school's flow of evaluation and judgment then became a tool for her mother to reinstate and reify the mission of the school to civilize and marginalize her. She was verbally and physically punished and disciplined for transgressions. And as another example of the multinodal processes of neocolonization, her mother did not just punish Ana for her failure to play the "good student" in Spanish class, but she also berated her for not being an authentic Spanish-speaking Colombian.

Authenticity

What does it mean to be authentically Colombian? Authentically White?

> *I get teased by other people, for example, "Oh, you don't speak Spanish? Like, you're Colombian and you don't speak Spanish?…. They'll be like, "Oh, hey, like, that's your Colombian side." It's always, "Hey, you're Colombian, you should do this." Or, "Why can't you do this, you're Colombian?"*

Ana's Colombian appearance is seen as signifying some sort of biologically determined, pure and authentic core. Her friends (see example above), family, and school (see examples below) remind her when she is and is not exhibiting an authentic Colombian identity. The construction and maintenance of the authentic "other" is one of the ways that the neocolonizer can marginalize minoritized students. It is the unwavering fixity of a stereotypical authentic Colombian as Spanish speaker that allows the neocolonizer to pigeonhole Ana as "other" (Bhabha, 1994).

The pressure placed on Ana by her parents and the school to achieve in the study of the Spanish language echoes colonialism's desire to pin down minoritized students, in this case, as authentic Spanish speakers. Somehow, Spanish should naturally flow out of Ana's mouth, a language genetically written into her body.

> *And so, I was really grateful when my mom only said to me in Spanish, "How could you? You're Colombian. You should be able to speak Spanish. Why can't you speak*

it? This should seem natural to you." And I thought to myself, "Yeah. Okay. The only time you hear mom speaking Spanish is on the phone. Yeah, I totally know Spanish, right?" My parents went and told her to stop tutoring me. My mom came out and told me, "You're so stupid...but it doesn't make any difference. You should be able to speak it. You should be fluent."

Ana's response to being demeaned for not being authentically, indeed, biologically Colombian enough (as evidenced by her lack of Spanish language achievement) is clever, and allows her to reclaim the Spanish language, gathering it up so that it is under her control:

After that, I decided, "I'm not taking Spanish. I'm going to continuously fail Spanish and cry over everything. My parents will demean me. I decided, yeah, screw Spanish. I think if I travelled abroad and stayed in a country for six months and picked it up, instead of being forced to learn it in school, I'd have learned more.

Ana's is such a powerful response, turning neocolonialism inside out and right side out again. First, in kindergarten, Ana is denied Spanish, her linguistic birthright, purportedly so that she can succeed in the neocolonial school context. Next, she is tutored in it—forced to learn it by both her parents and the school (notice, the school mission always has primacy). Then, academic support is yanked away. She is denied help to learn her mother's language, and is declared deficient because she is not more essentially, purely Colombian. Finally, in a not-so-expected turn, she folds back on her mother's language and her mother and decides she will never take Spanish if it means she will be demeaned—even though it is a key to her culture that has been denied her. Interestingly, Ana knows that even her mother, who is claiming to be the source of Colombian authenticity in this case, may not be seen as an authentic Colombian: "*when she goes down* [to visit Colombia]*, she has to be careful because people might think she's not Colombian anymore—or they can tell she's not Colombian enough.*" Ana recognizes that the definitions of what makes a Colombian are fluid, and she refuses capture by any one of them if it means she will cry and be demeaned.

Contrast the fixed conceptions of an authentic Colombian above with Ana's more nuanced descriptions of authentic Americans:

Being American is different. If you're born here, you're an American. You're not more American if you have White skin. If you're born on this soil and you're raised here since day one, even if your family is from Mexico or wherever else, you're American. My mom is American now. She has had her citizenship for the last 5 years, and that took 10 years for her to convince her to get her citizenship. She's American now, but I don't think she's American—and it's okay. She's not American to me. She has citizenship because of my dad's marriage, but other than that, I don't think so. I don't see her as an American. I can see my Aunt Rena (my mom's oldest

sister), who I'm really close to, who lives here—I could call her American…but not
my mom. From what I've heard, it takes three generations of living somewhere in a
country to be considered that ethnicity. So these two generations, to be born, it's a
standing that you have to grow.

Ana seems to describe three distinct hierarchical levels of authenticity of Americans:

1. An American by birth or legal citizenship (i.e., of any skin color, by birth, by marriage—her mom).
2. People who seem American (her aunt).
3. Longtime Americans of special standing.

At first, Ana claims there is no authentic American based on physical appearance, but there is a gut sense of who an American is when you meet them. Her aunt is and her mom is not. In describing the third category of American, she says it takes time to become American. It is as if there is an exclusive club you enter when you become American for which the rules for entry are not written and remain unclear. It takes at least 60 years to accomplish this *"standing"* so that no one individual can actually join the club unless many before them have toiled endlessly on the nebulous task of becoming an American. This gives a great deal of power to the hegemonic system of schooling and society, and lets the multinodal neocolonial system do its work to marginalize "inauthentic Americans." The neocolonial system is thus left alone, without surveillance or critique, unquestioned and accepted. Separately, all three tiers of Americans make Americanness look freedom loving, desirable, and earned. However, when noting the tiered system, it is obvious how this neocolonial structure promotes the naturalness of a hierarchy of human worth based on (in)visible rules of becoming an authentic and legitimate American. One of the subterranean rules of becoming American is related to what an authentic American body looks like, which I will now describe.

Mimicry

As discussed in the introduction, mimicry is a powerful flow of the neocolonizer. The neocolonizer requires the minoritized (who also develops the desire) to look and act more like European American Whites—to show that they are a reformed but recognizable "other." Mimicry plays out on Ana's body. In a neocolonial context, the differences between the minoritized body and the European American body are seen as proof of the supposed natural inferiority of the minoritized body. Frantz Fanon's groundbreaking psychoanalytic work about the minoritized body's visual difference foregrounds the anxiety and self-loathing engendered by colonialism's "othering" of non-White physical attributes. In *Black Skin, White Masks* (1967), Fanon described Black or mixed race women's desire to whiten and bleach themselves and their lives—indeed to be more essentially White. Ana's parents' and her own desire to look more like the neocolonizer with blond hair is illustrative—even though the situation that necessitates the lightening upsets her:

> Growing up, I was always angry about these things. Why is America like this? Why is it that my country is supposed to be one way, but then in high school, everyone makes decisions based on looks and what you're supposed to look like?

Here, Ana recognizes colonial ambivalence: the contradiction of what the United States says and what it does. In the next sentence of her testimonio, she seems to acquiesce but, perhaps, is engaging in a mockery of European American White blond imagery by dying her hair a color that so contrasted with her dark skin:

> I was always wanting to dye my hair a lighter brown. Eventually my mom said, well, let's go get it professionally done. And so we did. I came out blond. For two years my hair was blond, like platinum blond. And I hated it—so badly. The first six months I was like, "Okay, it looks cool. It's fun, it's different." ...I was done. I wanted to change the color of my hair back to brown. I wanted my natural hair color. My parents and I got into the biggest fight, and they were just like, "No! You have to go back...the blond looks so good on you. Why would you want to change it?" I said, "Are you serious? Like, I want my natural hair color. How many people are fighting for their kids to keep their natural hair color? I want my natural color back. I don't want to be blond anymore. I don't look good." Two days later, I was back in the salon getting my hair dyed blond.

Ana's wanting to return to her natural color after experimenting with dying her hair from dark brown to blond was denied by her Colombian mother and her European American father. She acquiesces to her parents, but in a reversal of the flow of mimicry, Ana questions her parents' desire to lighten or whiten her. "*Why would you put someone who is super tan to the point of black tan in blond hair?*" She asks, "*Where do I fit?*" She recounts a talk with her White father about President Barack Obama that shows her parents have contradictory expectations of Ana (that mirror those of the neocolonizer) based on her skin color:

> My dad says, stupidly, "He's only half black." I just looked at him, and said, "Are you serious right now? Do you know who you're looking at? Like you're always telling me to put Hispanic on my application. Are you saying that I'm not Hispanic and I should just do it because I'm...I look Hispanic? So, like, what am I Dad?" He realized that he made a huge mistake and just shut up after that.

Ana's parents reify the expectations of the neocolonizer to mimic a White European appearance. She is powerfully analytic about her parents' lack of recognition of the solidity of her brownness. She notes that her White identity is all they legitimize, but then they double back and punish her for not being able to conjure a Colombian identity that is more based in her body and her biological makeup. As a native with blond hair, Ana may look like a reformed but recognizable "other," but in her mimicry she also mocks the neocolonizer with the incommensurable display of dark skin and platinum blond hair (Ashcroft et al., 1995; Bhabha, 1994).

Colonial Desire

Robert Young (1995) described colonial desire as sexualized colonialist discourse. The neocolonizer seeks to define minoritized people as performing stimulating or exciting difference that both marginalizes and minimizes the "other." At times, in her testimonio, Ana seems to reify the image of a sexualized native other in describing herself: *"there are times when that crazy flirtatious Colombian person comes out"* and *"we'll be going out to the bars and I'll start dancing and I definitely do dance a little bit like 'Hispanic' with a lot more booty than most people."* The sexualized and exoticized colonized body is evident in postcolonial literature. The history of putting the newly discovered native "on display" for Europeans to judge and categorize as sexually primitive, exotic, and uncivilized is much documented. A most disturbing and well-known example is that of Saartjie Baartman, a Xhosa woman from South Africa who was brought to London in 1810 as a 20-year-old. She was displayed in a show as an example of a primitive sexual physique and became known as the "Hottentot Venus." After her death from smallpox, her genitalia were compared to that of an orangutan and they were then preserved and placed on display in the Musée de l'Homme in Paris. Baartman's body parts were finally returned by the museum to her homeland in 2002, but a casting of her genitalia still remains on display at the museum. Ana, because of her Colombian heritage and appearance, is expected to act and to be sexual:

> *I think it's just mostly the Spanish side where there are expectations. I think a lot of it is like, you should dance. You should be able to look like Shakira. You should be able to know how to move your hips. When I go out with my friends and we go dancing, my friends say, "Your hips don't stop moving." But I think it's like.... It's an annoying situation. Some people are like, "Oh my God, you really know how to move." And some are like, "You're such a whore." So does that mean then that if you're Latina, you are somehow promiscuous? My roommates are always like, "Oh, you're Colombian so you're naturally totally sexy," because they don't have the curves. But there are Colombians who are not—like my cousin who is 25.*

When reflecting upon it, Ana is able to recognize that there is no natural connection between being of Colombian descent and being able to dance or move in a sensuous way. Her peers' characterization of her as sexually deviant reproduces the neocolonizer's need to sexualize and put the "other" on display. Ana is able to both refute and perform the flow of essentialized Colombian colonial desire—an example of how both the neocolonial and the colonial flows are concurrent processes (Ashcroft et al., 2000; Willinsky, 1998).

Power in Homelessness

> The man who finds his homeland sweet is still a tender beginner; he to whom every soil is as his native one is already strong; but he is perfect to whom the entire world is as a foreign land. (Hugo of St. Victor, as cited in Said, 1979, p. 259)

One of the conditions of minoritized youth living in post-colonial times, is that of homelessness. Because of the historical, physical, and emotional displacement of minoritized youth in the United States, youth may find themselves searching for what constitutes home for them. Minoritized youth may be miles, years, and/or generations removed from their homeland(s) and are often not accepted as full citizens in a colonial or neocolonial nation. This may yield an experience of homelessness. By homelessness, I mean an internal place that is characterized by fluid, shifting, evolving, and negotiated meanings of home (Giroux, 2009; Sirriyeh, 2010).

Once youth recognize their homelessness, it can become a postcolonial flow of strength, wherein they have a unique and perhaps less muddled perspective as an outside observer of their homeland(s) and of their current "home." As Hugo of St. Victor claimed above, someone who sees all places as a foreigner, with the perspective that this distance brings, is in a desirable position. Likewise, Sintos Coloma (2008) discovered that his homelessness—living between American and Filipino identities—brought him both pain and pleasure. In her testimonio, Ana expresses both confusion and pride in her homelessness, and begins to recognize it as a *talent*—a postcolonial flow that she can use to her advantage.

Ana's inability to completely fit in as a White European person or as a Colombian person is clear when she describes walking with her brother in a street market in Colombia. Although they look Colombian, her brother "*stands out.*" Likewise, although Ana feels White and describes herself as White ("*I was the only White kid in this class*"), she is repeatedly seen as Colombian by her friends:

> *There's definitely that hole of where do I fit? It's kind of a joke between my friends. A lot of my friends here are White. They always say, "That's just Ana's crazy Co-lombian side coming out." Or when I don't do something that should be Latina…like, like dancing, cooking, or making really spicy foods…whatever people think Latinas should do, I'll be like, "Oops, I guess my White side is popping out!"*

Ana bends her White friends' stereotyping of her Latina or Colombian iden-tity back on itself, strategically utilizing her White background to claim status after it has been lowered by her White peers. She's effectively saying, "I'm White too," harnessing the power of her homelessness through recogni-tion of a White culture as an outsider-insider. At the same time, Ana is able to articulate the betweenness of her homelessness and recognize the ability to move between two or more worlds as a skill, rather than as the sad and pow-erless state often associated with the concept of homelessness:

> *I'm either A or B at the moment. Where do I fit? What do I call myself? I'm half Co-lombian or I'm just a regular American White person. A lot of people always ask me, "What ethnicity are you?" What do I say? I look Colombian but I feel like I act more White most of the time, but there are times where that crazy flirtatious Colom-bian person comes out. I can see my mom coming out. Homelessness is a good way to call it. I'm not just one or the other, I'm all of it. I always looked at it as negative, but it's a positive thing—a talent, that you're able to go in and out, a talent.*

Later, Ana applies the concept of homelessness as a talent to Obama, who she believes "*can think outside of the box,*" given he grew up in both the United States and Malaysia. Ana recognizes the goodness in being able to see from multiple perspectives—a condition of the postcolonial homeless person. As I will now show, homelessness is closely connected to being a hybrid per-son in post-colonial times.

Hybridity and Nationalism

Ana's multiple identities wherein she's "*able to go in and out*" is also de-scribed as hybridity. Her hybridity is evidenced in many ways, sometimes serving to decolonize and at others to reflect neocolonial flows. "*I do think of myself as half Colombian. But I do definitely think of myself as White, Ameri-can, and Californian, too.*" These many forms of identity (i.e., half Colom-bian, White, American, Californian) are negotiated in complex ways; they are produced by the neocolonizer interacting with minoritized people and deconstructing essentialist categories of identity (e.g., American). As seen above, Ana separates her identities as a Colombian and as a White person but also identifies with additional identities, sometimes separately and sometimes concurrently. She uses her hybrid identities strategically: "*I can go from A to*

B, and I take advantage. Where do I fit and how am I going to use my heritage? I unconsciously do this." Ana describes how she answers questions about her identity according to the questioner:

> *If asked where I am from, I usually say I am Californian, but if my mom asked what I am I would say half Colombian. If my dad or my family asked it's always, "I'm half Colombian." That's what I know people are asking for…because I'm darker. If I looked more White, they wouldn't be asking me that question at all.*

Unfortunately, this identification as "the reason why I am not White" reproduces neocolonial hierarchy of races where Whites don't have to explain their origin and people of color do—an outdated notion that if you are a person of color in the United States, you are unique given the census data that estimated that the 2009 U.S. population was over one-third non-White. But her response also shows that she recognizes the neocolonizers' essentializing gaze.

As Ana claims multiple national affiliations, she also essentializes herself as an eccentric Colombian. At the same time, she is aware of racism and will tell a "*creeper*" she is Californian, a more nebulous definition that strongly states her identity as White American—White Americans born here, when asked where they are from, give the specific state of their birth. She is also working to take pride in her Colombian heritage, which she claims has been essentially stripped away from her by her family and never acknowledged—except in neocolonial ways—by her school, family, and herself.

She emits a flow of hybridity by claiming multiple national affiliations of both Ireland and Colombia. This is a denial of the nationalistic farce of the American melting pot. As Subedi and Daza (2008) stated, "notions of (white) U.S. citizenship are constructed at the expense of local and global Others, which clearly subsumes the alternative ways minority subjects negotiate cultural citizenship" (p. 2). Ana does not want to "melt" and describes the United States as a "*cupcake" or a "fruitcake.*" She chooses identities that allow her to self-define and explains that she has a hybrid identity: "*I definitely do feel like I'm part of two worlds, the American side and the Spanish side.*" The examples she provides in this instance are of her Colombian family, who exhibit more physical love when she visits with them as compared with her dad's European White family that is more distant, individualistic, and intermittent in their expressions of care.

When explaining what she would like to do as a teacher based on her own experience of having hybrid identities, Ana said she would want to talk about the requirements for becoming an American citizen: "*You have to know more than an actual American does. So, it's hard to pass that test.*

Americans can't pass the test." Ana's exploration reverses the gaze back onto the neocolonizer, and again reveals a double standard: naturalized citizens are required to know more about the United States than Americans born here. Indeed, it is essential to ask, what makes a *real* American?

Urgent Messages for Teachers

Teachers can lead the way in decolonizing. Ana's second-grade teacher did this by telling Ana's mother:

> *"Why have your children not gone to Colombia? You need to take them to enrich them and enculturate them." That's when my mom really started making us travel. She started to speak Spanish to us, but I think at that point my brother and I were so removed from it that we'd respond with, "Mom's speaking Spanish. We don't understand you." And then we kind of pushed it off. But Mrs. Tohsaku was the one that said...they're your kids and they're different and that's a good thing.*

Teachers can be a source of reclaiming culture, heritage, and identity. The teacher here is an important and remembered part of decolonizing the hierarchy of races that seemed to be a defining part of Ana's family's and her own identity.

However, teachers must remain vigilant of their tendency to colonize. Even well-intentioned teachers can reify and essentialize cultures in their curriculum. For example, Ana's sixth-grade assignment to bring in food from her country of origin essentializes and diminishes Colombian culture as merely foods, fashion, and folklore. One could also ask why Ana chose Colombia rather than Austria or Ireland for her culture project and how Ana's project may have reified an essentializing conception of her Colombian culture: "*my mom...she made a juice cocktail. That's the only thing she's ever done Colombian in my school. I never ate Colombian food until I went to Colombia my sophomore year in college.*"

When Ana talks of her plans as a teacher she explains that she will bring students' cultures into the classroom: "*I would bring parents in and have them teach—because they are supposed to know.*" This is a direct acknowledgement of the value of the cultural flows of students' parents, and a proposal that they be invited to bring their knowledge into the neocolonial classroom as knowledge producers, rather than participate only as knowledge consumers of sanctioned Western-centric curriculum and teaching. She admonishes teachers to make student culture the center of their curriculum, saying that the lack of culture in her life was the cause of much pain and her figurative death—"*it killed me*"—at school and at home:

Let students' cultures be teachers' main focus. That's what America is about: letting cultures be what they want to be here. We're not a mixing pot, we're a cupcake…or a fruitcake. You want to bring everything in but still preserve more—not melt them down.

Further, Ana tells teachers to reverse the hierarchical flows they may wield to categorize and determine the futures of students:

Look at their culture and how that benefits them as a resource, but don't think, "You're Mexican; therefore, you're gonna flunk school." Kids shouldn't have to think, "I'm not gonna excel in anything" or, "I'm Asian; I'm book smart and socially awkward." That doesn't mean anything. Look at the history of the Chinese and how we discovered firecrackers. Look at Mexicans and how amazing the Mayans were. Use that, but don't use, "I'm Hispanic. I'm really dumb," or "I'm European. I'm smart." That's how I would be as a teacher—using culture as an advantage, not a disadvantage.

Teachers' use of a hierarchy of races in their judgment of students is completely evident to Ana. For as much as educators may like to deny that we don't teach that way—with hierarchies—we often do. It is the unfortunate hidden curriculum of the neocolonial classroom. For example, when I asked a group of preservice teachers to order random lists of people that I gave them (e.g., Blacks, immigrants, Europeans, etc.), they had similar responses to arranging the different groups according to perceived rank:

I learned that *I* am biased in my own way. It's hard to teach that we are *all* equal when society puts these stereotypes in our minds.

It was surprising how some just popped out as "better" than others. It was easy to let the places and people that were important to me guide my thinking. Seeing from a different perspective would really help this.

It made me recognize my bias and I felt so bad. We don't want to think we think that way. (Gallagher-Geurtsen, 2005)

Here, in Ana's recommendation to teachers, she is disrupting the tenets of biological determinism and a hierarchy of races. She recognizes that in her own education these hierarchies and binaries were institutionalized and, in fact, written onto her body, limiting her life possibilities and splintering her sense of self.

Ana closes her testimonio with a story of hope and redemption, wherein Ana's cousin is now being supported in reclaiming her identities that the neocolonial flows might obscure from her if she were not vigilant:

My cousin is the youngest; she's 15, half Austrian and half Colombian. She's being forced to learn German, so she's in honors and she's in a German class and a Span-

ish class right now. My aunt actually took her to Colombia last summer, and she can now speak Spanish because she had gone to Columbia and learned Spanish. She's going to Europe this summer to learn German. So I think that she, out of anyone, is the most culturally diverse, in a sense. She's always telling me about Colombian culture. I think, finally, my uncle and aunt thought, "You know what, this is who we are, it's part of you. And we want our family to grow from it." I think she's definitely benefited from everyone else making mistakes. Now she's starting to learn both languages. She can speak Spanish now; at 15 she could speak it because she's had the experiences.

Notes

1. Ana Smith is a 20-year-old college student from an upper middle income family who is studying to become a teacher. She is of Colombian and European descent, and physically appears more Colombian than White European.

2. All quotations from the testimonio are placed in italics with quotation marks in text and in italics for block quotes.

Chapter Three

Cynthia's[1] Testimonio

"When I Walk In to Tutor Them, They Think, 'A White Person Is Tutoring Me. I'm Brown. I Must Be Dumb,' so, if I Could Tan, Yes, I Would Definitely Tan."

People started pointing it out in sixth or seventh grade. I went to a small private school with all White people, so I fit right in physically but when my dad came to one of my games my friends said, "Oh, who's that? Is that your dad?" They had no clue. I grew up knowing that I had a White mother and I didn't even see my dad as darker—it didn't click until I was older. It dawned on me, "Oh yeah, I guess that whole side of the family is really, really dark."

Family

Most of my family is from California. My dad's side is from Mexico, but he was raised in Los Angeles. My parents were on vacation visiting my grandmother here when I was born. Then they just stayed here because neither of them graduated from high school, so they didn't have jobs. So they kind of just followed wherever the family was. I was raised by my grandmother, who got custody of me when I was five, but I was with her from two on. My grandmother was an educator who worked with a lot of inner city schools in child development. Her coworkers and all of her friends were different races, so I was raised with all sorts of cultures—people from the Middle East, African Americans, and a lot of Hispanics from Colombia and Mexico. That's why when growing up I didn't even realize that the people I was talking to and those in my family are brown-skinned. I went to a private school with a little more diversity but not as much as would be in the public schools.

I have two older brothers and we moved all of the time. My two older brothers lived with us for a couple of years and moved back and forth between my dad and my grandma—they got to choose because they were older. My oldest brother is actually really dark, like my dad. The next brother is a little bit darker than me and I'm the one that just doesn't fit in because I don't tan. I'm the one with lighter hair. I took my mom's side, the European side.

Spanish

My grandmother encouraged me to take Spanish from fourth grade on and I hated it, so I never really picked it up. My dad lost a lot of his Spanish. He was raised speaking Spanish, but he never spoke it, so the only real Spanish I had was if I would speak to his mom. She was from Mexico and she would speak to me every now and then, but it never really clicked. I didn't see my dad very often.

I hated Spanish in elementary school because all of my friends hated it and it was hard. Since I was learning English, I didn't see the point of learning another language because it didn't even dawn on me, again, that I had half of a family that spoke Spanish. I started taking Latin and Spanish in sixth and seventh grades and I didn't like the teacher. When I got into high school, I was forced to take a language and my grandma pushed me to continue through four years of high school; whereas, all of my friends only took two years. My tenth-grade year I had a great teacher and I really liked listening to the language. At that point, it dawned on me that I'd really like to speak to the other half of my family that didn't speak a lot of English. Through the last two years of high school and through college I just continued with it. My junior year I was offered a volunteer opportunity to go to Honduras for the summer and work. I really wanted to teach and work with children, and then when I found out it was an all Spanish-speaking community in the middle of nowhere, I jumped on it, and that's really where I started picking up the Spanish.

I was placed with another girl in Honduras, two and a half hours away from the closest city. No running water, no electricity. We taught classes on everything from English to concepts like what's biodegradable and what's not biodegradable, games, science, math—basically everything that they wouldn't get in the schools there because their schools are just basically concrete rooms with a couple of desks. We lived there for almost seven weeks with a host family learning the language and interacting with the culture there, cut off from anything technologically advanced. We ate a small amount of beans and rice three times a day, so I had a lot of peanut butter in my bag. I was only 17, so I loved it. It was a great experience. Now I have a Spanish minor that I just finished. I also realized if I'm going into teaching, I'd really like to work in inner city schools, and I thought Spanish would be helpful.

Being American

From my travel to Honduras and other traveling throughout my life, I have a different perspective on what makes someone an American. I have a really hard time with people saying that an American is someone who is born on American soil—from California to the Northeast. An American is someone who lives, works and contributes to society in some way, whether it's landscapers or custodians or paying bills. I don't think you need to be documented to be an American citizen. Part of the reason I think this is so is because North America, so much of it, was considered Mexico, or it was Mexico to begin with. Anyone who is living here, trying to make a living and giving back to society is an American. Voting and not complaining about the way the current situation is unless they've actually tried to have a say in it, makes you an American. If you have family ties here, you're American. Unfortunately, some people think, especially here, that an American is someone who pledges allegiance to only one specific country and who should not have a tie with any other country. The mindset is, "It's just us and everyone should just worry about themselves." I don't think an American is someone who offers justice to those living within a certain area, rather, Americans are people who are willing to help those in other countries. Part of being an American and being called an American and an active citizen is knowing when to jump out of our own shells and help other people in other countries, like Haiti.

Cross-Cultural Experiences

My ideas come from my experiences observing cultures and traveling. Most of the contact I've had with my dad was when I was little. As I got a little bit older and it started dawning on me that I have another half of the family that's from another country, I actually made more of an effort to have a relationship with them, whether it was talking to them or visiting with them more often. When I went to Honduras people would say, "Well, where is your dad from?" And I would say, "Oh, my dad's side is from Mexico," then they'd ask me about it. Then they'd say, "Well, why are you so pale? What do you know about your family?" I realized I had no idea. So, my junior and senior years I started making more contact and talked to them on a weekly basis. I went back a couple of summers to stay with my grandma in Mexico. I felt kind of ignorant not knowing about the Mexican side of my family. By watching them, staying with them for a couple of weeks or just visiting with them and watching their day-to-day life, that's where I've gotten the majority of my ideas. Also, growing up, my grandmother was really into traveling. From her perspective as a teacher, she didn't think you could really get everything from just the textbooks, so I had a lot of opportunities to travel to Europe and all over. I'm really observant, and would stand back, watch, and see how people lived their day-to-day lives.

Being pale never bothered me because I knew I couldn't change that. I actually really liked it when people pointed it out, because it showed that I did have a little bit more diversity. If you could go up to someone and assume someone's background off of skin tone, that means that you really don't know much about genetics or anything. When people would say, "You're so pale but your dad's so dark," I actually learned to really like it because it showed that I was a little bit different. But I didn't want to be different when I was younger. It wasn't until the seventh and eighth grades that I started really embracing it.

Identity

When I describe myself, I like to say that my dad's side is from Mexico. On the stupid little test forms that we have to mark off, I usually just put "other" because there's never really anything listed that's appropriate, because I'm a little bit of everything. I'm half Hispanic, but then the other half is everything. When I self-identify, it also depends on the situation. If someone says, "Oh, where are your roots from?" then I just say, "My dad's side's from Mexico and my grandma's is from Europe and is Native American," but if it's not brought up or anything, they can think what they want, I guess. I have called myself Mexican American, especially when introducing myself to people if I'm around my dad or my two older brothers. They don't see a resemblance, so I'll introduce myself as Mexican American. If I'm by myself and no one asks or no one cares, I don't feel I need to say anything if no one else is saying anything because around certain groups it just doesn't matter. Then there are times when I know not to self-identify. Because of my Hispanic last name, people would ask when I'd apply for scholarships and for interviews and I think there's a lot of stuff I didn't get awarded. It always made me wonder if it's because I did identify as Mexican American when they asked about my last name. In high school, especially my freshman and sophomore year when they would tell me, "Join this club. It's for Hispanics" or "This scholarship going out is for Hispanics," I never really felt I could apply for Hispanic scholarships unless I had known something about my background. I use my Hispanic background to my advantage in application essays when I would actually start reflecting on what it was like to grow up in a White society but be half Hispanic. I've never used it to my advantage where I've said I'm all Mexican. I couldn't say, "I completely identify with being Mexican and this is a scholarship that I'm applying for just because I'm Mexican American"—those scholarships I just haven't filled out.

Education

On my dad's side of the family, no one graduated from high school. In fact, most of them didn't even go on to high school. They're very poor and they made their money, the little that they have, through hands-on labor and hard work that a lot of Americans aren't used to. I'm quite different because I don't do hard labor. I have a job and I go to school, which is already different from them. In my dad's eyes, it's not necessarily that I'm becoming more of an American, but I'm becoming more of one of those Americans that are more educated and want to be more educated and learn things; whereas, he really has no interest in that. When he found out I was going to college, he asked me why. I said it was because I wanted to be able to afford things, because part of the reason my grandma got custody of me was because they just couldn't provide for me. I also wanted an education so I could work with kids that had to grow up like my brothers and I did for my first years of life, in very low poverty—shoes with the holes in them, no shoelaces. A t-shirt and tights in the middle of the winter, stuff like that. When he asked me that, he was actually quite offended, because from his perspective, if he had provided, whether it was the very minimum, he still had provided. Part of the reason for him being upset was that my two older brothers didn't go to college and barely finished high school. Since they're the males, I think the providing was always for them, especially in the Mexican culture, where the males provide and the women stay home, but in this case it was completely different. I was the one that was getting an education and I was the one that would be able to provide for myself. Whereas, they were the ones that were sitting back, not able to get a job.

Biculturalism

I'm the Spanish Club president at my college. I try to give people the perspective that you don't have to have that physical appearance or you don't necessarily have to live up to the idea of a specific country; that women are lesser or women do this or men do this. I would call myself bicultural now, but three, four years ago, I probably wouldn't have, because I hadn't gone to explore my other culture, my Mexican American or my Mexican culture. I wanted to explore, so I read about it and I learned the language. Now I would consider myself bicultural because I wanted to be in that culture because I wasn't.

My White grandma, not my parents, showed me that I had that other side. Just two years ago I went to Mexico and that's what began the process. I decided I wanted to go to Mexico because I wanted to see where my family is from, because some of them are still back there in Guadalajara and the

Mexico City area. I also just wanted to go for fun, to be honest. I went for fun with some friends for a week. When I was growing up, my grandma was always saying, "Well, you need to learn this part of the culture, too," and she was always giving me books by Hispanic authors and Hispanic illustrators. I thought, "Oh, more books after more books." And then when I went back to Mexico, I realized why she had done it. She wanted me to have some sort of bond with the Mexican side as well. But I couldn't really do that until I wanted to do it. If it would have come from my dad's side, it would have been different, because it would have been coming directly from the Mexican side rather than from a White woman earnestly and lovingly channeling that Mexican side. Even though my grandmother was born and raised outside of L.A., she always spent time with Hispanics and was always growing up in various racial areas. You can't really become bicultural unless you want to. I've also wondered, if I was raised with my dad, I probably wouldn't have been in college and I probably wouldn't have considered myself Mexican American. If I was raised with my dad, with the appearance that I have, with such pale skin, I don't know how that would have worked out at all because I would have looked so different than the rest of the family.

Something similar to that has happened before. My boyfriend's side is actually from Mexico. When I was first introduced to them, his family just didn't believe it. I'll ask him about what it's like to be raised in a White society with an all-Hispanic family and actually looking Hispanic and going to college. I have plenty of friends and people that I talk to that actually have a more typical Mexican appearance and are growing up in a White society, but then I also have a friend here who is studying abroad from Mexico, but she's very pale. She's got blond hair and blue eyes and only speaks Spanish. The fact that I am bicultural is really important to me, especially growing up in this state, where there is a lot of diversity that you may not see all the time—if you don't know where to find it. I love being more than one culture, and I love being able to say that. I love the educational background I've had growing up.

Working in Schools

I've also used my last name to my advantage. When introducing myself to a lot of the kids in schools, first they just see me as another White person that's going to come in and change them. I had a sixth-grade placement last semester for one of my education courses in an inner city Title I school. Every single student in the classroom, except for two of them, were English as a Second Language learners, and that didn't just include Hispanics. They were from everywhere. Out of 27 kids, 17 or 18 were from Mexico, specifically.

But as soon as I walked into the classroom, one of the sixth graders—he was probably one of the darkest kids in the class—turned to one of his friends and he said, "Of course, another teacher that they'll get us is White." Their teacher was the only Hispanic in the school—but she was pale, like me. I didn't talk to him until I had introduced myself. When I went around to each group and introduced myself, I said, "I don't want you to think that I'm just another White person walking into your classroom trying to change your ways or trying to get you to be more like me," and then I went into, "I'm actually half Hispanic myself." I was also a substitute at a lot of the preschools in the city area, and all of them were inner city Title I schools—even with four and five year olds—they get it.

If one of the Hispanic parents walks into the room, it doesn't even phase them. But if I walk into a room, they'll just stare me down, because they know, whether they're thinking it or not, they still know that I look different than them. I use it to my advantage to relate to them and get their attention and, especially in the inner city schools, to try to reassure them that no one's here just to "diss" you or to insult your culture. That's not why I'm here. When they hear my last name, they say, "Oh, Ms. Guzmán," then they know for sure.

Kids can tell that White people are trying to change them. There is such an emphasis on learning English, for example, White people trying to get the kids to read books that they don't want to read. Whereas, if they were reading books in Spanish, they'd probably be more interested. They know White people are trying to force English on them when none of their parents even speak English. Even the White nurses and school personnel that will come in and say smoking is bad, drugs are bad, and alcohol is bad, and you know at their house, a lot of them have parents that smoke or drink or do drugs. From my experience in schools, watching them and talking to some of them, they know that schools wouldn't go over some of the same information with White people. One kid said to me, "There's not anyone in my family that's gone past junior high." Kids think, "I know it's just White people who are educated telling me what to do, so I don't even bother going to college. I'm just going to join the army." I can pick that up. When I walk in they're probably thinking, "Oh, it's probably just another nurse telling us not to do drugs, even though my dad does it," or, "I know she's just here to show off her college degree and she's not gonna actually relate with me because she has no idea that I'm raising my five siblings at home and my parents are working four jobs."

Growing up in poverty, I remember looking at some of the people and thinking to myself, "Oh, they have a whole basket of groceries; they'll be able to pay for them all." Whereas, my mom would often get to the front and then she'd have to put stuff back. I know what the kids are thinking because I would think that myself; even at four and five I could pick it up. Or, when I would go spend the day with my dad, he would say, "What do you want to do, go to the park?" And he would list the stuff that was a little bit cheaper. We'd drive past the movie theatre and there would be lots of White people going into the movie theatre. Having that experience as a child, I know what they're thinking when I walk into a classroom.

When I walk in to tutor them, they think, "A White person is tutoring me. I'm brown. I must be dumb," so, if I could tan, yes, I would definitely tan. I often wish my pigment was a little bit darker. Up until this last summer, when I'd just bathe in sunscreen and I'd get made fun of all the time, even from my pale friends who will tan, it always bothered me, until just recently, I just don't care. I get teased from my brothers all the time. I don't think it's about wanting to look more Mexican American. I think it's about looking less Caucasian in this state. When I go to California, when I've gone to Europe, or when I was able to go to Spain for four weeks, it didn't bother me at all because in those countries there's every color. In this state and city, it's a little bit harder to find. You're automatically considered Caucasian if you have pale skin, unless you have an accent.

Identities

I do feel like I have two identities, especially when I'm with my boyfriend's family; or my friends from Mexico, Central, or South America; or when I'm with my dad's side. Sometimes I talk like what they call a gringa. I don't have the specific pronunciation that they use, so if you don't speak Spanish fluently and you're considered Hispanic, then it is kind of a disgrace. My Mexican grandma is always getting on me about how I need to go to Mexico and learn Spanish much better. Whereas, if I'm in America, sometimes it's good to be bilingual, but if you're talking with specific people, they don't see any need for you to speak Spanish. They need you to speak only English. They really could care less that you are bilingual. At least I speak some Spanish. I speak English and Spanish, which is more than a lot of people can do. When I'm with my Hispanic family, hey, I just laugh with them. I've noticed that when I went to Mexico and I would try to order something or I tried to speak in Spanish, they would just completely blow me off and turn to my boyfriend and have him speak instead. Before we started dating, he would just translate over me because, they would automatically assume I was just a White person trying to learn Spanish, and it was really frustrating for them if they were busy and they were trying to do something to give me the opportunity to actually speak in Spanish. Whereas, here, I worked in retail and we had a lot of Hispanics coming in and out to buy stuff. I would try to speak Spanish if I said something in English and they didn't understand, I would ask in Spanish and they spoke Spanish. Then they would look at me like I was being rude; that I was just trying to practice my Spanish with them, because I'm White. I just have to take it with a grain of salt and have a sense of humor about it. I laugh with them. I say, "Oh yeah, I know I look White, but I can speak some Spanish." Or when I'm with my Hispanic family I'll say, "Yeah, I'm White, but at least I'm learning your language; it's better than nothing." Neither of my brothers speaks Spanish, and they look like they should speak Spanish.

If a bicultural child can identify, at a young age, that she's a little bit of both cultures, and she can speak more than one language, it would help her confidence when she gets older. Rather than keeping it quiet, and thinking, "I don't know which one to put down on paper because I don't want anyone to get mad at me," she can be willing to put both of them down on paper in school. It would seem to me to be a really positive thing.

I was lucky enough to get a scholarship to a private school, which is unfortunate at the same time because within that private school I do not remember reading anything in class that was diverse. In all of our text books it was White people. And so I think the role that the teachers played, I don't even know if it was conscious, but they didn't try to increase the diversity within the classroom in any way. They just tried to keep it all the same. For example, with my last name, my principal, through six years, always refused to spell it right. She spelled it wrong, even when it was right in front of her, when she was showing me how to write my name when I was little, and I wrote it and then she rewrote it. Then I would write my last name and then she would rewrite it. One of my teachers actually took a point off of my last name because there's an accent over the "a" in "Guzmán." She would actually take off points every time I put the accent in. And so, even from a young age you can tell that if you're White, you probably should act White.

It's really weird to have that sort of last name, because I was the only one in my class when everyone else was Smith or Jones. I was always putting the accent on my name. My grandma was actually the one who looked it up. My dad didn't know there was an accent on it, and she actually said, "start putting it on there," so I did. I think the role that teachers played was trying to change it, because it was weird for them to have a White Mexican American in their classroom.

Cynthia: Rebel with a Cause

Cynthia's testimonio is a story of decolonization in action. There are different ways to decolonize, but they all reveal and dismantle forms of neocolonial power. When the neocolonial flows that govern the school and classroom are revealed, resisted, or reversed, those forces are weakened, allowing minoritized youth to begin to take more control of their destinies in school and society. At every turn, Cynthia is able to identify and interrupt neocolonial flows that pervade her life and the lives of the minoritized youth for whom she works in schools. Drawing upon her experience growing up in poverty and among minoritized people as well as upon her biculturalism, Cynthia consciously rebels against the structures of neocolonialism and "choose[s] the margin" (hooks, 1990) from which to live and carry out her work. Moving beyond recognition of what has happened to her and to minoritized youth and their families in schools, she takes action to disrupt the persistent fallacies of the neocolonizer. For example, Cynthia defines an American as anyone who *"works and contributes to society in some way,"* This plays havoc with neocolonial flows of nationalism that say that the borders of the United States are naturally occurring, therefore unquestioningly defining citizenship. Cynthia's exacting analyses of her own and others' perceptions and actions serve to make sense of both postcolonial and neocolonial flows, therefore prying them open to critical surveillance.

(In)commensurable Identities

> *My oldest brother is actually really dark, like my dad. The next brother is a little bit darker than me and I'm the one that just doesn't fit in because I don't tan. I'm the one with lighter hair. I took my mom's side, the European side.*

As a light-skinned Mexican American, Cynthia does not "fit in" because her appearance does not mesh with the neoocolonizer's essentialized images of a Mexican American. Similarly, Stephanie Lynn Daza (2009), also a "not-so-dark person of color," explained how she is (mis)recognized by her White adoptive family as White, and by acquaintances as heterosexual when she identifies as queer. Daza showed how she lives between refusing to be (mis)recognized through norms that essentialize all Mexican Americans as brown and all women with children as heterosexual, and being recognized as an essentialized Mexican American and queer woman, coping with the negative associations that come with those designations. Daza later stated that "'to be' means to be and not to be recognizable" (p. 340). This state of both being and not being recognizable as a Mexican American is lived by Cynthia, as evidenced by the weaving together of pieces of her testimonio:

> *I usually just put "other" because there's never really anything listed that's appropriate, because I'm a little bit of everything. I'm half Hispanic, but then the other half is everything.*
>
> *When people would say, "You're so pale but your dad's so dark," I actually learned to really like it because it showed that I was a little bit different.*
>
> *If someone says, "Oh, where are your roots from?" then I just say, "My dad's side's from Mexico and my grandma's is from Europe and is Native American," but if it's not brought up or anything, they can think what they want, I guess.*
>
> *When introducing myself to a lot of the kids in schools, first they just see me as another White person that's going to come in and change them.*
>
> *When they hear my last name, they say, "Oh, Ms. Guzmán," then they know for sure.*
>
> *My boyfriend's side is actually from Mexico. When I was first introduced to them, his family just didn't believe it.*
>
> *I've noticed that when I went to Mexico and I would try to order something or I tried to speak in Spanish, they would just completely blow me off and turn to my boyfriend and have him speak instead.*

In her testimonio, Cynthia has written herself as a kind of new Mestiza who is "not only here and there, is not only Mexican or American, or Mexican American, or even Chicano/a, but more, much more, [and] is always recreating the unimagined, the unknown, where mobile third space identities thrive" (Pérez, 1999, p. 79). The third or liminal space is where minoritized youth express their dynamic, fluid, and conflictual identities that as a whole are more than an either/or self or a simple biculturalism. I think that because of Cynthia's acceptance of the third or liminal space where she resides, she is able to strategically, but, more importantly, self-reflexively, deploy aspects of her identity to her cause—working for social justice for minoritized youth. Cynthia's performance of identities, some recognized, some not, is one way of answering Bhabha's (1994) question, "How are subjects formed 'in-between,' or in excess of, the sum of the 'parts' of difference (usually intoned as race/class/gender, etc.)?" (p. 2).

It must be acknowledged that her willingness to live among and between American White, Mexican, and Mexican American identities in a third space did not go unpunished by the school. Recall Cynthia's teacher's refusal to accept the accent mark on her name: "*I think the role that teachers played was trying to change it* [my name], *because it was weird for them to have a White Mexican American in their classroom.*" Teachers were unwilling to accept Cynthia's (in)commensurable identities. One teacher even disciplined her by taking off a point when she would include the accent mark on her last name, Guzmán. But, as we will see, Cynthia, in her own way, is able to discipline those who try to restrict who she is.

Disciplining the Neocolonizer

As educators, we are used to hearing the word "discipline" when talking about the structures of schools and classrooms (e.g., suspensions, turning a card, leave without pay, etc.). The concept of discipline is also utilized by postcolonial theorists. They often draw upon Foucault's (1977) work to describe how discipline works in a neocolonial context. To begin thinking about discipline we must first start with flows or discourses. Cannella and Viruru (2004) explained how neocolonial and postcolonial flows, or discourses, function. As you read the following, think of the neocolonial flow of minoritized students deemed to be lacking culture and education:

> Discourses are rooted in human ideas, institutions, and actions, making it difficult for individuals to think outside of them…. [S]ince the nineteenth century the dominant structures of Western society have reproduced themselves through such discourses. Human beings have internalized the systems, conformed to them, and submitted to their power. Further, discourse as a mechanism of power functions in the creation of systems of knowledge governed by rules of exclusion for what can and cannot be spoken, acted upon, thought, or tolerated. (p. 61)

As the deficit discourse of the lesser worth of minoritized youth became accepted in educational circles, researchers attempted to prove the discourse was fact (Solórzano & Yosso, 2002). Thus, the neocolonial flow of minoritized youth as lacking is accepted as everyday knowledge by many in education. Because discourses are rules for how to think, behave, and be, they describe what is "normal" for whomever or whatever the discourse targets. So, for this example, it would be considered normal for teachers to assume minoritized youth are deficient, or it would be acceptable to hear a minoritized student say that they are not that smart. Citing Foucault (1978), Cannella and Viruru (2004) stated: "*Disciplinary power* is imposed on bodies by creating the *desire to be 'normal'* (a normality created by the discourse). Individuals construct standards through which they judge themselves" (p. 62). In this case, minoritized students may also discipline themselves by thinking they are not that smart. Similarly, the desire to be a "good teacher" or a "good student" is also an example of disciplinary power imposed on us in Euro-American society.

Thankfully, Cynthia is able to create her own postcolonial flows that negate and discipline neocolonial flows. For example, in the classroom, she explains to children that she is not a wolf in sheep's clothing, and normalizes White educators as wielding undue, hegemonic power over others:

> *I use it* [my last name—Guzmán] *to my advantage to relate to them and get their attention and, especially in the inner city schools, to try to reassure them that no one's here just to "diss" you or to insult your culture. That's not why I'm here.*

Cynthia shows that she is not White, but Mexican American, and will not disregard or denigrate students' minoritized cultures as she knows they would normally expect from White teachers. She is adept at disrupting the harmful essentializing flows of the neocolonizer:

> The falsity of the colonialism-constructed identities where all of the derogatory labels (savages, uncivilized, lazy, irrational, uneducated, untrustworthy, unreliable, unpredictable, etc.) were fabricated by colonial powers, was primarily designed to achieve two important objectives in the overall project of colonization. The first was to justify the conquest and subsequent exploitation of foreign lands; and the second was to induce in the native population a self-unworthiness so these become willing participants in their marginalization and attached mass deprivation (Ghosh, Abdi, & Naseem, 2008, p. 58).

Likewise, she consciously dismantles disciplinary powers with her colleagues in her Spanish club:

> *I try to give people the perspective that you don't have to have that physical appearance or you don't necessarily have to live up to the idea of a specific country, that women are lesser or women do this or men do this.*

She reverses the flows of essentialized physical signs of difference, nationality, and gender, making those discourses too simplistic and clear-cut to be considered a rational "norm." Because Cynthia changes the rules of recognition—for example, one's physical appearance does not have to match one's country of origin—she threatens the neocolonizer by posing Trinh T. Minh-ha's (1995) question, "If you can't locate the other, how are you to locate yourself?" (p. 217). If we can no longer believe the discourse that says "all Brown people are from other places" or "all Whites are American," then who are we?

Cynthia continues her rule-breaking with a description of three ways to be bicultural:

> *I'll ask him* [her Mexican American boyfriend] *about what it's like to be raised in a White society with an all-Hispanic family and actually looking Hispanic and going*

to college. I have plenty of friends and people that I talk to that actually have a more
typical Mexican appearance and are growing up in a White society, but then I also
have a friend here who is studying abroad from Mexico, but she's very pale. She's
got blond hair and blue eyes and only speaks Spanish.

One can have bicultural heritage, like Cynthia, but appear more typically White American than Mexican and speak more English than Spanish; one can have both Mexican and American heritage but look Hispanic; and one can be a Mexican "national" living in the United States who is a monolingual Spanish speaker but appears White. In offering these examples of different kinds of biculturalism, Cynthia creates a shell game of sorts wherein all forms of biculturalism are legitimate no matter the degree of authenticity of the bicultural subject. If all three people are bicultural, then what does bicultural mean, and, excitingly, what does American mean? She also refuses the stereotype of appearance and language: *"Or when I'm with my Hispanic family I'll say, 'Yeah, I'm White, but at least I'm learning your language; it's better than nothing.' Neither of my brothers speaks Spanish, and they look like they should speak Spanish."* Cynthia confuses the hierarchical list of ethnicities from lightest to darkest, showing how her dark-skinned brothers don't speak Spanish and she does with her light skin. Her family contorts the rules of recognition and authenticity.

This last example of how Cynthia disciplines neocolonial flows or normalizations is striking in its brazen contempt for the powers that be:

The fact that I am bicultural is really important to me, especially growing up in this
state, where there is a lot of diversity that you may not see all the time—if you don't
know where to find it. I love being more than one culture, and I love being able to
say that. I love the educational background I've had growing up.

Cynthia takes a strong, subversive stand by saying that she is proud of her biculturalism, especially in a state where diversity and multiculturalism are marginalized and diminished. As a Latina appearing White, it is as if she is saying, "Surprise! I'm here, I'm Latina, and you didn't expect a minoritized person to come in this package and show up here." In many ways, as a native English-speaking, White-appearing preservice teacher in schools, she has infiltrated the neocolonizer's command post. Although minoritized people are made invisible by the White European majority, she has been here all along. Further, the neocolonizer's denial of the minoritized's existence is futile, given that the U.S. Census projected that by 2040 half of the U.S. population will be non-White (U.S. Census Bureau, 2009a, 2009b).

In sum, Cynthia's ability to recognize when and how she is being disciplined, and her contention that even very young children are aware of being disciplined, offers great hope to those who work in support of the decolonization of the school and classroom. However, her transgressive, anticolonial work will likely not go unpunished. As she states, *even from a young age you can tell that if you're White, you probably should act White.*

Unfortunately, part of the flow of acting White includes maintaining the status quo of a neocolonial, accentless existence. Because visual difference is the key to keeping minoritized people in their assigned hierarchical roles, border crossing and status lowering are not allowed for Whites because of the flow of the inferiority of Spanishness and Brownness. Whites are protecting Whites in order to maintain the "us/them" binary and the associated hierarchy of races. Yet, again maintaining her ability to discipline the colonizer, even amidst the neocolonizer's disciplining fog, Cynthia disqualifies the neocolonizer. Cynthia explains that her teachers desired her to be an accentless, "normal," White person whereas, although she was yet to speak Spanish, she was comfortable writing her surname with the correct Spanish language spelling—refuting the disciplinary power of the flow of normalized Whiteness.

The Borderless American

How is the idea of a nation constructed? Many accept the concept of nation without question—our nation is the United States of America with clearly defined and acceptable borders. Troublingly, the concept of a nation with its clear-cut descriptors—for example, the United States as a freedom-loving land of opportunity for all—does not come close to capturing the complexity, experiences, and, at worst, examples of our selective freedom and opportunity for a few. The publicly accepted stories of nations "usually represent and consolidate the interests of the dominant power groups.... Constructions of the nation are thus potent sites of control and domination within modern society" (Ashcroft et al., 2000, p. 150).

Cynthia's conception of a borderless nation, or a nation that considers the first peoples to live on the land as still having the right to live there no matter who has colonized it, flies in the face of our national allegory of Christopher Columbus and the founding fathers having civilized and improved this land and its people for everyone's good:

> *I have a really hard time with people saying that an American is someone who is born on American soil—from California to the Northeast. An American is someone who lives, works and contributes to society in some way, whether it's landscapers or custodians or paying bills. I don't think you need to be documented to be an American citizen. Part of the reason I think this is so is because North America, so much of it, was considered Mexico, or it was Mexico to begin with.*

Cynthia interrogates the assumption of the nation-state. She challenges the idea that the United States was meant to be—a natural and unquestionable result of human progress. Cynthia's definitions of an American are reminiscent of the Chicano/a Movement's concept of Aztlán—a metaphorical and physical Aztec homeland occupied by "an Anglo-centric, patriarchal, imperialist United States" (Moraga, 1993, p. 173). The idea of Aztlán refuses to accept the U.S.-Mexico border as a permanent divider that determines national identity and citizenship (Pérez-Torres, 2000), given "the oft-cited [Chicano/a] mantra, 'We did not cross the border, the border crossed us'" (Villenas, 2009, p. 55).

Cynthia's drawing upon the violent history of the United States' occupation of Mexico points to the importance of teaching the history of colonization—the violent capture and taking over of lands, peoples, and ideas. Without an understanding of the historical context of what is now the United States, would Cynthia be able to question flows of nation as natural? In her ability to affiliate with, extend her loyalty to, and express her concern for Mexico and beyond, Cynthia performs the flow of a transnational identity. Because Cynthia's real and imagined social life transcends national borders and is characterized by constant reformulations, adaptations, and abandonment of categories, her identity reflects this transnationalism.

> *Unfortunately, some people think, especially here* [in this state]*, that an American is someone who pledges allegiance to only one specific country and who should not have a tie with any other country. The mindset is, "It's just us and everyone should just worry about themselves." I don't think an American is someone who offers justice to those living within a certain area, rather, Americans are people who are willing to help those in other countries. Part of being an American and being called an American and an active citizen is knowing when to jump out of our own shells and help other people in other countries, like Haiti.*

Unveiling the prevalent national and curricular neocolonial, binary construction of us/them, Cynthia believes that one should have the freedom in this country to pledge allegiance to more than one country—or have multiple national affiliations (Dimitriadis & McCarthy, 2001). This is an anticolonial posture and an aspect of identity often associated with postcolonialism. Further, Cynthia defines an *American* as transnational, one who knows when to offer assistance to people who need support—like Haitians after the devastating 2010 earthquake. Cynthia's disregard for the borders of the United States as a determination of national loyalty, allegiance, and humanitarian action destroys nationalism as it is typically construed, lived, and often "woven into the very fabric of education" (Said, 1994, p. xxvi).

We're Watching You

Kids can tell that White people are trying to change them.

Cynthia lets the reader of her testimonio know that students are surveilling teachers and measuring the extent to which they are being civilized and surveilled. Cynthia's work in classrooms, disrupting neocolonial flows with straight talk about the neocolonizer with young children, shows her commitment to making change in early childhood and elementary classrooms: "The work of decolonization entails not only our self-reflexive efforts to work through mind-numbing alienation and essentializing divides, but also the commitment to transformation in social and educational contexts" (Asher, 2009, p. 75). Cynthia's comment (which she later retracts) that she would like to appear more brown recalls Daza's (2009) experiences as a light-skinned Mexican American: "My journey and desire to speak *and live* Spanish was wrapped up in my search for legitimacy as a brown person of color and, of course, my presumption, grounded deep in humanist ideals, of what an authentic brown subject ought to be" (p. 327). Cynthia explains that she no longer feels like she needs to look authentically Mexican American to work effectively with minoritized youth. She seems to have gained a level of comfort with her (in)authentic identities, biculturalism, and ability to get her message across to students.

Cynthia's dialogues with youth in classrooms mesh nicely with the disrobing aspect of postcolonial theory:

> Postcolonial theory helps to uncover and rebuild the autonomous yet hybrid identity of those dispossesed by imperialist dominance, its exploration and probing of indigenous, local, and creole or blended knowledges. It challenges, counters, and can reshape political structures that have their roots in colonialism and imperialism. (Hickling-Hudson, 2009, p. 366)

The project of neocolonialism is one of attempting to civilize minoritized groups into White European ways of thinking, acting, and being. Cynthia is keenly aware of this:

> When I walk in they're probably thinking, "Oh, it's probably just another nurse telling us not to do drugs, even though my dad does it," or, "I know she's just here to show off her college degree and she's not gonna actually relate with me because she has no idea that I'm raising my five siblings at home and my parents are working four jobs."

Cynthia is willing to base her classroom pedagogy on the lived realities of minoritized youth and make the postcolonial flow of student family life central to her understanding of students. Her actions disrupt the flow of the essentialized minoritized student living in poverty. Cynthia reveals a binary of "responsible White/irresponsible non-White." In so doing, instead of endorsing the discourse of poor minoritized students as irresponsible (their families doing drugs), she shows that although that may be happening, students may also be responsibly raising their younger siblings—something I often saw with my own Mexican American fifth and sixth graders. Again, the neocolonial discourse could stereotype and demonize the parentification of children (a long-term role reversal where a child sacrifices their needs to care for adults or siblings) (Jurkovic, 1997) in large, Latino families, but would this even be a question in large, Irish Catholic families, for example, the Kennedys, whose family tree is riddled with alcohol and drug abuse? The persistent double standards of neocolonial discourses that systematically denigrate the real and imagined practices of minoritized families are overturned by Cynthia's testimonio. Like postcolonial theory in action, Cynthia is able to "explore multiple ways of knowing the world, and enable us to refine the goals of emancipatory social action in ways that take the needs, aspirations, and practices of specific cultures into account" (Hickling-Hudson, 2009, p. 368).

Cynthia's message is not only that "the students are watching teachers," she also explains how she has used observation to gain an understanding and respect for diverse groups when she is traveling: *"I'm really observant, and would stand back, watch, and see how people lived their day-to-day lives."* While traveling abroad, Cynthia, too, engages in observations of the "other," but she uses these as a learning tool, not as a means of surveilling and disciplining the "other." Her true goal seems to be to discipline the neocolonizer by making it acceptable for young children to acknowledge teachers' intent to encourage their mimicry of the neocolonizer. She tells students, *"I don't want you to think that I'm just another White person walking into your classroom trying to change your ways or trying to get you to be more like me."* Cynthia is making the neocolonizer's flows evident to very young children. She assumes that even preschoolers are aware of the civilizing mission of the neocolonial school: *"They know White people are trying to force English on them when none of their parents even speak English."* Cynthia recognizes colonial ambivalence and engages in decolonization by listening to and talking with elementary students about their distrust and disapproval of educators' double standards in a tiered system that is founded on the binary of White/non-White.

Disqualifying Binaries and Hierarchies

I was raised with all sorts of cultures—people from the Middle East, African Americans, and a lot of Hispanics from Colombia and Mexico. That's why when growing

up I didn't even realize that the people I was talking to and those in my family are
brown-skinned.

One might be tempted to say that because of her Whiteness Cynthia did not notice color, but she explains that her life was so color-conscious that she did not see color as non-White. Her understanding disrupts the White/non-White binary and shows that she was operating under a color/no-color binary—disqualifying imperialistic hierarchies of race.

Cynthia is able to recognize binaries and how they have played out in her relationship with her family (i.e., mind/body; rich/poor; male/female), but, most importantly, she is able to see how cultural differences make the perspectives real and valuable. She reifies the cultural worth of her father's and brothers' perspectives and life choices:

> *When he found out I was going to college, he asked me why. I said it was because I*
> *wanted to be able to afford things, because part of the reason my grandma got cus-*
> *tody of me was because they just couldn't provide for me. I also wanted an educa-*
> *tion so I could work with kids that had to grow up like my brothers and I did for my*
> *first years of life, in very low poverty—shoes with the holes in them, no shoelaces. A*
> *t-shirt and tights in the middle of the winter, stuff like that. When he asked me that,*
> *he was actually quite offended, because from his perspective, if he had provided,*
> *whether it was the very minimum, he still had provided. Part of the reason for him*
> *being upset was that my two older brothers didn't go to college and barely finished*
> *high school. Since they're the males, I think the providing was always for them, es-*
> *pecially in the Mexican culture, where the males provide and the women stay home,*
> *but in this case it was completely different. I was the one that was getting an educa-*
> *tion and I was the one that would be able to provide for myself. Whereas, they were*
> *the ones that were sitting back, not able to get a job.*

Instead of condemning the perspectives and positions of her Mexican American father, Cynthia is able to understand his position, based on his experiences and cultural background. However, she takes her own route that strays from the cultural norms she has identified. Cynthia is quite independent in her thinking, but her ability to see from multiple perspectives and critique neocolonial flows in her life did not occur without support.

Grandma's Decolonizing Support

My White grandma, not my parents, showed me that I had that other side.

Key people can help to decolonize one's experience. In this case, Cynthia's White grandmother encouraged the reclaiming of her Mexican American culture. For example, she encouraged her to study the Spanish language in school, read traditional Mexican folktales and literature, and visit her Mexican American family. Given that her grandmother grew up or lived in various ethnic communities and worked with and for minoritized youth, she was able to *"earnestly and lovingly channel* [Cynthia's] *Mexican side."* Throughout her testimonio, Cynthia gives credit to her grandmother for preparing her for the journey to choose to reclaim her Mexican heritage.

Cynthia states: *"I never really felt I could apply for Hispanic scholarships unless I had known something about my background."* Cynthia wanted to earn her Mexican American identity through cultural understanding, observation, and study. Her grandmother modeled identity-affirming actions when she counseled Cynthia to start putting the accent on her last name. *"My grandma was actually the one who looked it up. My dad didn't know there was an accent on it, and she actually said, 'start putting it on there,' so I did."* Again, Cynthia's grandmother was and is a key supporter in decolonizing her education—showing that youth do not have to go it alone in their quest to be valued for their identities, histories, experiences, and selves.

Urgent Messages for Teachers

Cynthia offers no charity for educators. In her testimonio, she calls them out for their neocolonial actions and tendencies. This is her message for teachers: Not only is Cynthia watching, but so are even the youngest of minoritized students, who know that Whites, consciously or not, intend to remake them in their own image; marginalize them by steering them away from the academic paths that could access power and self-understanding; and demean their cultures and languages.

> Postcolonial educators remain implicated by their participation in systems of education that are rooted in Eurocentric, colonialist, and oppressive traditions. How then do we break out of recreating, recirculating, and transmitting colonizing educational structures and practices when we ourselves are enmeshed in the same? (Asher, 2009, pp. 72–73)

In her testimonio and in her work with children, she "stand[s] up for knowledges and people who have been perpetually placed in the margins...challenging the limitations of Western perspectives that may be hurting people in the real world" (Cannella & Viruru, 2004, p. 79). Cynthia is unafraid to reprove neocolonial ideologies and practices, making herself into a model of anticolonial action for teachers:

> *I was lucky enough to get a scholarship to a private school, which is unfortunate at the same time because within that private school I do not remember reading anything in class that was diverse. In all of our text books it was White people. And so I think the role that the teachers played, I don't even know if it was conscious, but*

they didn't try to increase the diversity within the classroom in any way. They just tried to keep it all the same.

Cynthia shows that the school curriculum was Eurocentric and that teachers marginalized minoritized knowledges and people, thus maintaining the neo-colonial status quo—something it seems she is sure to protest and upend in her own career in education.

Note

1. Cynthia Guzmán is a 20-year-old Mexican American college student from a low income, and later, a middle class family who is studying to become a teacher. She physically appears White European American.

Chapter Four

Nadya's[1] Testimonio

"I'm Sitting Right on the Cusp, and I Think, Do I Belong Here or Do I Belong There, You Know What I Mean?"

My story's pretty complicated. First of all, I'm adopted. I was born in Belarus, which is on the border of Russia. I was born less than 30 days after the fall of the Soviet Union—that whole area is White. I was the only Black baby in the orphanage—probably was the only Black baby for miles. When I was in the orphanage, I had been offered to Belarusian families who turned me down because of the color of my skin. I got lucky and had this great American woman come and she just thought it was so cool that I was half Gypsy and half Cuban. So, I came to the United States.

I grew up in a White family with a European background, German and Dutch, which is about as White as you can get. I grew up a biracial child. I didn't see race until, I would say, I came to New York and I started going to public school, where it was glaringly obvious to me that I looked one way and acted another way. Something went off in my brain that made me realize, I don't look the same as my mother. I don't look the same as the people I hang out with.

Biracial Identity

When I came to New York was the first time that I started having African American friends. I don't think I realized it then, but I think my mother actually sought African American friends for me because she knew that as a biracial child, growing up in a White family, it would be good for me to hang out with African American kids who looked like me—which was definitely a good thing. I think it paid off in the end.

When I was eight years old, I had a bit of an identity crisis because I acted one way and I looked another way. That's when I really started soul searching, figuring out who I was racially. As a child one of my biggest role models, my hero, was an Afro-pop singer, Angélique Kidjo. She has very, very dark skin. She's from Benin. She had short, short hair, cropped very close to her head. So when I went into third grade, I cut all my hair off—I wanted to look like Angélique Kidjo. It's interesting: I loved my hair when I was little; I thought it was great. But as I got older, I started to hate it. Look-ing back on it now, that is an indication to me that I realized I was different from other kids and didn't have long, blond hair. My hair was one of the first things that was indicative of that.

I still struggle a little bit, but most of that I think happened in middle school when I first started to see race, and I realized that I had to basically put myself somewhere because that's what I think you do, to be honest, is that you must have an identity racially.

Not many people like to say it, but honestly, if you look at it, it's true: When people look at me, they think one thing. When I open my mouth, it's totally a different impression, you know what I mean? People categorize. It might just have something to do with the human brain. It might just have something to do with human society, or history.

For me, being biracial is one thing, but being biracial and growing up in a White family is another. It was really difficult to find my place. I'm still looking for it—it's definitely a journey. I'm always jealous when I see people who have reached the end and found their destination because they seem so much more comfortable in their skin and they have a presence that is a little bit more confident. I think people pick up on that, and they interact with one another more easily. This is the case for people in general, but Black women are actually a really good example because Black women in particular have a lot of Black pride. I'm insanely jealous of confident Black women who have that sense of Black pride because I never had that growing up. I was never really exposed to that—until it was "too late." When I see Black women who are really comfortable in their skins and they love their hair and they can wear it this way and they can wear it that way, and they know what clothes to wear to flatter their bodies and they know how to talk and they know how to walk and they know how to act, I definitely have a lot of admiration for them. I shrivel a little bit inside because I feel like I'm never really going to get to that point, because I will always have a foot in each world, so to speak.

It's a double thing, for me because I am, number one, biracial, and, number two, I am dark-skinned, and I grew up and I live in an upper middle class, predominantly White environment. So, being biracial obviously I have, racially, two worlds. My birth father is Afro-Cuban, so he was probably very, very dark, and my birth mother is Russian, so apparently, she was Roma—a Gypsy—so she was probably a little bit darker than most Russian women but probably for the most part very White. It's weird to think about being caught in the middle like that because it's almost two polar opposites, and when you put them together you get me. I'm sitting right on the cusp, and I think, do I belong here or do I belong there, you know what I mean? There are elements of both cultures that attract me. I've never lost my sense of identity racially.

It's something that I'm incredibly proud of—being Russian and being Cuban and noticing things in myself both aesthetically (mostly) and personality-wise. I love noticing those things in myself from both cultures. I love being able to say that I come from where I do. The second part is being Black and growing up in a White family—growing up White. Because, again, people don't like to say it, but there is a way of acting Black and there is a way of acting White—stereotypically.

Black and White in School

I act White and you can tell because of my speech patterns. There are times when I have tried to act Black—especially when I was at my elementary school. It was pretty much racially segregated. All the Hispanic kids hung out together, all the White kids hung out together, and all the Black kids hung out together. I tried so hard to fit in with the Black kids, so hard. I did everything from trying to walk like them. I tried my hardest to talk like them, which means I would change my voice and change the way I spoke. I tried to dance like them and to like the kinds of things that they liked. It just didn't work, obviously. Looking back on it now, I just think, "Oh my God, I was a little oblivious at that point." The fact that they talked to me at all was a miracle. It just didn't work, at all. But I did try so, so hard. I must have just felt that this is where I belong. This is the way I look. Everyone who looks this way, hangs out together, so why don't I? You don't want to be different when you're that young. That comes later in high school where you're like, "Yeah, I'm a rebel and I want to be different." You don't want any of that when you're young, at the elementary and middle school level. You want to be the same as everyone else. Everyone else, to me, had their place, and I did not. So, I first tried to find my place based on the way I look. When that didn't work, I found my place based on the way I acted, and that was with the White kids. All my friends were White, all of them. I had Black friends, but I didn't hang out with them as much. My White friends were the kids I was having play dates with; were the kids I was eating with at lunch; were the kids I was playing with at recess—once I realized that I couldn't play with the other kids.

I went to a lot of different schools growing up, and up until third grade, I was probably the only Black kid in most of the schools or one of the only. I went to Tower for two years. There were 10 kids in the class and I was the only Black kid there. I think when I was that young I didn't really realize my teachers were discriminating against me. I have a memory of one of my teachers in third grade who just didn't like me, for some reason. I'm convinced it was because I was Black, but my mother tells me she was married to a Black man. I told her, that doesn't mean that she's not racist—because she hated me for some reason. I was kind of a wild child, but I wasn't that bad—I wasn't freakin' spray-painting things, you know what I mean? I had my moments but overall I was a pretty good kid. She just picked on me.

It was a dichotomy to me: to be Black you have to act this way; to be White you have to act this way. I look this way, I act this way, what do I do? It was rough. When I was in third grade I went up to one of the Black girls who was hanging out, probably dancing or something, and I said, "Hey, can I play with you guys?" Or, "Can I do whatever with you guys?" Maybe I was a little slicker than that, I doubt it.

She said, "No."

"Why not?" I said.

"Because you're a Black girl with a White mom," she says. I think I could be totally wrong on this, but I think that maybe most kids wouldn't have understood that quite as much as I did. It wasn't so much that she told me I couldn't play with her that made me cry, it was the racial jab. I cried and cried and cried, and the teachers didn't do anything about it, of course, because they don't know what to do. All of the teachers were White and they didn't really understand my pain. They had no idea what to do about that kind of a thing. This girl was totally insolent—I mean she was a problem. In the end, I talked to my mom about it. I've always been very, you know, confident about being adopted, and it always has been a topic for discussion in my family. It wasn't like a big shock to me. I realized my mother was White and I was not, but having it pushed in my face like that, I think, may have been what made me cry. It was difficult—especially for an eight-year-old to take. Looking back on it now, it's such an interesting kind of thing that goes on. Kids realize so young about race and who looks this way and who looks that way. It's wild to think about.

Hair

I'm going to go back to my hair for a minute, which I still have huge problems with. It's such a source of stress for me—hair for all Black women is, but some women figure it out. I just haven't because it has a lot to do with me being on the cusp. I don't want to straighten my hair permanently because I like the curls. I like the kink. I like, you know, the way it makes me look ethnic, the way it makes me look a little bit exotic almost. But I don't want an Afro, and whenever I wear my hair down, even if it's curly, I will make it as flat as possible. The first time I got my hair straightened I must have been very, very young. I came home and it was so weird to me that I started playing a game in which I was two people. I was myself and I was a White girl. I would be talking to the White girl and made up a whole story. And then I wanted to see what it looked like when it was straight, so I wet it. Obviously, it started to curl up again and I was devastated. I didn't get my hair straightened for a very long time. If I did, it was only for 10 minutes because I liked the curls. The last time I got my hair straightened was very recently where I seriously got it blown straight and flat ironed. I remember coming home and it was like, "Oh God." I was really worried about it getting wet because I really liked the feeling of it being straight. It was so new and it was like I could run my fingers through it and I could shake it down my back. Then I had a dream that night. It was a horrible, horrible dream, in which somehow I forgot that my hair was flat ironed and I got it wet. As soon as it started curling up again I looked in the mirror and I was horrified, and I started screaming, "Monster! Monster! Monster! I'm a monster! I'm a monster!" I woke up and I was like, "Oh my gosh, wow."

I definitely think it meant something. My hair is a huge source of stress for me because I think it looks horrible all the time. I felt really, really good when it was straight. The fact that in my dream when it curled back up I was calling myself a monster, was mind-boggling to me to think that being Black and having Black hair makes me think of myself as a monster. The next time I got my hair straightened, I had another anxiety dream like that in which I got it wet and it was just horrifying. So, my hair is definitely another thing that always constantly reminds me that I have not quite found, you know, that identity, that confident identity, that says, "This is me, I'm biracial and I'm proud of it." My hair is a constant reminder to me that I'm still looking for my spot. In my case, I don't think I can be in both worlds because I've tried it. I've tried it a long time ago. I've tried it recently and I've realized that I just need to be me.

Belonging

I definitely understand the idea of homelessness and not belonging here and not quite belonging there. I joke a lot about being the token Black kid because pretty much all my friends are White. Just by coincidence, I think. I joke a lot about being the token Black kid and then my friends tell me, "You're not Black. You're not Black." It's really upsetting to me, when they say I'm not Black, actually. I don't let it get to me too much because I know what they mean. I know they don't mean it in a bad way. What they're talking about is, "You are not the typical Black person. You act White," and I like being Black. I mean, I think everybody has this sort of secret desire to be an oppressed minority because it gives you a sense of pride to say, you know, I survived or whatever, or I'm, you know, pushing along and reminding people that I'm here and I'm powerful despite the fact that I'm oppressed. I mean, I'm a Black woman growing up in a White man's world.

Checking Boxes

I'm very proud of who I am, don't get me wrong. I enjoy the feeling when people are surprised when I exceed expectations. If you look in the working world, there aren't many women, for example, corporate jobs or engineers, there are not many Black women out there. I really enjoy being able to say, well, these are all options for me. It came up a lot when I was applying for colleges, in the demographic section and affirmative action. I checked every box except Asian. I even checked "other," because I am every box. I checked White, Caucasian, because I was thinking of my Russian birth mother—my blood. I checked Black/African American, which is a really crazy box, actually, because my North African friends can't check it. I didn't check Native American but I checked Hispanic because I'm Cuban. And I checked "other" and I put Roma. I checked pretty much all the boxes. It was just interesting having to check those boxes that said I have to quantify myself. Why am I checking these boxes?

I'm checking these boxes so colleges can look at them and say, "Oh, here's a Black woman who is half Gypsy and half Russian and half Cuban who wants to go into engineering. Oh, we don't see many of those." I hate affirmative action, but I'm going to check those boxes anyway because I know the playing field is already unlevel. There are so many variables: You've got your legacy kids. You've got your rich kids. You've got your athletes. You've got your musicians. Affirmative action was not designed for kids like me. I come from a relatively high income family. I have had every educational opportunity possible. When I check those boxes, they see that I checked Black/African American. They see that I checked Hispanic. But they do not know my background. They do not know what it means.

This is why the affirmative action is a little bit messed up. When affirmative action was created, if you were Black, chances were 98% of the time you were probably of low economic status. You probably did not make a lot of money. You probably did not have very good educational opportunities. Nowadays things are changing. I am part of the generation that steps out of what was when affirmative action was created. But the policy hasn't been changed yet, so I still benefit from it. I also got the National Merit Scholarship for Black high school students. When I got it, I said, "Great. This will look good on my college application," but I was also a little bit upset about it because I know I'm being compared against kids who didn't get SAT prep. I paid $90 an hour for my SAT prep every week, and I had a really good SAT *tutor. So, it's not fair. Honestly, it's not fair. But, I couldn't bring myself to not disclose because I just couldn't. Even though I knew it was unfair. At the end of the day, how much does affirmative action really work? Probably just as much as it works to be a legacy kid.*

    Checking boxes is such a surface, imperfect thing. For example, my North African friends who are actually African American, cannot check that box because it says Black/African American. They are from Africa. My Egyptian friends, my Libyan friend, cannot check that box—which is crazy. Come to think of it, I'm not actually African American. I am Caribbean American—if you want to go into race about it. So, by African American you automatically think Black, but that's not always the case. Not all Black people are African American. Not all African Americans are from Africa. This is why you have affirmative action: You have a Black woman growing up in a White man's world. You have Hispanic women growing up in a White man's world. You have basically everyone except White men growing up in a White man's world. There's the sense that "we're trying to even things out," but is this the case? And, do you want to do that? Do you want to give a special advantage to people of color or people who are not of European descent? What does that say about our society and what does that say about what we think about race? I got it all the time, "Oh, you're gonna get in because you're Black," or, "Oh, you got in because you're Black." I cannot tell you how furious that makes me—I rip people's heads off, I do. I give them the full, "I got in because…well, I like to think it's because I worked my ass off for four years and had a 4.2 GPA, and, you know, a full resume, but hey, who knows?" Maybe it was because I am Black. When I got my acceptance letters back, Yale rejected me, but I got into the other six schools. I almost put myself down thinking, "Would they have accepted you if you were White?" We'll never know the answer to that question. But I like to think that, "Yes, they would have." I don't know.

    Stereotyping did not enter my radar entirely until I was in public school. I spent three years in public school, then when I went back to private school, it was an international school—so those stereotypes didn't exist. Everyone was from everywhere. All of my Black friends are Caribbean or African. They just radiate Black pride, which is beautiful. How does it make me feel when I think people judge me based on the way I look? I think the only answer I can give to that is that I really look forward to dispelling whatever they are thinking, challenging their perception. I'm doing it, too. When you look at somebody on the subway you automatically—it's just something that happens in your brain. You're not doing it on purpose. Honestly, I think it is something about the way the human brain works that we put things into categories. What happened ever since our culture became literary rather than oral is that, instead of seeing bigger connections and bigger ideas, we started quantifying things and putting things more in categories. Science did that as well. Apparently there was really a switch in the brain where we went from talking to reading. You look at someone and you think one thing or you think another thing. I've had it happen to me so many times, where my impression is just blown out the window when somebody opens their mouth. I realize it probably happens to other people, too, when I talk to them. It makes me try not to impose those categories on people, especially living in New York City and going to an international school where you never know. New York is an incredibly diverse place. My school's an incredibly diverse place. If I end up going to school in Atlanta, am I going to be faced again with a bit of a division between Black and White and very little in the middle? What am I going to make of that and where am I going to belong? Am I going to be back in third grade again saying I act this way and I look this way, what do I do?

Part of the reason I rejected Duke, one of the schools on my list, is because I heard it was racially segregated, and I can't do that. I will not go to a racially segregated school; it's not my scene, not after growing up the way I have. I think mostly it has to do with living in New York and going to an international school where there is no minority. Obviously you still see race. We make little quips at each other and this or that, but honestly, I am in some ways sheltered—because New York is a different planet compared to the rest of the world. Being in an environment where people don't necessarily base so much of their impression on a race or based on the way they look is pampering. The rest of the world is not like that. That's going to be a pretty rude awakening in college. What I would hope is that it has taught me not to make those judgments of people when I look at them or when I talk to them, because you never know, honestly.

It's just not possible to judge too much at One World High School (OWHS) because in one class you'll have the entire United Nations—kids from everywhere. Is OWHS predominantly White? Maybe. But, I don't think all the students there that you look at as White would necessarily self-identify as White. Of course, you have your share of them, but for the most part people come from all over the world and identify from their country, not necessarily as White or Black or Hispanic or whatever. Going to an international school, it's just a salad bowl. Our teachers come from all over the world. They all have funny accents. Being different was normal. Being different was great. If you were from a cool place, cool.

As far as the curriculum goes, I think at OWHS, it's an international school and part of its goal is not based in the United States. I'm pretty sure that it's a European program, actually. Kids all over the world take it and there are a range of courses offered. In my philosophy class, for example, we learned about philosophies from all over the world, because my teacher says it's best to include non-Western perspectives as well. He told us he actually had to push for that—that it wasn't originally part of the curriculum. We took world history. Our teachers were very passionate about it. Most of them were not U.S. Americans—most of them are from the UK. Obviously, this is a kind of "manipulation" that you don't realize is happening, right? I have a multinational perspective now. But, I think if I had stayed at Tower, that would not be the case. I don't know.

I think if I had stayed at Tower, I would be a lot more pretentious. It is one of those prep schools where you are getting a lot more of this colonization effect. I think that this is purely speculative, but I happen to have friends who go there. At a lot of these schools when you see so many of these pretentious kids who come out of them who think they're better than everyone else, you get this immediate idea, "Why do you think you're better than everyone else?" I don't think I'm better than everyone else or at least I don't think I do or act like I do. I had a friend who went to and graduated from Tower. He was my friend. He was a nice kid, right? But there was some stupid social thing that happened. He was supposed to call and he didn't and I was waiting for him all night or something stupid like that. I saw him on the train the next morning, and I said, "You didn't call."

He's like, "Oh yeah, I got caught up," or whatever.

And I crossed my arms and did that kind of pouty thing, and I'm like, "I'm still waiting for you to apologize."

He goes, "I don't apologize."

I said, "What are you talking about?"

He's like, "Apologizing is not something I do. Like I just don't apologize to people."

And it was kind of like, what? How do you not apologize to people, you know what I mean? Later he just stopped talking to me, and my whole group of friends. He just stopped talking to us because he decided, "Well, I'm better than them," I guess. He didn't need to answer to anyone else. He's White—very White. He's Jewish and both his parents are White and I was his only Black friend. Most people would say, I don't even count. He went to prep schools his whole life—he hadn't seen the other side of the world. In the same way that he was very White, you could say someone is very Black in that they have not or do not acknowledge or see the other side of the world. They're very caught up in their own culture, their own box. He doesn't see the things that other people do and acknowledge them and say, "Hey, that's cool. I wish I could dance like that," or, "Hey, this is nice. I wish I knew how to cook that kind of food." He's grown up White and never really had that much exposure to anything else, to my knowledge. His elitist and pretentious attitude has something to do with "colonization." Because what ends up happening is that you get this idea of yourself, the idea of the way things should be, which is a definite symptom of pretentious people—that things should be this way. There's no other way for things to be. I don't think I have had that kind of education—I had it to some extent, but at OWHS you get an international perspective, but I don't consider myself to be better than other people. I look at other people and I have great admiration for them, great admiration. My friend, Tom, who got into Princeton, was telling me he went to this Princeton reception. He comes from a pretty pretentious family, let me tell you. His parents are assholes, I'm sorry, but they are. Everyone will back me up on that. He was like, "Yeah, it was disgusting. The kids were pretentious. The parents were pretentious. They were all filthy rich. It was gross." I'm thinking, "Wow. If you thought they were pretentious, man, they must have been pretentious." So I asked him,

"So, like, if you're not gonna go to Princeton, where do you think you might like to go?"

And he's like, "Princeton."

I'm like, "Why?"

"Because it's Princeton."

Why did he choose his school for the prestige like that? Because everybody else thinks they're better? That's a little gross to me. Those are his values. It's not his fault, it's kind of his parents' fault.

Advice for Teachers

What I would say to teachers? I can't emphasize it enough: talk to the kids, learn their story. There is no other way for you to know who these kids are, what backgrounds they come from, and what their story is than for you to talk to them and to their parents. Know your kids. Know your kids of color. Know your minorities and know your White kids, too. Know all of your kids because we love to categorize things, but it's not so easily done, especially nowadays. Consider, there is some projection that says (don't quote me on this) that in 300 years, everyone's going to be my color. There won't be race anymore. Everyone's going look like me because we'll just have all mixed and meshed. Nowadays, there are going to be kids like me who look one way and act another way. You think they're one way and they are another way. You've got to go with the flow a little bit. If you have a kid who's coming fresh off the boat from Ethiopia, if you get to know them, maybe read a little bit about their culture, talk to them and if it's at all possible, try to integrate some of that into your curriculum, and say, "Hey kids, we have a stu-

*dent here from Ethiopia, we'll learn a little bit about his or her culture."
Have the kid talk to their peers a little bit about what it's like to be from another place—it just enriches the entire environment for the teachers, for the
kids, for everybody.*

*It's sad, but even if you tell teachers not to see color, they're gonna see
color. Everyone sees color. The point is not to beat yourself up about it, but
be aware of it. Be aware that you see color, and based on your upbringing,
based on the way you have lived your life, when you see someone of a certain
race you are automatically going to make a judgment. The key is to be aware
that you are making that judgment and to be open to having that judgment
completely thrown out the window. Then you need to really pull out your
teaching skills and not differentiate. Especially if it comes to a public display
of discipline in front of the class, because that's going to rub off on the kids
too, and then there's going to start to be an imbalance within the classroom
kids. Have the same expectations.*

*I'm not saying that everyone has to reach the same bar and if they're
not, it's a failure, but, it goes back to—know your kids. I think it's inappro-
priate, even if the circumstances fit your judgment, to act only on that judgment. Be prepared to be surprised. For example, as a kid, I was not a good
student at all. I don't think that surprised many of my teachers. But as I got
older, my grades started moving up and I started becoming much more academically adept. If my third-grade teacher saw me now, she wouldn't know
who I was. My mother tells me that I was always driven. I knew I always had
a certain sense of drive, but I don't think I ever cared as much about doing
well as I did after, say, sixth grade—that changed because of my environment—everyone else was doing it, too. It might have been something that was
just geared to turn on in me at that point. The best advice I could give to a
teacher is "know your kids, and do not, do not, do not treat them based on a
judgment you have made, even if it's confirmed. Constantly work on dispelling that judgment, dispelling that idea you have in your head. Because
chances are, it will be. Kids change so much, so much."*

Future

*In 10 years I'd like to be more confident. I want to know where I stand be-
tween my "two worlds" and have firm footing. I want to be focused on being
me and trying not to be anyone else because I've tried that and, believe me, it
doesn't work out as well as people think it does. I think most of all, I would
like to earn people's respect, whether I was White, or Black, or Hispanic, or
Eastern European. The way you do that is through your actions. I think that
actions speak louder than race. I would hope that 10 years from now my ac-*

tions will do the work for me, and whatever judgments people make of me based on the way I look, I can, you know, help them understand that it's not always that easy to determine who someone is. I need to understand myself that it's not always that easy—that it's constantly a struggle and you should never give up that struggle because working at it harder makes you stronger. But I also want to understand that I have cause to be comfortable with who I am. I guess that's it. And my hair: I hope it's long. I hope I know how to deal with it. And I hope it doesn't make me cry anymore. And I hope that it is curly but not too curly.

Nadya: Finding Her Place

Nadya seems to be searching for her place, a home or location of sorts amidst both neocolonial and postcolonial flows that pervade her life at school and in her city. She wants to, "*know where I stand between my 'two worlds' and have firm footing.*" Her testimonio moves back and forth, never quite settling in any one place, rather, shifting between sure-footed denunciation of neocolonial categorizations and discourses, tentative reflections about being "*caught in the middle,*" and painful retellings of being captured and pinned down by others and by her own neocolonial desires. She feels a sense of loneliness about her struggle to find her place: "*Everyone else, to me, had their place, and I did not.*"

Neocolonial and postcolonial flows emanate from her, her peer groups, and her schooling—but Nadya remains highly analytical and reflective about her determined journey to understand and be comfortable with who she is. Nadya is able to clearly articulate how neocolonial categorizations are formed and damage people, and how she is part of at least two worlds. Ultimately aware of her alterity, or the way her identity has been deemed "other" by neocolonial flows, Nadya tried very hard to fit the school's and society's conception of one's place. She recognizes the state of being different among normalized White Europeans and searches for her location in the world (Ashcroft et al., 2000).

Hybridity: A Foot in Both Worlds

It's a double thing, for me because I am, number one, biracial, and, number two, I am dark-skinned, and I grew up and I live in an upper middle class, predominantly White environment. So, being biracial obviously I have, racially, two worlds.

Nadya struggles to find a home for herself while moving back and forth between Black, White, Russian, Cuban, and Roma identities. Although identity comes about for an individual, it is also determined by larger social and political flows that give meaning but also can distort and damage. Identities are carefully produced by the neocolonizer to perpetuate the agenda of dominance of minoritized groups (Ghosh et al., 2008). Such fixed and narrow rules for what it means to be and act White and what it means to be and act Black make it virtually impossible for Nadya to be accepted and to comfortably accept herself as both White and Black. Unfortunately, the neocolonial discourse does not allow for a person to be both: one must fall into the either/or binary of Black/White. To defy these rules is to be seen as impure:

> In colonial discourses of the Other—as in official multiculturalism—each national (or racial/ethnic) group is viewed as pure and homogeneous, representing an authentic and unified culture. In this knowledge paradigm, any deviation from the "norm"—assertions or display of strong individual experience or "multiple identities"—would be seen as impure, even betrayal. (Singh & Schmidt, 2000, p. 23)

Although Nadya's identity is necessarily impure, there is no one pure culture or cultural identity for anyone. All cultures are involved in one another and form one another, and to say otherwise is to ignore the dynamic and sometimes damaging neocolonial and postcolonial flows of culture, nation, politics, economics, etc. Nadya's intense need to find a singular place repeats the neocolonial mandate for a singular, pure identity:

> *I still struggle a little bit, but most of that I think happened in middle school when I first started to see race, and I realized that I had to basically put myself somewhere because that's what I think you do, to be honest, is that you must have an identity racially.*

Given what postcolonial scholars might call her hybridity, Nadya may find it difficult to settle within the current popular conceptions of identity as fixed and singular. Because of both postcolonial and neocolonial flows circulating in school campuses and society, Nadya's sense of who she is racially and culturally will remain in motion, conflictual, and ambivalent. She will therefore feel both attraction to and repulsion for the ways in which she has constructed her identity (Bhabha, 1994). Still, Nadya feels "*caught*," although proud of her identities:

> *It's weird to think about being caught in the middle like that because it's almost two polar opposites, and when you put them together you get me. I'm sitting right on the cusp, and I think, do I belong here or do I belong there, you know what I mean? There are elements of both cultures that attract me. I've never lost my sense of iden-*

tity racially. It's something that I'm incredibly proud of—being Russian and being Cuban and noticing things in myself both aesthetically (mostly) and personality-wise. I love noticing those things in myself from both cultures. I love being able to say that I come from where I do. The second part is being Black and growing up in a White family—growing up White. Because, again, people don't like to say it, but there is a way of acting Black and there is a way of acting White—stereotypically.

Nadya's analysis of being "*caught in the middle*" is similar to Gloria Anzaldúa's (1999) poem in which she described her ambivalence about living in the borderlands between five different and narrow neocolonial discourses targeting five different races:

> To live in the Borderlands means you
> are neither *hispana india negra espanola*
> *ni gabacha, eres mestiza, mulata,* half-breed
> caught in the crossfire between camps
> while carrying all five races on your back
> not knowing which side to turn to, run from. (p. 194)

Like Anzaldúa, Nadya's worlds are incommensurable, incomplete, and incomprehensible to the neocolonizer. Therefore, they are difficult for Nadya to understand without feeling as though she is caught or struggling for solid ground.

While Nadya utilizes the neocolonial categorizations available to her (i.e., Black, White, Russian, etc.) to define "*a way of acting Black…and a way of acting White,*" she also disqualifies them, denying them any power to define her. At the same time, she offers the example of demographic checklists on college applications to show how her racial and ethnic roots do not meaningfully identify her. "*When I check those boxes, they see that I checked Black/African American. They see that I checked Hispanic. But they do not know my background. They do not know what it means.*" In other words, she claims that you cannot know someone based solely on their ethnicities. To try to do so results in essentializations of each category such as, "all Blacks are this way," or, "all Whites are that way."

Seeming to advocate the normalization of difference as opposed to the neocolonial discourse's normalization of sameness, Nadya explains how difference, ethnic difference in particular, was commonplace and accepted—even venerated—in her high school. "*Being different was normal. Being different was great. If you were from a cool place, cool.*" Although this comment shows that difference was normal in Nadya's high school, she still must contend with an identity that is more than "different" from White European. Her identity construction may require multiple consciousnesses, as well as recognition of the fluidity and conflictual nature of belonging to many ethnic groups in neocolonial spaces (Singh & Schmidt, 2000). Nadya performs the postcolonial flow of a multiplicity of homes, heritages, and hybridity, thus denying the "'*fixity*' [emphasis added] in the ideological construction of otherness" (Bhabha, 1994, p. 66). Although the neocolonial discourse would like to pin Nadya down as a cut-and-dried Black woman, she is not. Therefore, Nadya's fluid and dynamic, hybrid identities disrupt the neocolonizer's systems of oppression and fixed identity categorization. Nadya's quest for her place in the world will necessarily be incomplete and characterized by an internal otherness. This may mean that her feet may always be in two or more worlds, for this is how postcolonial hybridity seems to work. Perhaps Nadya may find her home where she seems to be: with feet not so firmly planted and often dancing between many tangled worlds (Bhabha, 1994).

Messages from Monstrous Places

But as I got older, I started to hate it [my hair]. *Looking back on it now, that is an indication to me that I realized I was different from other kids and didn't have long, blond hair. My hair was one of the first things that was indicative of that.*

During European exploration and colonization of the Americas through the nineteenth century, people of color were put on display in museums and world's fairs for their "abnormal" physiology, and were described as primitive, monstrous, and hideous (Willinsky, 1998). Nadya's desire to resemble the White European neocolonizer physically, along with her ambivalence about her naturally textured hair, repeats colonialism's discourse of the Black person as monstrous. In her testimonio, she tells about her association between her desire for straight hair and her desire for Whiteness:

The first time I got my hair straightened I must have been very, very young. I came home and it was so weird to me that I started playing a game in which I was two people. I was myself and I was a White girl. I would be talking to the White girl and made up a whole story. And then I wanted to see what it looked like when it was straight, so I wet it. Obviously, it started to curl up again and I was devastated. I didn't get my hair straightened for a very long time.

The next time she got it straightened, she had a dream that she got her hair wet and it started to curl.

As soon as it started curling up again I looked in the mirror and I was horrified, and I started screaming, "Monster! Monster! Monster! I'm a monster! I'm a monster!" I woke up and I was like, "Oh my gosh, wow."

Nadya's reinscription of neocolonialism's denigrating and dividing discourse is shocking when we think about it as a colonial flow that is at least 500 years old. That such monstrous messages are replicated by and arise out of a young Black woman in 2010 is evidence of the pervasive invisibility of neo-colonialism. Nadya is perplexed by her self-neocolonization:

> *I felt really, really good when it was straight. The fact that in my dream when it curled back up I was calling myself a monster, was mind-boggling to me to think about that being Black and having Black hair makes me think of myself as a monster. The next time I got my hair straightened, I had another anxiety dream like that.*

Nadya's explanation of why she had such a powerfully negative response to the image of her "White hair" returning to "*Black hair*" is a decidedly rational, humanist, and recolonizing analysis:

> *I think it is something about the way the human brain works that we put things into categories. What happened ever since our culture became literary rather than oral, is that, instead of seeing bigger connections and bigger ideas, we started quantifying things and putting things more in categories. Science did that as well.*

Nadya identifies the turn towards colonial thinking as when the colonizer's culture began its project of civilizing through imposing socially constructed Western literacy and scientific categories on the peoples, animals, plants, and cultures of the world. This is when the authority of "the book" was used to inspire awe in colonized [read: *minoritized*] peoples in order to subjugate them (Bhabha, 1994; Willinsky, 1998). But, Nadya sees this shift as a good and civilizing move when, in fact, it may have helped her to view herself as "monstrous" with her Black hair. In her dream, when she was no longer mimicking the White colonizers' straight hair, she somehow was taken up by the neocolonial flow of a monstrous Black woman. In this case, Nadya uses science to reify, and comes close to justifying, or at least excusing, the colonizers' civilizing, quantifying, and categorizing mission. Nadya's explanation that "*it is something about the human brain*" that may contribute to this horrific construction of the monstrous Black denies that the imperial mindset was one of "bringing civilization to barbaric peoples" who deserved to be controlled, given their inferiority (Said, 1994, p. xi).

Nadya does have affinity for her Black hair but, again, performs a neocolonial flow of self-exoticism related to her hair that could be traced to colonial discourses. "*I like the kink. I like, you know, the way it makes me look ethnic, the way it makes me look a little bit exotic almost.*" Nadya's exotification of herself because of her "*Black hair*" is nothing new. The phenomenon of "a black person…being reduced to the sensual and the sexual" has been in place "since the beginning of American history" (White, 1999, p. 13). Indeed, the neocolonizer's exoticizing gaze upon the "native" has extended its reach to Nadya. She explains how she strives to feel confident about her physicality given the exoticizing and monstrous messages in the form of neocolonial flows that she has incorporated into her self-perceptions.

> *I'm insanely jealous of confident Black women who have that sense of Black pride because I never had that growing up. I was never really exposed to that—until it was "too late." When I see Black women who are really comfortable in their skin and they love their hair and they can wear it this way and they can wear it that way, and they know what clothes to wear to flatter their bodies and they know how to talk and they know how to walk and they know how to act, I definitely have a lot of admiration for them. I shrivel a little bit inside because I feel like I'm never really going to get to that point, because I will always have a foot in each world, so to speak.*

Ghosh, Abdi, & Naseem (2008) might call Nadya's self-neocolonizations "identity deformations" that are certainly the goal of a neocolonial project (p. 59). The monstrous messages that Nadya must examine have been accepted by her to some degree in order for them to have taken root, negating Nadya's fluid, hybrid identities. Her "*Black hair*" has become emblematic of her struggle: "*My hair is a constant reminder to me that I'm still looking for my spot.*" For Ghosh et al., Bhabha's (1994) third space where identities emerge is a process of negotiating meaning wherein, "one has to hope [minoritized youth could] redeem some deformed identities over time and space" (2008, p. 64). This seems to be Nadya's intention: to be a confident Black woman.

Overlooked and Overdetermined: The Imposition of Categories

> *People categorize. It might just have something to do with the human brain. It might just have something to do with human society, or history.*

Nadya concedes that, in addition to the possibility of a biologically-based urge to sort people, history has shaped people's need to categorize—a uniquely postcolonial perspective. One of the legacies of colonialism is the use of seemingly natural and scientifically-based categories, specifically, hierarchies and binaries, to sort and place people in rank order, often by the color of their skin. This is troubling, as can be seen over and over in this book. Indeed, "the nightmare of the ideologies and categories of racism continue to repeat upon the living" (Young, 1995, p. 28). When a rigid race-based category is placed on someone, it can do damage by both overlooking the person and by overdetermining who they are. Both of these experiences are described by Nadya in her testimonio (Bhabha, 1994; Said, 1994; Young, 1995).

Nadya is wrestling with multiple categories based on her ethnic backgrounds and what they mean to her and those around her. We've discussed Nadya's incommensurable identities. She looks Black but acts White. However, Nadya can also be described as a transnational subject who is tied to her Cuban, Russian, Roma, American, Black, and White identities and who is being raised by a White mother and surrounded by White friends. As we will see in this section, Nadya deploys the different aspects of her ever-shifting, conflicting, and overlapping identity categorizations for different and complex purposes. In the process, she "constantly reformulates, adapts, and abandons categorizations" (Khagram & Levitt, 2007, p. 215), disobeying the neocolonizer's rigid system of classification and marginalization.

Nadya's sudden realization that she is not White came as a shock to her, and began a journey of realizing that her teachers also saw her through the lens of a marginalizing and firm neocolonial flow of the troublemaking Black girl.

> *I didn't see race until, I would say, I came to New York and I started going to public school, where it was glaringly obvious to me that I looked one way and acted another way. Something went off in my brain that made me realize, I don't look the same as my mother. I don't look the same as the people I hang out with.*

> *I have a memory of one of my teachers in third grade who just didn't like me, for some reason. I'm convinced it was because I was Black, but my mother tells me she was married to a Black man. I told her, that doesn't mean that she's not racist—because she hated me for some reason. I was kind of a wild child, but I wasn't that bad—I wasn't freakin' spray-painting things, you know what I mean? I had my moments but overall I was a pretty good kid. She just picked on me.*

Nadya is sure that her teacher didn't like her because of the color of her skin. In this case, Nadya feels overdetermined—as if her Black skin somehow only signified a "*wild child*." Interestingly, she claims she should have been more accepted by her teacher, given that she did not fit into the neocolonial flow of delinquent Black youth "*spray-painting things*." This shows how Nadya may have internalized the colonizer's overdetermined images of what makes a "good Black" and a "bad Black" person. However, she is also able to pinpoint the clean-cut neocolonial binary of Black/White that was deployed at her school. She was performing both categories: "*It was a dichotomy to me: to be Black you have to act this way; to be White you have to act this way. I look this way, I act this way, what do I do? It was rough.*" She is able to identify the colonizer's binary categories, and feels the pull in each direction—to act White and to act Black. In essence, she is mocking the White European neocolonizer by looking Black but acting White (Bhabha, 1994; Fanon, 1967). This was not comfortable for Nadya because not only did her teacher not accept her performance of a White flow, her peers did not accept her performance of a Black flow.

As a young child Nadya disciplined herself by desiring to be a "normal" Black kid. She was aware that her actions did not fit the flow of a Black person, and she tried to perform her conception of the part. *"But I did try so, so hard. I must have just felt that this is where I belong. This is the way I look. Everyone who looks this way, hangs out together, so why don't I?"* She decided if she had Black skin she needed to be Black and associate with Black students at school. Nadya was harshly rebuked by a Black peer who told her she could not play with her because she had a White mother. As we can see, repeatedly, Nadya is denied her hybrid identities because she does not fit neatly into the neocolonial slots and categorizations placed before her—essentially she is overlooked or ignored due to her Black skin.

Despite being overlooked and over determined, Nadya is proud of her postcolonial flow of multiple ethnicities and national affiliations. She seems to enjoy upending the categories:

> *I'm very proud of who I am, don't get me wrong. I enjoy the feeling when people are surprised when I exceed expectations. If you look in the working world, there aren't many women, for example, corporate jobs or engineers, there are not many Black women out there. I really enjoy being able to say, well, these are all options for me. It came up a lot when I was applying for colleges, in the demographic section and affirmative action. I checked every box except Asian. I even checked "other," because I am every box. I checked White, Caucasian, because I was thinking of my Russian birth mother—my blood. I checked Black/African American, which is a really crazy box, actually, because my North African friends can't check it. I didn't check Native American but I checked Hispanic because I'm Cuban. And I checked "other" and I put Roma. I checked pretty much all the boxes. It was just interesting having to check those boxes that said I have to quantify myself. Why am I checking these boxes? I'm checking these boxes so colleges can look at them and say, "Oh, here's a Black woman who is half Gypsy and half Russian and half Cuban who wants to go into engineering. Oh, we don't see many of those." I hate affirmative action, but I'm going to check those boxes anyway because I know the playing field is already unlevel.*

There are times when Nadya is utilizing her hybridity to her advantage. At other times her fluid and changing identity overwhelms her because of others' unyielding measurements and judgments of her, based on her lack of authenticity as one or the other.

> *I joke a lot about being the token Black kid because pretty much all my friends are White. Just by coincidence, I think. I joke a lot about being the token Black kid and*

then my friends tell me, "You're not Black. You're not Black." It's really upsetting to me, when they say I'm not Black, actually. I don't let it get to me too much because I know what they mean. I know they don't mean it in a bad way. What they're talking about is, "You are not the typical Black person. You act White," and I like being Black.

It's as if Nadya's friends are trying to help Nadya continue performing the flow of normalized Whiteness and be confident in her White identity. Black is constructed as an insult. Black can only be one thing—an essentialized deficit model of a Black person. Nadya's Blackness is both overlooked (i.e., her presence as Black is not acknowledged) and overdetermined (i.e., her Blackness is somehow indicative of a negative stereotype of, or flow about, Blacks (Bhabha, 1994). But we need to see how Nadya has also benefitted from acting White. Fanon (1967) showed how acting White garners power in a neocolonial context:

Every colonized people—in other words, every people in whose soul an inferiority complex has been created by the death and burial of its local cultural originality—finds itself face to face with the language of the civilizing nation; that is, with the culture of the mother country. The colonized is elevated above his jungle status in proportion to his adoption of the mother country's cultural standards. He becomes whiter as he renounces his blackness, his jungle. (p. 18)

No matter what Nadya does, she can not escape her friend's reinscription of neocolonial categories about her Blackness. When it serves her White friends, they claim she is not Black, meaning she is accepted and does not fit the negative stereotypes of Blacks. Alternatively, her friends claim she is Black when she is accepted into prestigious universities, as if she were simply handed the acceptance letter based solely on the color of her skin:

"Oh, you got in because you're Black." I cannot tell you how furious that makes me—I rip people's heads off, I do. I give them the full, "I got in because…well, I like to think it's because I worked my ass off for four years and had a 4.2 GPA, and, you know, a full resume, but hey, who knows?" Maybe it was because I am Black.

Examining the source of these damaging neocolonial flows, Nadya identifies the hegemonic thinking of the neocolonial White European. One of her White male peers, who she describes as "*very White*" claims he never apologizes. She attributes his behavior and thinking to his Whiteness.

He's grown up White and never really had that much exposure to anything else, to my knowledge. His elitist and pretentious attitude has something to do with "colonization." Because what ends up happening is that you get this idea of yourself, the

idea of the way things should be, which is a definite symptom of pretentious peo-
ple—that things should be this way. There's no other way for things to be.

Her peer's sense of impervious rightness echoes White Europeans' domination of minoritized youth by consent. In other words, his *"elitist and preten-*
tious attitude" represents power structures that serve neocolonial interests
that are accepted as normal and natural by many. But Nadya is able to wrest
her identities away, standing apart from the neocolonizing identity deformations that intend to afflict her with low self-esteem.

Nadya explains how categories do not tell us much about people, but she
also uses them to make sense and (non)sense of herself and the people
around her. Her complex dealings with categories imposed by both herself
and others serve to perpetuate neocolonial conceptions and disrupt them
through her hybrid performance of unsanctioned combinations of identities.
It is troubling to acknowledge that if one's language(s), one's culture(s), and
the color of one's skin do not represent the dominant culture's rigid categorizations (even if you mimic sanctioned identities), you, as minoritized, do not
feel whole, one, validated, or even "real," perhaps. It is disheartening that our
schools and institutions are unaware of, and continue to proliferate, the
mechanisms that perpetuate the neocolonization of our youth. Nadya is mis-
identified through overdeterminations and overlookings by others and herself. These historical and present moments result in "less confident beings
who will actually collaborate with their oppressors in the project of oppression" (Ghosh et al., 2008, pp. 64–65). An example is Nadya's self-
identification as having monstrous Black hair. Nevertheless, Nadya, as evidenced throughout her testimonio, has begun to engage in a process of decolonizing her life and education (Abdi & Richardson, 2008; Kanu, 2009).

The Long and Winding Roads of Decolonization

I'm here and I'm powerful despite the fact that I'm oppressed. I mean, I'm a Black
woman growing up in a White man's world.

Although she knows how to "act White" Nadya understands that the neocolonial structures that govern her life will see her skin color first and judge
her based upon it. She also knows that she places some of those monstrous
messages on others and herself. *"I'm doing it, too. When you look at some-*
body on the subway you automatically [categorize]—*it's just something that*
happens in your brain." Her acknowledgment that she is minoritized in the
colonizer's world gives her a starting point from which to begin to unmask
the multinodal workings of neocolonialism in her schooling and in her life.

She analyzes how her White friends construct their choices that perpetuate the neocolonial power structure. For example, a White friend who describes a Princeton University reception as "*pretentious*" and "*gross*" still decides to attend that school:

> *And he's like, "Princeton."*
> *I'm like, "Why?"*
> *"Because it's Princeton."*
> *Why did he choose his school for the prestige like that? Because everybody else thinks they're better? That's a little gross to me. Those are his values. It's not his fault, it''s kind of his parents' fault.*

Nadya's identification of how power is maintained and passed from White European parent to child and so on opens the door for "escaping dominant Western philosophical and intellectual orientations that tend toward the colonizing of others" (Cannella & Viruru, 2004, p. 78).

Her disdain for the imposition of categories in her life motivates her to disable them. "*It makes me try not to impose those categories on people.*" However, while wanting to defy essentialist discourses based on biology as socially constructed, she also reifies them by saying that our need to categorize is biologically brain-based—something we can't help doing based on our heredity. Together, this is evidence in Nadya's case of the complexity and long-term project of decolonization. It seems as if Nadya has two tapes playing in her head. One plays the neocolonizer's flows. The other validates her experience as the recipient and wielder of categories that often do not mesh traditionally, and whose incommensurability leaves her and others in awe. Nadya intends to suspend judgment, because one can and should expect that judgment may be wrong: "*What I would hope is that it has taught me not to make those judgments of people when I look at them or when I talk to them, because you never know, honestly.*"

Urgent Messages for Teachers

> *It wasn't so much that she told me I couldn't play with her that made me cry, it was the racial jab. I cried and cried and cried, and the teachers didn't do anything about it, of course, because they don't know what to do. All of the teachers were White and they didn't really understand my pain. They had no idea what to do about that kind of a thing.*

Teachers' inaction after Nadya's painful experience of being narrowly categorized as an inauthentic Black girl because she was being raised by a White mother gives this book a purpose. Unless teachers can come to terms with the wider world's history of colonization and the history of neocolonization in American schooling (as well as in their own personal lives, however unintentional), the number of "casualties" of neocolonialism will continue to grow. Reading the testimonios of youth and understanding how they may represent neocolonial and postcolonial flows may be a way to begin identifying and arresting damaging messages in schools.

Though Nadya mentions it only briefly, teachers who bring non-Western perspectives into the curriculum can be role models for anticolonial praxis:

> *In my philosophy class, for example, we learned about philosophies from all over the world, because my teacher says it's best to include non-Western perspectives as well. He told us he actually had to push for that—that it wasn't originally part of the curriculum.*

A focus on non-Western knowledges and ways of thinking can be placed on the reform agenda for additional subject areas such as history, literature, science, math, and art (Merryfield 2008; Willinsky, 2009). Nadya also calls for a conscious anticolonialism. I believe that Nadya is compelling teachers to acknowledge their own neocolonial, essentialized, hierarchical, and binary categorizations, so that they can begin to actively resist them in their thinking and actions. Nadya says: *"The best advice I could give to a teacher is 'know your kids and do not, do not, do not treat them based on a judgment you have made, even if it's confirmed.'"* Her powerful anticolonial mantra is: *"Be prepared to be surprised."*

Note

1. Nadya DeLange is an 18-year-old Black high school senior with Russian, Cuban, and Roma heritage. She was adopted and raised by a White European American upper middle class single mother.

Chapter Five

Amelia's[1] Testimonio

"I Always Feel Filipina First...
It's Okay to Be Both Filipina and American."

I'm from the Philippines. I'm about to have been here two years. My dad is a mechanic. I have an 11-year-old brother who is in the fifth grade. I came here because of my future—I want to live here to be more successful, to be a good nurse. The United States is the best country in the world: you can speak another language like English, Spanish, or French here. I want to be here. I have only lived in the Philippines and now, here.

Languages

My first language is Tagalog—it's from the Philippines. We also have a language in the Philippines called Kapampangan. I speak English, but I also speak Kapampangan. My family speaks more Tagalog than English at home, but outside we speak English. We speak English outside so many people can understand us. Kapampangan is different than Tagalog because we're from a different state in the Philippines, so we spoke that. In school I learned Tagalog and English.

Being American and Filipino

Americans are nice. They talk to me a lot, so I can speak English a lot in school. How are Americans and Filipinos different? Language is one difference. Another is that Americans take leave of their family when they're younger. But Filipinos can live with their family up into their 20s. Americans look different: their hair, eyes, etc. I am both Filipino and American, because of language. I speak English and Tagalog, so I'm both. Americans are friendly and nice. They're my friends at school. No, you don't have to speak English to be American. You can still be friends with Americans, even if your English is not that good.

If someone asked me where I was from I would say, "I'm from the Philippines." I've lived here for about two years. I feel American when I'm with my friends, when we're watching TV. Sometimes, we go outside. My friends

*are Mexicans, Hawaiians, Filipinos, Americans, Koreans, and Vietnamese—
I have a lot of friends—but I don't feel American when I am at home.*

*I feel Filipino at home because we're eating Filipino foods. We're
watching Filipino TV. We're talking Filipino—we eat together and we watch
together. We go to church together. We play together with my brother. And
we love together. We stick together. In the Philippines we have family reunions. You are Filipino if you speak Tagalog, are friendly, and you probably
go to church. My church is mostly Filipino but there are Americans, Mexicans, and Hawaiians. It's Catholic. Church is good. There's a lot of Filipinos and there's no Filipino Father there. There's an American and an
African Father. It would be nice to have a Filipino Father because he could
speak in Tagalog to the others that can't really speak English and be able to
hear all their problems. When you're at home you speak your own language,
but when you're with your friends you speak English, so it's kind of weird.
For example, when I'm with a group of people, I say "Hi," and they teach
me. If I eat food like sushi, I feel American.*

*Most important to me as a Filipino is family. My dad and my mom are
separated so my mom is living in the Philippines with my half brother and
I'm living here with my dad. It's hard. My mom is not coming here. No. My
mom is married in the Philippines. My dad said we can go visit after high
school—I've got two more years. Friends are also important in Filipino culture. I have Filipino friends. I talk to them about my problems, school problems and homework problems or projects. Usually it's science, math, or
history.*

*I always feel Filipina first. It's kind of hard to explain. Like when we're
at school, we do team projects. We talk together and stay after school to
work on our project—that makes me feel American. I feel American because
in my classes there are a lot of Americans or other Asians that speak English.
They don't speak my language, so when we work together we speak English.
Also, through communication, for example, the phone or texting, with my
American friends in English makes me feel American. It's okay to be both
Filipina and American. For example, yesterday we had a Filipino American
church function where we were serving food to Americans. Filipinos serve
food to people at the church every Sunday.*

*At the grocery store I feel Filipino and American. When I'm with my
family, we speak Filipino, but we're in an American store. But when I'm with
Americans or other kids, for example, Hawaiians, I feel American. When I'm
with Filipinos at the movies, I feel more Filipino than American—it's the
people I'm with. If my friends go to my house, my Filipino friends and others,
like Korean, my Filipino friends and I will speak English so they can understand us.*

Being American

Some ESL students want to be very American. When Asian people grow up here, they tease the new kids because they don't know a lot about English. They ignore them, then do something mean to them. For example, they'll say, "That girl or guy doesn't like you very much." They'll say that to me, to an American, or to other people. They want to be good at school and be very American.

African American girls like to hang out with American guys, White guys, to be their boyfriend, to be more American. They change their voice, how they dress, their hair. They change their car. They put blond in their hair, and make it straight. But some African Americans are not like that. I have a friend, she's simple. She's always playing video games like a guy. She's nice. She's herself. She brings video games, like Nintendo, and always says, "Hi," to us.

How are Filipinos like Americans? They are similar because they can read, speak American, and do math. They are educated and athletic. What's important to me about being American is friends—having American friends. School is important because of my academic subjects and friends. All my subjects matter because you have to learn them for next year.

I feel more Filipino than American—I'll always feel that way. How I look when I see myself in the mirror and my family is Filipino. We're always eating Filipino food with my dad. I'll always be a Filipino. Some Americans say that my English isn't really good. But Filipinos say I'm full Filipino because I can speak Filipino and I can be friends with them because I'm Filipino. I want to be friends with Filipinos.

Classes

My first subject is geometry. It's kind of hard because it's shapes, but my teacher is nice. She has been my teacher since I was a freshman. My second period, Mr. Parks, my ESL teacher, is nice and we're close. He teaches me and he teaches us about English—so that's kind of an easy subject. History is kind of hard because of the projects. We learn of the history of America or other countries and read it section by section. My fourth period, choir, is not hard because we just sing. I don't really need help in algebra because I already took that subject last year. My last period is biology. It's hard and we're doing projects now. There are a lot of pages to read, but my teacher is nice—so nice. She teaches us how to be responsible, to do our work, and be respectful.

Learning English

What makes it hard to learn languages? When kids are saying bad words, it's kind of hard, I don't want to say it. But they're saying it to me, but I won't say it. I don't like to say bad words. Asian people have teased me. To me, Asian is Chinese, Korean. Other Asians are bad because they feel they're better than Filipinos because they can speak English, so they can tease us. But they grew up here. There are a lot of Filipinos who speak English, who were born here and they speak English. What makes it nice and easy to learn language is being able to talk to my friends—they teach me. Last year, I was really shy but now I can speak English a lot. I'm so nice in the class now, but last year I was too quiet. It makes it hard when teachers talk too fast. They'll say hard words and I'll think about it and later on I can probably figure it out.

Advice for Teachers

What advice would I give teachers who are teaching students learning English? I would tell teachers to speak slowly so students can understand. Explain it carefully to them. For example, in history, explain why it happened or what it is that happened. Give them enough time to think, and help them to do the work. Teachers should know that kids tease us. For example, someone teased my friend, a girl that is half Thai and half Russian, so she's not that nice. That day, there was a poem to read. The teacher gave it to the students, then my friend said, "What's this?" but she knew what it was. Then that girl said, "It's a poem." Then she called her a bad name: "Bitch." She was really mad. That girl is an ESL student, too, and she knows the poem, but she pretends that she can speak English very well and she teases me, too, on the bus. She told me on the bus, "I know more English than you." She said that to me. I was really mad. She's sitting with me and she said that to my face. Me and my friends want to talk to Mr. Parks about that, but I don't know if she wants to talk about it. There's a lot of competition in ESL class. When we are having a class discussion about something and the teacher asks a question, and a student raises their hand but they get the answer wrong, another student will raise their hand to feel like, smart, and to make you feel bad. Some Mexican and Korean people do that. By raising their hand when you don't know the answer, they're saying, "I know that one and they don't know it." Japanese people, for example, my teacher said, "Who knows that?" and a Japanese student said, "I know it. I know it," but he doesn't know it, and some other student really knows it. He wants to be the good one—to be the best student in the class, to be close to their teacher, for it to be more likely to get a high grade. But teachers don't do that. In the Philippines, they teach saying, "You can do it"—encouragement. They help you.

I would tell teachers don't teach Asian, or Pacific Islanders, or Mexican people that they're not good at English. Teach them to speak English, to understand English, to feel like they can speak English very well so they can do well in school. They should talk to students a lot so they can know and understand what the non-American people feel about their school and friends.

They should teach Tagalog here, because some Filipinos, they know only a little bit of English. If American teachers and students knew Tagalog, they could speak with American people because right now they are too shy to be with them. They could answer their questions. So they should have it here. But just translation, not a Tagalog history class.

Forgetting Language

My brother will not remember Tagalog after a while. Because he has American friends and he always speaks English—and sometimes he speaks English to me, so I think he'll forget it. It's okay, because he can still understand Tagalog, he can't speak it, but he can understand it. And I can teach him, if I can still remember it. He forgot our language, Kapampangan. It's sad because when my mom is calling, my mom speaks Tagalog but my half brother speaks Kapampangan, so my brother is speaking Tagalog and my half brother is speaking Kapampangan, so they can't understand what they're saying to each other. He can understand Kapampangan, but he can't speak it.

Amelia: Transnational in a Neocolonial Smog

Amelia's testimonio reveals performances of many flows of transnationalism. In other words, her conceptions of the United States, Americanness, and language transcend, transform, and redefine traditional or neocolonial borders and boundaries (Khagram & Levitt, 2007). For example, instead of highlighting our lingua franca, American English, she claims that the United States is "*the best country in the world*" because of its multilingualism. She explains that one can be an American even if they don't speak English, abandoning the citizenship requirement of English proficiency. Offering a poignant example of how Amelia sees the United States as a multicultural transnational space, she explains, "*If I eat food like sushi, I feel American*"—

a dish brought to the United States by Japanese. These assertions deny the neocolonial flow that posits that an American is someone who is of European-American heritage and an English speaker. What is eye-opening about Amelia's testimonio is her perspective as a transnational subject who seems to be seeing the United States for what it is: an intensively multilingual and multicultural place where being American is defined in complex and, perhaps, unexpected ways that easily reveal "the fading of America" (Spiro, 2008, p. 40). Similarly, Spiro (2008) claimed that for people to perform and display their Americanness, fluency in popular culture is probably a more meaningful gauge of common knowledge than is familiarity with the United States Constitution, for example, It is not difficult for transnational subjects to prove that any rigid definition of an American will unravel once we take into account who people are and how they actually live and think in this "unbounded" place called the United States of America.

Amelia's testimonio seems to ask us to consider, what is *distinctively* American (Spiro, 2008)? Amelia's positive and dynamic notions of linguistic diversity, friendships across ethnic boundaries, and Americanness as multicultural, are set against a distinctively American backdrop or smog of neocolonial schooling that encourages English acquisition at any cost and subtractive assimilation into a mythical American ideal. Amelia confronts some of these flows and smog with postcolonial flows of hybridity, strategic nationalism, and multiple national affiliations, all the while struggling to make sense of and manage the neocolonial flows that attempt to bind and limit her and her peers.

Filipino First: Complex Hybrid Flows within Neocolonial Policy

Like the other youths' testimonios in this book, Amelia's narrative expresses a shifting and fluid identity that can sometimes feel American and sometimes feel more Filipino, depending on who she is with and where she is. A hybrid identity, as discussed in previous chapters, is the result of the intersecting, clashing, and joining of the incommensurable identities and meanings of multicultural youth. As a more recent immigrant, having resided in the United States for less than two years, Amelia at times expresses a strong fondness and patriotism towards the United States, but remains primarily affiliated with her Filipino identity. She often echoes the welcoming and meritocratic flow of the neocolonizer, but remains true to herself—her Filipina self.

Amelia's statement, *"I always feel Filipina first"* is a denial of the neocolonial project of Americanization in schooling (Said, 1994). Our current educational policies still promote a national ideal of monolingual English proficiency and a push towards immigrants blending into American society (U.S. Department of Education, 2001, *No Child Left Behind Act* (NCLB)). For example, the "Emergency Immigrant Education Program" of Title III of the Elementary and Secondary Education Act provides emergency funding for school districts that experience a sudden influx of immigrants. The purposes of the funds are to improve instruction of recent immigrants and assist "with their transition into American society" (U.S. Department of Education, 2001, NCLB, Section 3241). How might an immigrant to the United States be "transitioned" into American society? What is "American society" and who defines it? Why is a "transition" necessary according to federal policy? These unanswered questions seem to bring us back to the beginning of this book, making space for educators and policymakers to act upon unexamined ideologies about what it means to be an American and, indeed, what it means to Americanize someone. Is Amelia, after two years in this country, sufficiently transitioned into American society if she "*feels Filipina first*" and claims that "*it's okay to be both Filipina and American*"? The flow of a bicultural identity with an emphasis on one's Filipina identity clashes with the myth of the unitary and pure American identity that requires one to shed meaningful connections to countries of origin in order to blend into European American flows. The reality of minoritized youths' identities is much more complex than we might imagine—lending credence to the concept of hybrid identities that are more dynamic and difficult to define. For example, notice how Amelia's perceived nationality shifts depending on who she is with and what she is doing:

> *At the grocery store I feel Filipino and American. When I'm with my family, we speak Filipino, but we're in an American store. But when I'm with Americans or other kids, for example, Hawaiians, I feel American. When I'm with Filipinos at the movies, I feel more Filipino than American—it's the people I'm with.*

Complicating matters, language often plays a momentous role in determining minoritized youths' fluid identity constructions.

Amelia's contention, "*No, you don't have to speak English to be American*," flies in the face of the neocolonial project of Americanization through English-only proficiency. The NCLB Act required that English learners show yearly progress in their acquisition of English and "meet the same challenging State academic content and student academic achievement standards as all children are expected to meet" (U.S. Department of Education, NCLB, 2001, Section 3102)—goals that although seemingly equitable at first glance, are unattainable by many English learners, given that the research is clear that it takes five to seven years to achieve academic proficiency in a second language (Thomas & Collier, 1997). This policy sets up an unreasonable national standard that, in essence, guarantees that many English learners will be categorized as failures, reifying the hierarchy of races with White European native English speakers at the top of the rank order. Further, the *Immigration and Nationality Act* of 1952 required that,

(a) No person except as otherwise provided in this title shall hereafter be naturalized as a citizen of the United States upon his own application who cannot demonstrate—

(1) an understanding of the English language, including an ability to read, write, and speak words in ordinary usage in the English language: Provided, That the requirements of this paragraph relating to ability to read and write shall be met if the applicant can read or write simple words and phrases to the end that a reasonable test of his literacy shall be made and that no extraordinary or unreasonable conditions shall be imposed upon the applicant; and

(2) a knowledge and understanding of the fundamentals of the history, and of the principles and form of government, of the United States. (U.S. Citizenship and Immigration Services , 1952, Section 312)

Clearly, federal law requires English proficiency at more than a basic level where one could, in English, demonstrate understanding of "the fundamentals of the history, and of the principles and form of government." Amelia's contention that someone can be American without speaking English seems to draw upon a national narrative of an unquestioningly welcoming land much akin to that described in Emma Lazarus' 1883 poem engraved on a bronze plaque and mounted within the pedestal base of the Statue of Liberty: "Give me your tired, your poor, Your huddled masses yearning to breathe free, The wretched refuse of your teeming shore." Rodriguez (2007) reminded us: "Public figures, opinion writers, and lawmakers at all levels venerate the English language as the glue that provides cohesion in an otherwise impossibly diverse immigrant society—what makes *e pluribus unum* possible" (p. 36). Further, Willinsky (1998) claimed that English's position at the top of an invisible hierarchy of languages not only exists, but makes the United States unwelcoming for speakers of other languages. He said, "My concern is that the linguistic chauvinism embodied in this notion of the native speaker sustains a colonizing division of the world that ultimately makes countries where English is the mother tongue less welcoming for those from other lands and languages" (p. 197).

However, Amelia's hybridity is displayed, as is characteristic of hybridity, in contradictory fashion, with elements of neocolonialism and minoritized experiences that protest neocolonial rules (Bhabha, 1994). For example, displaying a rigid tie between language and nation (e.g., Americans are English speakers), Amelia claims her Americanness comes from her ability to speak English: "*I am both Filipino and American, because of language. I speak English and Tagalog, so I'm both.*" But in her claim to being American, she does not shed her Filipino identity by saying something like, "I'm American now." Rather, she insists that she is both. Clearly, what it means to be American is not so clear. Amelia shows there are layers of meaning that create a complex matrix of identity constructions. For example,

> *I feel American when I'm with my friends, when we're watching TV. Sometimes, we go outside. My friends are Mexicans, Hawaiians, Filipinos, Americans, Koreans, and Vietnamese—I have a lot of friends—but I don't feel American when I am at home.*

Interestingly, she feels American when watching TV with her multicultural and multilingual group of friends, displaying an American identity that crosses borders and boundaries, dismantling a neocolonial hierarchy of races and a mythical pure identity—all of this in a young woman who is "*Filipina first.*"

Naming Nations: The Uses of Nationalism's Rigidity

The meanings of nations and how they label or name particular people and actions play a significant role in Amelia's testimonio. Using a nation (Canada, for example) to identify a person, their characteristics, and culture is a dangerous practice and one that perpetuates the divisions and categories upon which neocolonialism thrives. Nationalism has not just been utilized as a tool of the colonizer to exclude those who do not fit into national narratives of, for example, the United States or Americanness. Recall that nationalism is "often based on naturalised myths of racial or cultural origin" (Ashcroft et al., 1995, p. 183). However, it can also be used as a tool of political resistance, allowing colonized groups to forge a unified identity in opposition to a dominant colonizing group. For example, intertribal alliances and efforts among Native Americans to recover their cultures and languages, partially destroyed by colonial and neocolonial schooling policies, is one way that a heterogeneous group can claim its "national" ties and come together to gain political and social power (Spring, 2004). Amelia seems to draw upon a more essentialized, although positive, notion of national Filipino identity as family-centered, Tagalog-speaking, Filipino food-eating, and friendly in order to show strength and solidarity in the face of an often hostile school and learning environment.

I feel Filipino at home because we're eating Filipino foods. We're watching Filipino TV. We're talking Filipino—we eat together and we watch together. We go to church together. We play together with my brother. And we love together. We stick together. In the Philippines we have family reunions. You are Filipino if you speak Tagalog, are friendly, and you probably go to church.

Despite the advantages of forming a positive, unified Filipino identity, I have discussed at length the dangers of homogenizing cultures and nations as singular, fixed, and knowable (i.e., *"You are Filipino if you speak Tagalog, are friendly, and you probably go to church."*) There is a problem with identifying by national origin, without recognizing the fantastic complexity and fluidity of what it means to be, for example, Filipino—it can serve to build stereotypes that allow the neocolonizer a system wherein essentialized identities can be trapped and classified according to hierarchies and binaries. Although minoritized youth retain aspects of group flows—for example, Filipinos as family-centered—postcolonial theory stresses that because of the past and current clashes of cultures, one's identity will be hybrid. This may be the case for Amelia. Hybrid identities are a way of refuting the colonizer's categories and possibly "developing new anti-monolithic models of cultural exchange and growth" (Ashcroft et al., 1995, p. 183). Without recognition of the hybridity of identity in a neocolonial context, stereotypes seem to abound. Nadal (2008) described the harmful stereotypes that Filipino Americans may encounter in the United States:

> Like most people of Color, Filipino Americans are taught that White America is the norm and the standard of beauty in the U.S., and that their own brown skin and almond-shaped eyes are less valued. Like most Asian Americans, they are taught that they are never "American" enough and that they might always be viewed as foreigners or immigrants. And like various people of Color, they may learn that they will always be the recipients of racial discrimination based on a range of stereotypes, including model minority, a perpetual foreigner, a criminal, unintelligent, and/or an uncivilized savage." (p. 155)

Amelia's postcolonial flow of essentialized Filipinoness is double-edged. Naming herself in this way can serve to help her gain and maintain solidarity with her Filipino school and community members, but it could also promote a more fixed identity that she might adopt and others might force upon her—restricting life's possibilities.

Dispelling the myth of essentialized identity and fixed definitions of American nationality, Amelia knows, as she says, that *"it's okay to be both Filipina and American."* She displays many instances of hybridity, as discussed in the previous section. Her choices of friends span many nations and languages: *"My friends are Mexicans, Hawaiians, Filipinos, Americans, Ko-*

reans, and Vietnamese—I have a lot of friends." Also, her contention that multilingualism is what makes America great—"*The United States is the best country in the world: you can speak another language like English, Spanish, or French here,*" is an example of how she sees America as a nation accepting of multilingualism—she even sees it as a defining aspect of its greatness, which contrasts with a national and pervasive educational narrative of a monolingual English-speaking nation.

Through the troubling use of nation as a meaningful and unyieldingly rigid identifier, Nadal (2008) explained that Filipino Americans are often discriminated against by other Asians, possibly as a result of "a darker skin tone of Filipinos, the stereotype of Filipinos as inferior due to socioeconomic or educational history, or a common view of Filipinos as not being 'Asian' enough" (p. 157). This seems to be the case for Amelia.

> *Asian people have teased me. To me, Asian is Chinese, Korean. Other Asians are bad because they feel they're better than Filipinos because they can speak English, so they can tease us. But they grew up here. There are a lot of Filipinos who speak English, who were born here and they speak English.*

The colonizer's hierarchies of nations, races, and languages persist as minoritized youth further categorize and rank one another—embodying the colonizer's system of subjugation. Nadal (2008) related how discrimination often leads to Filipinos restricting their relationships to Pacific Islanders, Latinos, and other Filipinos. Furthermore:

> Filipinos and Filipino Americans may develop a "colonial mentality" due to Spanish and American colonization. …[C]olonial mentality is defined as a form of internalized oppression, in which the colonizer's values and beliefs are accepted by the colonized as a belief and truth of his own. (p. 158)

The use of nation to categorize is also a part of Amelia's lexicon:

> *Some Mexican and Korean people do that. By raising their hand when you don't know the answer, they're saying, "I know that one and they don't know it." Japanese people, for example, my teacher said, "Who knows that?" and a Japanese student said, "I know it. I know it," but he doesn't know it, and some other student really knows it. He wants to be the good one—to be the best student in the class, to be close to their teacher, for it to be more likely to get a high grade.*

When students categorize one another by nation, we are seeing the global pervasiveness of pigeonholing "others" by nation—a designation with limited and *limiting* meaning.

Peter Spiro (2008), in his book *Beyond Citizenship*, critiqued the myth of American nationalism in all its forms (from new nativist nationalism to liberal nationalism), pointing out its inability to comprehend transnationalism. In contrast, Amelia's performance of this flow is quite fluid. Transnationalism can be defined generally as a world that is characterized by complex and dynamic processes brought about by contested, denaturalized, and hybridized territorial borders and cultural boundaries (Khagram & Levitt, 2007). Because of the difficulty of defining what makes the United States uniquely the United States, and our generalized lack of conformity, Spiro (2008) claimed that "an undertaking to impose American-ness on immigrants emerges as a hopeless enterprise. It is thus improbable that American citizenship will be resuscitated on conservative nationalist terms; there will be no turning back of the clock" (p. 115). Indeed, Amelia performs multiple national affiliations and alliances to an astounding degree as she claims an American identity based on being Filipina first, being trilingual, eating sushi, and having friends who are American, Korean, Filipino, and Hawaiian. She does not melt into the inflexible, national, stereotypical flow of a rigid European American monolingual English-speaking identity. With all her multiple national affiliations, Amelia claims an American identity in the *"best country in the world."*

Language Loss

Will Amelia need to lose one of her three languages to become American? "My first language is Tagalog—it's from the Philippines. We also have a language in the Philippines called Kapampangan. I speak English, but I also speak Kapampangan." Language loss is a common and even planned aspect of neocolonization:

> Language is a fundamental site of struggle for post-colonial discourse because the colonial process itself begins in language. The control over language by the imperial centre—whether achieved by displacing native languages, by installing itself as a "standard" against other variants which are constituted as "impurities", or by planting the language of empire in a new place—remains the most potent instrument of cultural control. (Ashcroft et al., 1995, p. 283)

The neocolonizer gains power by assuring that minoritized linguistic groups, like native Tagalog speakers, learn the neocolonizer's language and, thus, the neocolonizer's way of seeing the world. Because language is intertwined with culture, it constitutes the perspectives of those who speak it: "To name reality is therefore to exert power over it, simply because the dominant language becomes the way in which it is known" (Ashcroft et al., 1995, p. 283).

The aim of teaching in American schools is the achievement of English monolingualism, despite the existence of foreign language programs and limited bilingual programs. Amelia's experience is no different; Tagalog is not a part of the school's language offerings nor does her church have a Tagalog-speaking priest. Nettle and Romaine (2000) explained that the United States is "a graveyard for hundreds of languages," and quoting Glanville Price, they described English as a "killer language" (p. 5). Because our schools have done a poor job of teaching bi- or multilingualism, language loss for bilingual students is a common occurrence, despite the benefits bilingualism brings to individuals, their families and communities, and our nation. As *The Economist* (2001) noted in an article about the life of Kenneth Hale, this scholar explained that languages contain the intellectual wealth of a people and that when languages are lost it is like dropping a bomb in the Louvre. Although Amelia is currently trilingual, she seems to be prepared to lose one language. She also concedes that her brother's fate will probably be to become a monolingual English speaker:

> *My brother will not remember Tagalog after a while. Because he has American friends and he always speaks English—and sometimes he speaks English to me, so I think he'll forget it. It's okay, because he can still understand Tagalog, he can't speak it, but he can understand it. And I can teach him, if I can still remember it.*

Amelia seems to accept that it may be inevitable that she will lose her language but also carries the responsibility for passing it on if she "*can still remember it.*"

> Although it is natural for languages to change and even to die over time, the pace of this recent loss is not natural. In addition, it is the languages of the most marginalized people in the world that are at the greatest risk. A combination of factors has brought the world to this point, but three in particular stand out: colonialism, the hegemony of English as a global language, and the rise of public education systems that promote selected national or official languages. (Blair & Fredeen, 2009, p. 62)

Loss of one's mother language due to the pervasive neocolonial flow of monolingual English teaching in schools is a violent stripping away of intertwined flows of identity. Nonetheless, this loss does not mean that the speaker cannot use the neocolonizer's language itself to resist and reframe neocolonial flows. Although not as ideal as maintaining multiple languages, English can be utilized to subvert and disqualify the neocolonizer's far-reaching power. For example, Amelia can communicate in English, critiquing the overly competitive nature of ESL classes in her high school and the lack of support some teachers provide—disrupting the flow of English acquisition as a natural and neutral event: *"I would tell teachers don't teach Asian or Pacific Islanders or Mexican people that they're not good at English."*

Willinsky (1998) reminded us that, "languages are not lost by accident or unwillingly forsaken" (p. 190). Despite the research on the benefits of bilingualism, the United States' insistence on English monolingualism is a legacy of colonialism. The neocolonial practice of English-only policy and legislation in the United States weakens our nation and denies the rich heritages and lives of our multicultural youth and their families. Willinsky said that "we need to face the historical role of schools in expediting the loss of languages in one generation after another in a colonial project that needs serious reconsideration after the age of empire" (1998, p. 191–192). The repercussions of language loss are not only emotionally damaging, they can break up families, communities, and ways of knowing the world that are unique to that linguistic culture:

> *He forgot our language Kapampangan. It's sad because when my mom is calling, my mom speaks Tagalog but my half brother speaks Kapampangan, so my brother is speaking Tagalog and my half brother is speaking Kapampangan, so they can't understand what they're saying to each other. He can understand Kapampangan, but he can't speak it.*

The deleterious breakdown of interfamilial relationships due to linguistic colonization is a powerful tool of neocolonization. If one can't communicate with one's siblings, parents, and grandparents, how are culture, language, and connection retained? As is heartbreakingly described by Amelia, the far-reaching effects of the English-only policies and practices of American schools need to be questioned and reformed in order to decolonize education for linguistic minority students. Merryfield (2008) reminded us that "the inheritance of imperialism lives on in the information, underlying assumptions and filters of American daily life" (p. 88). Making invisible neocolonial flows visible offers educators the ability to begin a decolonizing process within schools and society.

"*Very American*": Striving for and Repudiating the "American Dream"

The question of what it means to be American is difficult to answer. Even more vexing is trying to define what it means to be American on a continuum of sorts—with "not-so-American" on one end and "very American" on the other. Amelia's definitions of Americanness shift and change depending on her purposes. Here, she critiques Americanness as overly rigid, based on White European native English speakers:

Some ESL students want to be very American. When Asian people grow up here, they tease the new kids because they don't know a lot about English. They ignore them, then do something mean to them. For example, they'll say, "That girl or guy doesn't like you very much." They'll say that to me, to an American, or to other people. They want to be good at school and be very American.

Amelia tells her reader that some students want to be "*very American*." She goes on to explain that being very American consists of speaking a lot of English, doing well in school, and ignoring or ostracizing people who do not know a lot of English. Americanness here is equated with academic prowess through intimidation and cruelty. The interests of the school are not questioned. Minoritized students marginalize one another through surveilling each other to make sure they are acquiring as much English as possible—punishing one another for failure to reproduce this neocolonial flow of English monolingualism. Those who have acquired more of the colonizer's characteristics (English, in this case) demote the groups who are more "native" or less colonized.

Being "*very American*," according to Amelia, also means having a White American boyfriend, changing how you talk, straightening your hair, and making it lighter:

African American girls like to hang out with American guys, White guys, to be their boyfriend, to be more American. They change their voice, how they dress, their hair. They change their car. They put blond in their hair, and make it straight. But some African Americans are not like that. I have a friend, she's simple. She's always playing video games like a guy. She's nice. She's herself.

Amelia is critical of Black girls who try to act like the neocolonizer—who are not themselves. Interestingly, as a White American, if forced to answer the question of what being very American might look like, I would agree with Amelia. I think many European Americans would agree that speaking English, doing well in school, having a White boyfriend, and looking as White as possible yourself would move you closer to the "very American" end of an imagined continuum of Americanness. However, if we look at American youth as a whole, they are not as White nor as academically successful. Neither do they speak English very well, according to national and international standardized test scores and U.S. Census data for both native and non-native speakers of English (Gonzales, Williams, Jocelyn, Roey, Kastberg, & Brenwald, 2009; U.S. Census Bureau, 2009a, 2009b). So why is it that Amelia and many others ascribe to and actually strive for the "American Dream"—Whiteness and social success? The "American Dream" is exactly that—a dream, but an unattainable one for so many. The "Dream" comes with media images saturated with happy, straight-haired, White people wielding power and smarts. Amelia, early on in her testimonio, states that *"the United States is the best country in the world,"* but later denounces her ESL classmates and Black girls who strive to be "very American." Amelia, as a transnational subject, is able to cross boundaries that may traditionally define Americanness and question what it means to be an American. Similarly, Orelus (2007) shows how "neocolonized subjects have been miseducated to internalize and reproduce old Western values, beliefs, and norms at the expense of their own" (p. xiii). Amelia, from her transnational perspective, is able to promote her own values even as she concurrently internalizes and reproduces neocolonial values.

Urgent Messages for Teachers

Teachers should know that kids tease us.

Amelia explains that teachers should know that kids tease them for not learning enough English or even for their attempts to learn English. This echoes neocolonial flows that punish minoritized youth for not fitting into the mold of a native English-speaking, White European American.

That girl is an ESL student, too, and she knows the poem, but she pretends that she can speak English very well and she teases me, too, on the bus. She told me on the bus, "I know more English than you." She said that to me. I was really mad. She's sitting with me and she said that to my face.

Clearly, the race to gain more attributes of the neocolonizer—the English language in this case—garners more status and power, whereas failure to acquire these attributes lessens one's power:

There's a lot of competition in ESL class. When we are having a class discussion about something and the teacher asks a question, and a student raises their hand but they get the answer wrong, another student will raise their hand to feel like, smart, and to make you feel bad.

Teachers need to understand that Amelia's testimonio is lending them insight into the lives of students learning English, showing them how, in some situations, a competitive and punishing system has prevailed. Amelia shows how minoritized youth compete with one another, forming a panopticon, or an internal all-seeing watchtower that expects everyone to acquire the colonizer's language as quickly as possible (Foucault, 1977). A public display of English knowledge is highly prized among Amelia and her peers. The shift from a collective and mutually supportive learning environment to an individually competitive one is a goal of the civilizing aspect of colonization. In other words, pitting students against each other is an effective way of elevating the status of the colonizer's language (Ashcroft et al., 2000).

Amelia also suggests that teachers should be encouraging in their teaching of English, and that they should not marginalize or label students by their nationality:

> *I would tell teachers don't teach Asian or Pacific Islanders or Mexican people that they're not good at English. Teach them to speak English, to understand English, to feel like they can speak English very well so they can do well in school.*

Amelia tells teachers that they should not use the neocolonial flow of the "other" as inferior learner or non-English speaker. She is well aware that she and her peers are categorized by teachers as either American or non-American, and she feels that this categorization should not be utilized by educators to predetermine educational outcomes. Further, she explains that students need native language support:

> *They should teach Tagalog here, because some Filipinos, they know only a little bit of English. If American teachers and students knew Tagalog, they could speak with American people because right now they are too shy to be with them. They could answer their questions. So they should have it here. But just translation, not a Tagalog history class.*

It should be noted that though she positions Tagalog literacy as a transitional tool for understanding, Amelia does not accord Tagalog the high status of an academic language worthy of study. In the end, Amelia explains that teachers need to know who their students are socially and academically in order to teach them well—echoing the youth-centered message of this book:

> *They should talk to students a lot so they can know and understand what the non-American people feel about their school and friends.*

Note

1.   Amelia Amparo is a 15-year-old Filipina American working class high school student who would like to become a nurse. She lives with her father and younger brother.

Chapter Six

Dung's[1] Testimonio

"I Have More Knowledge than People Who Live Here. I Learn Everything I See."

Most teachers don't understand what their students are doing, what they're thinking about, and what problems might sometimes exist in their families. Students have many issues. Kids from different countries have different kinds of family problems, so I think teachers need to know the children's backgrounds, so they can treat them in a way that makes it easy for the children to respond and show respect for the teacher. That way, the teacher can treat students perfectly and that would be so much better than students just going into class, listening, learning this and that, and then leaving.

My teacher right now is pretty good but not the teacher I had in another state. She was really bad. There, in class, she made it clear: "I teach you and you have to learn. If you don't learn, you fail. That's it." That's what happened to me two years ago when I was at McCarthy High. My teacher just didn't care. She had the attitude of, "Whatever." If I came to class, late or not, with my homework or not, she was like, "Whatever, turn it in and then erase it." That's why I failed a lot of my English classes. That's why, right now, I have to stay in school to rebuild that credit. I really want to learn, but nobody told me anything about how you get points to graduate high school or how it works—I come from another country.

Background

My name is Dan Tran. That's just my English name. My real name is kind of funny, Dung.[2] It means hero. My friends were calling me a pretty bad word, and it's okay. That's why I changed it to Dan. I'm 20. I come from Vietnam in the south, near Ho Chi Minh, Saigon. I've been here in America about five years already. I spent my first year here in this state and then we moved. I want to talk about the first year here. I had a very good teacher my first year here. She was very helpful and taught me and my little brother.

My teacher, I remember her name. She helped me a lot. She taught me step by step, really, really carefully. "Today, you learn this. If you don't understand, let me know, and I'll help you, however I can." I felt like I was her child. I felt protection and support, the way she taught me. I learned very fast at that time. I could write and read perfectly—really well. But then my family decided to move to look for a better life and job so I ended up at McCarthy High School.

McCarthy High

I didn't like the way the teachers taught students there. There were many Mexican children and they spoke Spanish—that's why I felt like I didn't belong there. They spoke Spanish in class even though there were some other Asians and students from different countries too. The teacher spoke Spanish with the Mexican children. So I'm thinking, "I'm learning English right here so why do you have to speak Spanish in class?" That was not okay with the different students. It was like, wow.

Every time we had homework, projects, exams, or essays, I didn't understand what I had to do. They just gave us the topic and that was it. Then she would just, "Blah, blah, blah," at the class for a little bit, and then sit down at her desk and do whatever she wanted to do. And I'm sitting right there and I don't know what to do. The other kids would speak Spanish and I didn't feel like being friends with them. Sometimes, I would look at them and they would be laughing at me or something because I wasn't talking very much. When I was sitting there I just wished I could have the teacher come to me and talk with me a little bit to explain what to do, or ask, "Do you have any problems with the work I gave you?" That might have been helpful to me. But she didn't even come over to me to talk or show me how to work. I'm just there and I could do whatever. Then the problem is, when I went to talk to her and I said, "I don't know how to do this work. I kind of missed something in my school year, how to connect B to C," or something, but she wouldn't even care. She would just, "Blah, blah, blah. Okay, you have to do this, do that"— she'd just give me a little bit of information about it and then say, "Okay." Then I would go back to my seat and do nothing—because I still wouldn't know what to do. I would try but it's hard because nobody would teach me.

My family can't speak English. That's why I am going to school to learn a little bit, and then I can help my family. It just depends on people, I think. Maybe I learn a little bit slowly. My brother, he's a better learner, I think, because he's younger. He knows how to do school, but I don't. I ask him sometimes, but, you know, my brother cannot show me everything. I have to figure it out myself. So it's kind of hard. That's why, right now, I am staying in high school to get enough credit to graduate.

I didn't feel good at McCarthy. That was a horrible time for me. We came back here last year because I thought the school here was better than McCarthy. The teachers get along better with the students and more people are more friendly than there. My English teacher here is pretty good and I learn better now. And I have friends here. My counselor here told me, "You're missing that credit. You need to redo that, take that, and take that class to graduate."

Students from Different Countries

In all the districts in America, if a student from a different country comes to school they will have different problems. I had to work. Some people have an issue related to their family, but they cannot tell the teacher because it's a family thing. They will feel, "I cannot talk to anybody about my family thing." I have a friend in Michigan, who told me, "I had to come here and get married to live in America." So, there are many kinds of problems. That's why sometimes students don't go to class or can't pay attention. They may be worrying about getting kicked out and being sent back to their country. It's scary. Sometimes students go to class and they look overwhelmed. They are feeling very bad about something but the teacher thinks that student is being lazy—but it's not true. They are worrying about something. Not all students that come from our country have the legal paperwork to live here. Someone may have tried to get the legal paper to live here—that's why sometimes they may miss school for a week or a month and then come back to school. Sometimes students have to help their family, so they work after school until night, so they don't really have a chance to get their homework done. There can be all kinds of issues. Sometimes they've had an incident with their family, for example, or maybe they've fought with their father.

Future

I speak Vietnamese and English. I learned a little bit of French, but I can't really remember all of it. I've lived in Vietnam, and in three states. I lived in California for six months, but in California, they do not allow you to go to high school if you are over 18, so that's why we moved here. I don't want to go to college when I don't know anything. I will go to college when I know what I want my career to be and what I'm going to do. I will go to college for a good reason—not wasting money or wasting time. Now I know what my career will be. I want to go to a technical school and be a car designer, an engineer, fixing cars, building cars, going fast like in NASCAR—sports cars. My goal is to be an engineer for Lamborghini or Mercedes. I want to do hands-on work. I don't want to do something boring—I want to do something active.

Comparing Americans and Vietnamese

What is an American? When I was still in Vietnam, America meant money and a better life. America meant whatever you want, it happens. I watched a lot of American movies about big cities and people living with very luxurious things and nice cars. My family knew that America had better schools and could build us a better future, so that's why they gave up their company. We were not very poor in Vietnam but we were not very rich. We had a very big house. We had a shipping company. We'd send mail, even cars, motorcycles, whatever customers wanted, from south to north and north to south. Then my parents gave everything up just for me and my brother to come here. When they came here, they had to work in a restaurant, washing dishes, but in Vietnam we'd never do that. There they'd tell people, "You do this. You do that." They didn't have to do anything. But when we came here, we had to do it—for my future and a better life.

Americans just have more. People make connections. You want anything, America has it. Just go online, eBay, you can have everything. Americans have freedom of religion, freedom of speech, and freedom of the press. In my country, they hide everything. There are many secrets. The government doesn't let their citizens know what they're doing or how they make money. There, we felt like we lived in a country with freedom, but it was not really freedom. We were in a kind of jail that is under the government control. In Vietnam, if we say anything about the government, they put us in jail and then nobody knows. So when I came here, I looked back at my country, and I said, "Wow, they do that?" Yeah, it was surprising. Oh, wow. In Vietnam, I didn't know anything. They all say, "America is bad." They just want to mess around with our country and start a war. When I came here, I saw America is a universal country. I felt pretty good. People in America, when they see another country has needs, they go with all their heart. I feel I'm human now. In Vietnam, I didn't feel at home. Now, I know Americans are not rich. People still have to work very hard, day to night. They have to do work to make money. I think I missed something. When we were in Vietnam, we needed somebody to live here and come back to my country and tell how it really is. People would lie. They'd say, "Go to America and you can just lay down." When I came here, I understood that people have to work to make money—it was not so much like money falling down from the sky.

When I first came here and someone would ask me where I'm from I'd have a hard time because I knew nothing. I just knew Vietnamese, no English, so I'd say, "Vietnam," and then "Dan." That's all I'd say. People here don't get along with Vietnamese—they fight with each other. Vietnamese people in Vietnam, they connect together; they have each other. But people here, friends or family, they act separately—totally separately. Why? Money. Everything's about money. When we came here my aunt and her family— they're just looking for money. When we came here, we brought a lot of money. When we figured out that she just wanted to get our money, we moved to another state. We didn't want to live here any more. We didn't want to see her. For Vietnamese families here, if you have a big cow, they want to have a bigger cow—competitive. They don't want to get below each other; they want to get higher and higher. But in Vietnam, most people are very poor, so they have each other to live each day.

In Vietnam, they still act human and help each other. Not like here: "You do that. You do this, I don't care." I think family is key. In Vietnam you don't need to work every day—you work today and tomorrow then you don't have to work. You still live, but here you have to work. If you don't work, you don't have money to pay bills—gas bill, car bill, and insurance bill. There is more pressure here than in Vietnam. In Vietnam, we don't have social security. In Vietnam you live today and not tomorrow—but it's still good. White people here are still good. There's still the pool guy and the pool guy still lives like that until he dies—he doesn't worry about anything. Here we worry a lot—it's competitive. We might be friends, but just for talking—there's no borrowing money.

Feeling American

I feel American. The first year I was here I didn't feel American. I just wanted to go back to my country. Now, starting my third year here, I feel American. But it happened earlier than that: in 2008, when I went back to my country to visit for a couple of months I felt, "Wow, I cannot live in my country any more." It seemed different. The people there are still nice, but the government—I cannot live there. When I went back to Vietnam, I was just driving a motorcycle and the police tells me to, "Go this way." I got stuck in traffic with a lot of people. He says, "Turn," and then he hit me with his baton on my hand. Wow! That's not okay. You cannot hit me for that reason. I couldn't turn my motorcycle to the right side. I had to go straight. He hit me on my hand. I thought, "Wow, that's not right." Where's the freedom? I thought, "Wow, I cannot live in my country any more." I live here now and I have a lot of benefits, why would I come back to my country?

I feel American because I have the freedom to speak what is right. If somebody is doing wrong, I can speak out. Why do you do that? I can choose the people who I think are good for me and for a lot of people. You go to anywhere, and they smile at you. I feel very American. They are a lot of groups that help out. To feel American is to help people. Being Vietnamese is still in my heart. I still want to have my country and the people in my country, but I think because my country has freedom, I feel my country is America. Now it's kind of like in the middle. When I go out to school, to a movie, or to a restaurant, I feel American. When I'm with my family I feel Vietnamese. At home we have to speak Vietnamese with my parents.

So when we go out, we feel American, but when we go back home, we feel like we are back in our country, for example, when we have a Vietnamese television channel to watch. We don't want to forget our own religion or culture. We still, like, separate the two sometimes: today you have to do it the Vietnamese way and tomorrow you have to do it the American way. That way, we don't forget things in Vietnam. We're keeping our culture for the next generation.

Respect is important. People who were born here are not very respectful. They've lost that. In my country, I think because we see how hard our family is working, we respect our parents. My mom had to work day and night so why would I do a bad thing to her? I have to help her. But people here, they're texting all the time with friends, playing games, and they don't care what their family, their parents are doing. They've lost respect from their hearts—White American families. For example, when I work for my restaurant, I see parents put noodles on the table—no plate, nothing. That table is really dirty. We clean it a lot but it's still dirty. Their kid just grabs and eats—that's not right. A lot of young parents do it with their child. It's like, "Wow, it's not right." It's disrespectful. I think, "That's your child. You have to take care of them. How can you do that with your child?" When they grow up, say at 18, they still don't care about you—they still let you do whatever you want. They are basically saying, "I don't care." In Asian countries, families take care of their children. My mom always takes care of me. Anytime I come home late, she asks me, "Where were you? Where were you at? What were you doing?" I still feel love in my heart. They still protect me as if I was seven or eight years old. I feel like, "I know you love me a lot, so I'll never do anything wrong to you. Sometimes I go to a friend's family and I just can't believe it. I'm just laughing. Wow. The way they talk to their parents is unbelievable. Sometimes students here go outside and smoke dope, weed, stuff, and it's like, "Wow, man." Some of my friends they wonder, "Oh, I want to get married around 18." I say, "Come on man, you don't have a job. You don't have your career figured out yet." They are not responsible. When you ask them if they care about their parents, they say, "I do whatever I want." That's their opinion.

Language

When you come to America, you have to speak English. When I talk with my Vietnamese friends, some friends say, "Okay, why don't you talk Vietnamese?" But other friends say, "You know what? You want to learn English?

Speak English, man, don't speak Vietnamese with me." I say, "Okay. You want that? Speak English with you?" Sometimes I feel, "You know what, you're Vietnamese, man, just speak Vietnamese. It's easy for you." If you want to learn English, go to American people and go speak English. Don't speak English with me, no. You're Vietnamese and I'm Vietnamese. It's not right. I'm Vietnamese first. Your culture comes first, not your second language. That's your mom's language, your people's language, so you have to speak it. I get mad sometimes. It's okay that people do different things, but they can't make fun of me. I think they should try to help me. The first time, they tricked me a little bit about speaking English because I don't speak English well. I thought they were laughing at me a little bit, but I figured out they were not laughing at me, they were trying to help me. They try to tell me, "You have to say that," to make me remember that I said it wrong. Then I have to fix that, so next time I speak better. There's a girl named Mary Lynn who helps me with English. Sometimes I think she's laughing at me, but she's not. I can see it from her eyes, "Okay, you just want to help me."

My brother, he speaks Vietnamese at home. He's not going to lose it. When he's with friends, we speak Vietnamese all the time. But with American friends, we speak English. So we're still keeping our culture and language. We try not to lose it—that happened with my cousin because he came young so he lost it—he was about five years old.

Two Worlds

I kind of feel I'm part of two worlds. Sometimes they are together, sometimes they're different. I feel like they are together right now. I speak what I am feeling and then you[3] answer my questions and then you listen to my feelings of what I'm saying. But sometimes, you know, when you go somewhere, like to do paperwork or to do something—when I go to a restaurant, they're not really nice, like if they are serving an Asian or a Latino, they're like, "You're Asian, why do I have to serve you really well?" They are racist—a little bit. They say, "There you go." That's it.

I felt more Vietnamese in Vegas, because it's about money there, so they don't care about people. I didn't go anywhere. I just stayed home because I didn't want to get in trouble. In Vegas they can have a lot of gang stuff. But I still have two pretty good friends from there: one is African American and one is Latino. They helped me a lot, to have fun, play games, playing soccer, things like that. They were really helpful and fun. I felt American when I talked with them, sharing about our lives. Sometimes when they spoke with each other, I want to ask them, "What does nigger mean for you guys?" They were laughing and explained that among friends it's okay to say. But don't if you're Asian or White because if you go talk with Black guys and you say, "nigger" that would be a problem.

If I drew a portrait of myself and my two worlds, in one hand I would hold a Vietnamese flag and in the other, an American flag. ESL students, most of them, have the same issue, where they feel they are from another country, as they are learning English. English is good but our own language is still good, too. They want to keep both. The new language is for their life, their new future, how they'll work, so they have to have it, too. We have to do that. I don't want to lose anything I know. I want to keep English for my knowledge, for my future. Maybe sometime later I can use my old language for something good.

Learning

Everything you learn is for something, not for no reason. When I came here I felt smarter. I know a lot. I know two of the world's languages. I have more knowledge than people who live here. They just know one thing. Theirs is a little world. But I came from my country. I learn everything I see. But people here they don't learn. They just do whatever they like. They just watch people working and they don't even learn about it. They say, "Why do I have to learn?" But I'm not that way. Asians are different. When we see stuff, we want to learn. That's why most Asians are very smart, for example with math and calculations. We're very good at calculations. We're very good about thinking about the future. For example, we build the way for our child, our children, better than Americans. Americans just set up money for their children, but not really. Once their children spend it, they're done. But in our family, if you have some sort of problem with money or in school, we would help you. We don't mind spending our money—our retirement money—for our family. I don't care about retirement because family is our number one priority.

If I were to give advice to a teacher, I would say, first, you have to understand children better. Number one. Ask about students' lives and what has happened to them. If you want to teach children, you have to know your students, for example, what they are doing, what problems they have—this you must know first. Then it will be easier for you to teach them English. Next, understand that students want to have fun, so sometimes we may not be totally respectful. That's normal. We are growing up, so we want to have some fun. For example, I've seen some English teachers, who are just kind of boring, which is not so good. So make it fun. Next, know your students and if you see that a student is missing something a lot, like misspellings, for example, you have to go to the student. Go to them. Don't ask them to go to you be-

cause they may feel sorry about it but they are scared to go and speak Eng-
lish. The student may be thinking, "I cannot go and ask because I don't know
how to ask the question." So you have to come to them. Teachers need to
make sure that students really, really understand their work.

Dung: Disqualifying Neocolonial Structures Through Transculturation

In his testimonio, Dung critically analyzes how his countries, teachers, schools, peers, and parents act in the world. In the end, he requests that the school and society bend to immigrant students, not the other way around. Dung accomplishes this by being an actor in the process of transculturation. Transculturation is the process by which minoritized youth select and invent from the neocolonizer's flows. This reverses the typical flow of dominance and definition by the neocolonizer. Both neocolonial and postcolonial flows become enmeshed and transmuted, in turn diminishing the status and power of the neocolonizer. Transculturation is one of the processes that construct a hybrid identity, as discussed and described in previous chapters (Ashcroft et. al., 2000; Khagram & Levitt, 2007).

Transculturation is one of the ways in which youth take control in neo-colonial contexts and recreate reality based on their experiences inside and outside of schools. For example, Dung examines the neocolonial flow of the teacher/student binary, and instead of accepting that the teacher dominates and defines the learning process of the student, he claims that the student and their lived experiences should be central and primary to the teacher's peda-gogy: *"If you want to teach children, you have to know your students, for example, what they are doing, what problems they have—this you must know first."* In this way, the teacher is positioned as student, and the student be-comes the teacher.

Throughout his testimonio, Dung identifies the nodes of the multinodal roots of neocolonialism, and *he,* not the school, surveils the nodes in ways that reveal untenable educational and societal practices. He reverses binaries, disrupts hegemonies, and creates strategic essentializations—all in a project that brings the margin to the center of our attention as educators of immi-grants. Dung shows the reader that educators' persistent insistence on blam-ing students for failure while ignoring their resources and realities does a disservice to students. Dung's description of his experiences echoes the find-ings of Bartlett and Brayboy (2006), who said (with reference to the research of Ray McDermott) "we continually seek to explain minority school failure by asking what is wrong with 'those students' or their families rather than by examining how schools (and larger society) structure and produce the failure of particular groups" (p. 362). Next, I discuss how Dung disqualifies the structuring of failure through the application of inherently false neocolonial binaries, a practice common in society and in schools.

Reversing Binaries

As discussed in previous chapters, binaries are a way for the neocolonizer to create and sustain clear and rigid categories about people and ideas. Some examples of these binaries are: colonizer/colonized; White/Black; civilized/primitive; teacher/student; English/non-English. These categorizations miss the complexity of the people and ideas that they pin down. They serve the interests of the colonizer in that they "establish a relation of dominance" (Ashcroft et al., 2000, p. 24) and certainty about the colonized. Dung is adept at complicating the relationships encased in neocolonial binaries. Often in his testimonio he works against the teacher/student binary:

> *Most teachers don't understand what their students are doing, what they're thinking about, and what problems might sometimes exist in their families. Students have many issues. Kids from different countries have different kinds of family problems, so I think teachers need to know the children's backgrounds, so they can treat them in a way that makes it easy for the children to respond and show respect for the teacher.*

Dung upends the typical relationship between teacher and student, where the teacher is all-knowing and the student is the recipient of the teacher's knowledge. He defines the teacher as someone who lacks knowledge about their students. Much like Freire's (1970) scathing description of how the teacher/student binary plays out, Dung critiques teachers for their overbearing and presumptuous pedagogy. Freire stated that, in such an uneven relationship,

> the teacher knows everything and the students know nothing...the teacher thinks and the students are thought about...the teacher chooses the program content, and the students (who were not consulted) adapt to it...the teacher confuses the authority of knowledge with his or her own professional authority, which she and he sets in opposition to the freedom of the students...the teacher is the Subject of the learning process, while the pupils are mere objects. (p. 54)

Dung makes teachers' knowing their students primary over the typical, principal concern that the teacher first know the curriculum. The teacher's dominance over the students can be seen in educational practices and policy. For example, the No Child Left Behind Act (NCLB) mandated that teachers be tested to determine their subject matter knowledge through exams like the PRAXIS, exacerbating teacher concern for curriculum over the significance of students themselves (U.S. Department of Education, 2001). The question needs to be asked: What educational outcomes might result if teacher credentialing programs made knowledge of students a certification requirement with the same primacy as knowledge of subject matter?

Similar to his disruption of the teacher/student binary, Dung complicates the neocolonial binary of knower/known. In the neocolonial relationship, the *knower* is the school authority, who is understood to know automatically who minoritized students are. In this relationship, the *knower* has the power to define, and the *known* (the minoritized student) is the passive recipient of the *knower's* supposed knowledge. Dung paints the neocolonizing school representatives as unknowing about the *known*: "*I really want to learn, but nobody told me anything about how you get points to graduate high school or how it works—I come from another country.*" In his almost sarcastic and incredulous take on school officials, Dung shows that his obvious need to understand high school credit requirements was missed. He identifies the neocolonizer as blind to his desire to learn, and ignorant of his situation as an immigrant who is unfamiliar with the American public school system. This apparent oversight and withholding of information leads to an oppressive experience that restricts life possibilities, including limiting Dung's ability to graduate from high school.

The overarching theme of Dung's reversal of binaries is the disruption of the center/margin binary that typically positions minoritized students' knowledge, concerns, and experiences as marginal to a White European center and, indeed, in need of the influence of the supposedly superior White European center (Ashcroft et al., 2000). However, Dung shows that the periphery is central: "*I'm Vietnamese first. Your culture comes first, not your second language. That's your mom's language, your people's language, so you have to speak it. I get mad sometimes.*" He calls the reader's attention to the centrality of Vietnamese culture and language in his life. Although in the official high school curriculum Vietnamese language and cultural flows are positioned as marginal, Dung makes it clear that he wants to maintain his primary language and culture, bringing them front and center. Furthermore, Dung identifies when teachers may be utilizing essentializations about immigrants or not seeing them and their realities at all, thereby enforcing marginalization. He educates the uninformed "center" by explaining that the pressure of being an immigrant in the United States can be overwhelming to students:

They may be worrying about getting kicked out and being sent back to their country. It's scary. Sometimes students go to class and they look overwhelmed. They are feeling very bad about something but the teacher thinks that student is being lazy—but it's not true. They are worrying about something.

By positioning the margin as central to educators' concern and as the appropriate focus of pedagogical performances, Dung exposes the neocolonial flow of center/margin, unveiling it as a ruse that serves to elevate the status of the school and diminish the lived realities of minoritized youth. By reversing binaries, Dung shows that they do not capture reality, denying them pedagogical legitimacy.

Disrupting Hegemony: Surveillance of Teachers

Dung disrupts hegemonic ideologies. Hegemony means "domination by consent" (Ashcroft et al., 2000, p. 116). An example of a hegemonic idea is the generally accepted notion that schools are caring places that have the interests of youth at heart. Other seemingly obvious and natural beliefs about schooling are that teachers have a handle on what students should learn and what they need—therefore they are deserving of respect. Unfortunately, the unquestioned and normalized hegemonic practices and policies of schooling work largely to serve only those in power. "With educational intentions, structures, and contents mainly designed by and for the middle class, the outcomes of education favour middle and upper-middle class contexts, while marginalizing those segments of society that come from working and lower class families" (Abdi & Richardson, 2008, pp. 1–2). However, Dung is able to disrupt these hegemonic ideas and critique teachers by surveilling them (Foucault, 1977). Cannella and Viruru (2004), citing Foucault (1977), explained how surveillance works:

> Surveillance creates an always, everywhere disciplinary technology. Using predetermined standards of "normality," observation and judgment of oneself and others is accepted. Hierarchical observation is constructed as supervised supervisors observe others; discipline is effective because everyone understands that they are being observed and may be punished. Surveillance has been manifested in the creation of examinations, whether scholastic tests or medical exams. (pp. 63–64)

Although Dung may not be able to overtly punish his teachers for their inability to serve students well, his testimonio is one manner in which he can make public his critical evaluations of his teachers and schooling experiences. Therefore, instead of the neocolonizer's interests being positioned and accepted as the interests of all, Dung says teachers should understand that the interests of students are primary. Dung is very willing to critique his teachers and school if they do not meet the needs of students:

> She was really bad. There, in class, she made it clear: "I teach you and you have to learn. If you don't learn, you fail. That's it." That's what happened to me two years ago when I was at McCarthy High. My teacher just didn't care. She had the attitude of, "Whatever." If I came to class, late or not, with my homework or not, she was like, "Whatever, turn it in and then erase it." That's why I failed a lot of my English classes. That's why, right now, I have to stay in school to rebuild that credit.

It seems that Dung's home culture is not only primary to him but is the lens from which he sees the world and surveils teachers. In his culture, caring for youth and giving them what they need to succeed and achieve are paramount. This is also the assumed goal of schooling. We can see that Dung's experience discounts this normalized view of schooling as created for students and in their service. Dung reverses the typical direction of surveillance and denounces the practices of an entire school: "*I didn't like the way the teachers taught students there.*"

Dung's evaluation of teachers is not entirely critical. He also describes teachers whose pedagogy is effective and who are particularly supportive:

> She helped me a lot. She taught me step by step, really, really carefully. "Today, you learn this. If you don't understand, let me know, and I'll help you, however I can." I felt like I was her child. I felt protection and support, the way she taught me. I learned very fast at that time.

This approving portrayal of a teaching performance positions the student as judge of the teacher. Dung describes a maternalistic teaching pedagogy. For him it matters how the student feels and receives teaching. From Dung's culturally situated position(s), the teacher should show full regard for the needs of immigrant students.

Strategic Essentializations

> Asians are different. When we see stuff, we want to learn. That's why most Asians are very smart, for example with math and calculations. We are very good at calculations.

Here, Dung utilizes an essentialism about Asians—that Asians are good at math. Neocolonial categorizations, such as the stereotype that all Asians share the same characteristic of being good at math and calculations, serve to limit the life possibilities of Asians who do not fit the mold created for them. Much discussed in educational literature, the myth of the model minority describes all Asian Americans as hardworking, law abiding, and educated. "For Asian Americans, deviation from the model minority ideology implies not only a moral shortcoming due to their own individual failure, but also separates them from the American norm, thereby reinforcing their foreigner status" (Park, 2008, p. 136).

Ashcroft et al. (2000), referring to an interview given by Gayatri Chakravorty Spivak on the reception of her earlier work on the subaltern, summarized her argument on the need to opt for a strategic embrace of essentialist discourses (p. 79) in these terms:

> In different periods the employment of essentialist ideas may be a necessary part of the process by which the colonized achieve a renewed sense of the value and dignity of their pre-colonial cultures, and through which the newly emergent post-colonial nation asserts itself. (pp. 79–80)

Perhaps without being aware of it, Dung likewise utilizes essentializations in order to elevate the status of particular groups with defining features. Dung's recitation of a neocolonial myth that all Asians are good at math is evidence of the staying power of inaccurate essentializations to define whole groups of people (Wing, 2007).

Although Dung uses an essentialization that may concurrently raise the status of Asian Americans and serve to limit their possibilities, more often in his testimonio, he reverses the typical pattern of White Europeans defining the "other" and uses *strategic essentializations* to define White Americans in not so complimentary terms (Spivak, 1988). Some examples of Dung's strategic essentializations are:

> *Americans just have more.*
>
> *Everything's about money* [in America].
>
> *They've lost respect from their hearts—White American families.*

Thus, Dung forms his own strategic essentializations of the neocolonizer. This differs from how Spivak conceptualizes strategic essentializations that are utilized to raise the status and political power of minortized groups. For example, Dung explains that Americans and the United States promote individual competition over the collective, communal effort:

> *People here don't get along with Vietnamese—they fight with each other. Vietnamese people in Vietnam, they connect together; they have each other. But people here, friends or family, they act separately—totally separately.... For Vietnamese families here, if you have a big cow, they want to have a bigger cow—competitive. They*

*don't want to get below each other; they want to get higher and higher. But in Viet-
nam, most people are very poor, so they have each other to live each day.*

Dung's description of a hyper-competitive American society echoes neocolonialism's civilizing flow, wherein a superior society is defined as individualistic—one in which there is a movement away from collectivity and
cooperation.

In a related vein, Dung points to the excesses of American capitalism as
a weakness rather than as a sign of a civilized society. He strategically essentializes Americans and American life as revolving around money and mate-
rial goods. He homogenizes all Americans as having *"lost respect from their
hearts."* He offers a sad example of American disrespect and irresponsibility:

*Sometimes students here go outside and smoke dope, weed, stuff, and it's like,
"Wow, man." Some of my friends they wonder, "Oh, I want to get married around
18." I say, "Come on man, you don't have a job. You don't have your career figured
out yet." They are not responsible. When you ask them if they care about their parents, they say, "I do whatever I want." That's their opinion.*

Dung illustrates how Americans are irresponsible to their parents and to
themselves. In promotion of a postcolonial flow of immigrant sacrifice, Dung
explains that he has great respect for the sacrifices that his parents made to
come to the United States: *"Then my parents gave everything up just for me
and my brother to come here."* Dung strategically juxtaposes his respect for
his parents, himself, and his education with Americans' lack of respect,
thereby raising his status as a Vietnamese immigrant and diminishing the
power of White European Americans to define him as inferior.

*I learn everything I see. But people here they don't learn. They just do whatever they
like. They just watch people working and they don't even learn about it. They say,
"Why do I have to learn?" But I'm not that way.*

Dung uses strategic generalizations and stereotypes to define himself as superior to Americans. I contend that this is an aspect of transculturation, in
that tools of the colonizer (essentializations and their associated hierarchies)
are wielded in a manner that targets and diminishes the colonizer's power
and ability to define "the other."

Hybridity as Complex Cultural and Linguistic Maintenance

*If I drew a portrait of myself and my two worlds, in one hand I would hold a Viet-
namese flag and in the other, an American flag. ESL students, most of them, have*

*the same issue, where they feel they are from another country, as they are learning
English. English is good but our own language is still good, too. They want to keep
both. The new language is for their life, their new future, how they'll work, so they
have to have it, too. We have to do that. I don't want to lose anything I know.*

Dung explains that his hybridity is chosen and particular. His Vietnamese identity is central to who he is; however, he is also American. Sometimes his identities are separate and sometimes they coexist:

*We still like, separate the two sometimes: today you have to do it the Vietnamese
way and tomorrow you have to do it the American way. That way, we don't forget
things in Vietnam. We're keeping our culture for the next generation.*

Dung wants to maintain both his Vietnamese identity and his American identity. He speaks of two identities, but how they move and shift is complex. For example, he feels American when he goes out and Vietnamese when he is at home:

*I kind of feel I'm part of two worlds. Sometimes they are together, sometimes they're
different. I feel like they are together right now. I speak what I am feeling and then
you answer my questions and then you listen to my feelings of what I'm saying.*

The shifting nature of hybrid identities is complicated and does not yield a simple answer akin to something like 1+1=2:

[Neo]colonial hybridity is not a *problem* of genealogy or identity between two *different* cultures which can be resolved as an issue of cultural relativism. Hybridity is
a problematic of colonial representation and individuation that reverses the effects of
colonialist disavowal, so that other "denied" knowledges enter upon the dominant
discourse and estrange the basis of its authority—its rules of recognition. (Bhabha,
1994, p. 114)

Similarly, in a study of 46 Vietnamese American youths who were journaling about their identity development, the youths' paths were found to be extraordinarily complex and made up of different flows: "their writings and reflections indicated that career choices, academic grades, family relationships, ethnic identity, gender roles, and sexual identity were all intimately intertwined" (Vo-Jutabha, Dinh, McHale, & Valsiner, 2009, p. 686).

Interestingly, Dung shares an example where he has abandoned his "*Vietnamese first*" identity and Anglicizes his name from Dung to Dan:

*My name is Dan Tran. That's just my English name. My real name is kind of funny,
Dung.[4] It means hero. My friends were calling me a pretty bad word, and it's okay.
That's why I changed it to Dan.*

Dung's need to change his name to a name recognizable by the neocolonizer can be interpreted as an act of mimicry. As Singh and Schmidt (2000) stated, "mimicry remains subversive to the colonizer though the colonized may not be fully conscious of this effect" (p. 24). Dung's act of mimicry, the adoption of an American name, "is not a menace just because of its opposition to colonial discourse, but even more from its disruption of colonial authority, from the real possibility that [this] mimicry is also mockery" (p. 24). In other words, when a Vietnamese American–appearing young man is called Dan—a common White American name—he no longer fits the neocolonial mold of minoritized other with a foreign name and appearance. This name change breaks the colonizer's rules and mocks the ridiculous hierarchy that neocolonial flows strive to maintain.

Educators should also consider the reason why Dung changed his name. Though in Vietnamese his name means "hero," his friends were calling him by the derogatory term, "shit," because of the English meaning of dung. This is a perfect example of how colonization removes meaning from the lives of youth through the marginalization of non-English names. What does it mean to change your name to stay under the colonizer's radar and to fit into the neocolonizer's narrative? How do mimicry and mockery serve to concurrently colonize and decolonize? Dung is aware of and values both his Vietnamese and American languages and identities. While remaining critical of aspects of both, he consciously intends to maintain both, counteracting neocolonial schools and curriculum that actively promote Eurocentrism and "a monological interpretation of culture and identity" (McCarthy, Giardina, Harewood, & Park, 2005, p. 158).

Urgent Messages for Teachers

If I were to give advice to a teacher, I would say, first, you have to understand children better.

It seems that Dung's primary message to teachers is this: It is not that the students need to understand and adapt to the school, but that teachers need to understand and adapt to the students. The dominant focus needs to be reversed: instead of the center simply negating and dictating to the periphery, the periphery should be able to trust that the center will draw on the periphery's knowledges to shape the definition of what a teacher should be. Of course, this decolonizes the traditional center/periphery binary as it is performed in schools and classrooms.

Further, though it may seem obvious, teachers need to initiate one-on-one conversations with their students, to consistently check for understanding and to actively express care and concern for their immigrant students. For example, Dung says:

> *When I was sitting there I just wished I could have the teacher come to me and talk with me a little bit to explain what to do, or ask, "Do you have any problems with the work I gave you?" That might have been helpful to me.*

Teachers need to come to students and see if they need help. The teacher needs to reach out to students. No educator wants to see their pedagogical decisions and efforts result in a statement such as Dung's, "*I would try but it's hard because nobody would teach me.*" Troublingly, no one would teach Dung. Therefore, the only solution is for teachers to go to students and be in their service. This begs the question: What does it mean to take responsibility for teaching students, for helping them to learn? Dung explains that even when he attempted to work unsupported in class, he felt that his teacher "*wouldn't even care.*" Teachers need to express that they care about students and their learning—in essence, teachers need to take explicit responsibility for teaching their students.

Finally, Dung explains that there is a constant need for teachers to informally assess their students—a practice much promoted in the educational literature. Throughout Dung's testimonio he tells of incidents where his teacher had no concept of the extent of his lack of understanding. The teacher he felt was best and who allowed him to learn "*really well*" was always checking for understanding and telling Dung to let her know if he needed help. Conversely, with teachers who were out of touch with him and his needs, he describes a frustrated helplessness: "she didn't even come over to me to talk or show me how to work."

Dung's advice for teachers of immigrant students is for them to be physically, emotionally, and cognitively *with* their students, not apart from them.

Notes

1. Dung Tran is a 20-year-old Vietnamese American middle class high school student. He lives with his mother, father, and younger brother.

2. All names of persons and locations are pseudonyms. This particular pseudonym was chosen because it retains the meaning of the original story of name calling.

3. Dung is referring to me, his interviewer, in this quote. I did not edit this out as it seemed to be an important commentary on how hybridity can be experienced as a more holistic identity.

4. See note #2, above.

Chapter Seven

Now What?

Decolonization and Revolution in the Classroom

How can educators teach themselves and their students to become willful world citizens, fearless of and even inspired by the sense of homelessness that a decolonizing pedagogy requires (Giroux, 2009; Salvio, 1998)? In other words, how can teachers and students recognize and critique their own and schools' neocolonial flows, and then become border crossers who read and write the world from multiple postcolonial perspectives, even when this may mean letting go of cherished beliefs, ideologies, and power (Freire & Macedo, 1987; Giroux, 2009)? In recognizing and honoring the postcolonial flows of the youth who perform them in our schools, we have the opportunity to make schooling more relevant to our students. Conversely, if we persist in legitimating and cementing neocolonial conceptions of students and their lives, we narrow life possibilities, thereby doing real damage to minoritized students and their White European peers who will persist in displaying a warped and limited view of what it means to be educated in the United States of America.

In this final chapter I will attempt to further address the overall goal of this book—decolonization. By decolonization, I mean that I am offering analysis and ideas that should assist the reader in "thinking through and against the legacy of education's earlier and still persistent colonial mission" (Willinsky, 2008, p. vii). I first discuss the need to manage the tensions of narrative authority in testimonio research in order to work towards decolonization. Next I share the overall lessons that youth taught us in their testimonios, attempting to honor their experiences with suggested actions that may help to decolonize schooling. I follow this with a discussion of implications for education as a whole. And finally, I end with a call for a pedagogical revolution, given the embeddedness and violence of neocolonialism in educational practices.

Before moving into the chapter, it is important to acknowledge that decolonization is messy work. "Decolonial practice must be emergent while at the same time planned, must be individual while at the same time community based, must recognize dominant discourses while at the same time turning them upside down" (Cannella & Viruru, 2004, p. 124). Therefore, I submit that the analysis I offer is mine and is surely laced with my own Western-centric conceptions. The suggestions for practice are tentative. Given that I work with K–12 teachers in their classrooms, I feel it is necessary to present some ideas for educators to consider for school and classroom use. Teachers tell me that they have grown tired of academics offering only conceptual and theoretical challenges to their pedagogy without concrete ideas for them to make change and bring theory into practice—especially when they feel passionately compelled to make changes but need support to operationalize their drive for social justice. Although I do not provide a recipe for decolonization—as this would be an impossible and colonizing act—I would be doing educators (and their students) a disservice if I did not put forth something tangible for them to consider bringing into their work with youth.

Managing the Tensions of Narrative Authority Testimonio

Who listens to youth? When, why, and how? Where are the tensions of narrative authority when that authority is shared by youth and academics? Who has authority to read and write the world in testimonio research? In this section, I will address these questions in relation to utilizing testimonio as a method of narrative research. Because narrative authority is shared between the youth and the researcher, the power to name reality shifts throughout the research process, and through reading the research report—in this case, a book. I show that although testimonio research can be considered a decolonizing practice, it does not fully escape the traditional anthropological capture of the metaphorical "other," charging the researcher with the responsibility for managing the tensions of narrative authority (Olson, 1995).

Who Listens to Youth? When, Why, and How?

Originally, I set out to write a book that would report verbatim interview transcripts, in their entirety, of youths' experiences in neocolonial school contexts. What better way to be sure youths' voices were heard, and with my agenda in plain view? However, as I began collecting data and transcribing interviews, I recognized that the interview transcripts belied the wholeness of the youths' experiences and ideas, because they were unnecessarily punctuated by my questions and voice. They were also not easy to read, which I felt diminished youths' narrative authority.

I reflected on an article I had recently read that made immigrant youths' voices central through testimonios (González, Plata, García, Torres, & Urrieta, 2003). The youths' narratives were so powerful—more so, I thought, without the interceding voice of the academic's narrative. With narratives in the form of testimonios, I felt as though I got as close as I could to understanding students' urgent messages without having sat down in a room with them. Not only did they bring me to a fuller understanding of their educational lives as immigrants, they made me want to *think* and *act*, instead of merely attempting to watch from a distance or being content to empathize. This is exactly what testimonio should do. It "is an invitation to a tête-à-tête, not to a heart to heart" (Sommer, 1996, p. 143, as cited in Beverley, 2005, p. 555). As I read my interview transcripts, the intensity and violence of the stories that they shared seemed faded. During interviews I was bearing witness to stories of neocolonial violence and postcolonial struggle that students had never been asked about before. Therefore, I decided to construct the interviews into narratives, minimally editing them. In this way, they became testimonios.

One of the strengths of testimonio research is that it provides a powerful audience for first person accounts of present experiences of injustice. Although youths may be telling their stories of injustice and survival in their everyday lives, those who hold the power to make individual and institutional change may not be in the room. Troublingly, youths' stories and experiences are often discounted or overlooked by adults and people in positions of power. Educators listen to youth when they are utilizing neocolonial, school-sanctioned devices (such as formal speeches, essays, etc.) that are presented in Standard English, especially when the message is one that reifies the goodness of schooling and a standardized Western-centric curriculum. Because I edited the students' stories into Standard English and published them in a book to be read by educators, one could say that the youths in this study were given a microphone *and* a full room of educators to listen to their stories. In this way, youths have narrative authority, telling their full stories to a powerful audience in a language the audience understands without researcher interruption.

When reading a testimonio, we cannot ignore youths and their perspectives. Unlike typical decontextualized research—the reporting of interview data that only excerpts interview transcripts when it suits the researcher's needs—testimonio presents the content of the entire transcript. Additionally, when reading, the reader may feel compelled to respond, as if in the same room with the youth. The reader may feel the need to act based on the injustices witnessed during the reading, and may be compelled to interrupt what could be called a one-sided conversation. The one-sidedness of the conversation (for indeed it was originally an interview with the researcher) may be a key device that engages the reader, therefore increasing the youths' narrative authority. In this way, testimonio research is decolonizing, because we are forced to engage in youths' stories both of neocolonial flows and of how they negotiate and disrupt them (Beverley, 2005).

Where Are the Tensions of Narrative Authority when It Is Shared by Youth and Academics? The Ever-Present Absent "Other"

Although I could say that testimonio research gives primary narrative authority to the youths who share their stories, as the researcher, I am always there. I envisioned the research, created the protocol, centered my questions on postcolonial theory, and got the final word at the end of each chapter with my analysis of each testimonio—all giving me narrative authority. In the testimonios themselves, I have omitted my utterances that existed in the interview transcripts—feigning an absence that should remain ever-present in the mind of the reader.

However, there are various ways that I manage the tension between the youths' narrative authority and my own narrative authority that work towards decolonization. First, by reading youths' lives through the lens of the historical legacy of colonization in schooling, I hope to have opened possibilities for youth to move towards self-determination (Smith, 1999). The entire research project grew out of a postcolonial critique of schooling in the United States. Second, my analysis of each testimonio is separate, and is offered only after the testimonio is presented, giving youth primacy and allowing the reader to draw their own interpretations, which are surely different from mine. Third, the interview protocol itself is provided in an appendix and explains that challenges and disagreements with the ideas I present were welcome during the interview and for member checks. For example, Ana opens her testimonio with, "*You should know that I'm comfortable telling you my story and more than happy to disagree with you.*" Fourth, each testimonio ends with advice that youth have for teachers, turning the tables on the neocolonial power differential between teacher/student. Fifth and finally, I am "othered," in a way, as the ever-present absent other in the testimonio. Paradoxically, although I used to exist in the transcript, I am silenced as youths speak. The silence of the researcher as youths forcefully share their urgent stories may be essential to future decolonizing research, wherein the "subaltern" narrate their own lives.

Thoughts about the Future of Decolonizing Research

Who has authority to read and write the world in testimonio research? I look at testimonio research as a transitional research praxis between the dangerous practices of positivist research and the emancipatory practices of indigenous and subaltern research—a praxis that truly grants narrative authority to those who traditionally are denied it by people in power. I agree that "it is not ethical to walk away, or simply to carry out projects which describe what is already known" (Smith, 1999, p. 147). Because minoritized youths' descriptions of their experiences of schooling are not often heard, nor are postcolonial interpretations of youths' experiences currently popular, I feel that this work may help open ways for researchers, educators, and youth to see damaging neocolonial practices, begin sharing narrative authority, and eventually give up that authority, so that those who have yet to be heard can be. Not until those in positions of power (academics in this case) are utterly silent at strategic moments will the subaltern narrative achieve primacy. Academics will need to find ways to relinquish control (i.e., stop talking, writing, and building authoritative narratives) in order for decolonial possibilities to flourish.

Lessons from Youth

There is much to learn from the themes shared across the five testimonios in this book: minoritized youths' performances of complex hybridity; the fading of what it means to be American; decolonization in the form of contrapuntal readings (Said, 1994); and youths' urgent messages for teachers. I will address each in turn and outline tentative implications and actions for schools.

Minoritized Youths' Performances of Complex Hybridity

Youths' testimonios make visible how their hybridity, as conceptualized by postcolonial theorists like Bhabha (1994), is experienced and performed inside and outside of school. By analyzing youths' testimonios through a postcolonial lens, hybridity has come alive in compellingly dynamic ways that disqualify the veracity of singular and fixed derogatory neocolonial identities (Ghosh et al., 2008). For example, Ana's conflicts and clashes of both White and Colombian identities, Nadya's straddling Black and White worlds, and Dung's giving primacy to his Vietnamese identity are just the tip of the iceberg. We need to consider the complexity of what it means to perform the flows of unsanctioned identities within the context of a neocolonial smog structured by mythically pure, binary, and hierarchical identities. We have seen hybridity manifest itself in youths' testimonios in ways that fundamentally alter neocolonial and postcolonial flows, intertwining, disrobing, dissipating, and clashing with them. Colonial ideologies and postcolonial conceptions change one another throughout youths' testimonios, altering the face of schooling.

Youths' stories are evidence that neither neocolonial practices nor postcolonial practices are immune from one another. As Young (2001) stated, "Postcolonialism is neither western nor non-western, but a dialectical product of interaction between the two, articulating new counterpoints of insurgency from the long-running power struggles that predate and post-date colonialism" (p. 68). If we recognize that postcolonial flows affect all students and teachers in schools, we also realize that neocolonial processes are not immune to postcolonial flows; they are affected by one another and intertwine to create reality. We have seen that the results of the interaction of these flows have both positive and negative effects. On one hand, when a postcolonial flow of a hybrid identity (for example, Amelia's Filipino and American identities) comes into contact with a neocolonial flow of an American as native English speaker, Amelia's flow discounts the neocolonizer's contention that Americans must be native English speakers. In this instance, the neocolonizer is no longer a reliable narrator of Amelia's life, and the power to define and control is usurped. However, as youths show, the dance of postcolonial flows is not a benign process.

Despite instances of the creative intermingling of flows, intractable and damaging neocolonial schooling flows based in the myths of naturalized hierarchies, binaries, essentialisms, and nationalisms persist, limiting students' life possibilities. Some examples of the neocolonial smog that hybrid, minoritized youth must negotiate and survive are Ana's teacher asserting that her mother's Spanish is hurting her daughter's academic success; Cynthia's recognition of the persistent messages by White school authorities to Latinos that their families are deficient, dysfunctional, and defective; the assumption of Nadya's high school peers that being Black is equivalent to being socially and academically delinquent; Amelia's ESL teachers ignoring or remaining unaware of brutal competition in their classrooms; and Dung's high school counselors "forgetting" to counsel immigrant students on how to graduate high school.

As seen in the testimonios, youth are able to utilize their hybridity to work within and against damaging flows, but their critical reflections and decolonizing actions are uneven and, in many cases, unnecessarily hard-won. As educators become more aware of youths' hybrid flows and neocolonialism in schooling (a goal of this book), they can help them to negotiate their hybridity and critique neocolonialism in order to work against it. As Dung explained when I asked him directly about his different identities, he felt like his two worlds were together, diffusing the binary of American/Vietnamese:

I kind of feel I'm part of two worlds. Sometimes they are together, sometimes they're different. I feel like they are together right now. I speak what I am feeling and then you answer my questions and then you listen to my feelings of what I'm saying.

Listening to hybridity may allow students to feel whole and accepted. By eliciting experiences of hybridity from youth, we show them that all of their worlds are accepted. We surrender to the whole person and listen to all of who they are and what they experience—creating a more equitable and socially just schooling experience.

How can educators truly "hear" hybridity? By interviewing students and having them write their testimonios, we can bear witness to the urgent stories of their hybrid lives through oral, written, artistic, and/or video devices. These may be ways to hear hybridity. It seems that youths' worlds may come together when they feel they are listened to about their cultural and linguistic worlds, and when they are asked questions about who they are and how they feel with regard to their languages, nationalities, and cultures in different settings. In my experience, student cultural and linguistic identity is a neglected topic in classrooms. It is often overshadowed by the sanctioned, implicit flow of a murky "American" identity, which I discuss next.

What Does It Mean to Be an American?
The Fading of America

An American is someone who lives, works and contributes to society in some way, whether it's landscapers or custodians or paying bills. I don't think you need to be documented to be an American citizen. Part of the reason I think this is so is because North America, so much of it, was considered Mexico, or it was Mexico to begin with. Anyone who is living here, trying to make a living and giving back to society is an American. (From Cynthia's testimonio, chapter 3.)

The youths' testimonios urge us to see Americanness in a new way—one that questions a single and solid American identity so often unconsciously taught in schools. There is no easy answer to what it means to be American, and the youth in this book perform an astounding variety of flows related to the concept of Americanness. According to the youths' testimonios, being American and feeling American are two separate issues that sometimes overlap. Being American has a wide range of meanings for each youth. For example, Ana says you can be a citizen without being American. She considers her aunt, whose English is not as good as her mom's, to be more American than her mother. Cynthia constructs an image of a borderless American, viewing citizenship as unnecessary as long as you are giving back in some way. Amelia and Dung both describe Americans in positive and negative terms: English-speaking, multilingual, competitive, materialistic, free, and irresponsible. They describe themselves as American, but they are always Filipino or Vietnamese "first." Youth "feel" American when they *"go to the movies," "eat sushi," "do team projects"* after school, give back to the international community, compete for good grades, have the freedom to voice what they think, etc.

The complex negotiations of what makes up youths' identities and youths' array of definitions of Americanness demonstrate what Spiro (2008) calls the "fading of America" (p. 40). Youths' identities and lives are utterly complex. They extend beyond English language knowledge and understanding of U.S. history, as is required by citizenship exams. Thus, we cannot suppose that these sanctioned measures of "Americanness" are adequate measures of how "American" someone is or is not. Indeed, it is important to ask, has there ever been a singular and solid definition of an American? I contend that "Americanness" has always been a faded, hard-to-discern concept that is a complex and fluid patchwork of people, identities, and ideas. Neocolonial flows of a single, pure, and identifiable nation would have our minoritized students believe that there is a desirable American identity that they should strive to attain. However, as we have read in youths' testimonios, this mythical identity does not exist.

What does it mean for schools if there is no real American? How should that conclusion affect curriculum, policy, teaching, and overall pedagogy? If we are striving to make education more relevant for youth, especially minoritized youth, how can schools and classrooms listen to and respond differently to our students? The complexity of students makes the complexity of responding to them somewhat daunting, but it is our charge, nonetheless. In many ways, it seems as if educators need to create an individualized curriculum for each student that takes into account the fading of America, the blurring and blending of national boundaries, the imposition of colonial legacies, and, most importantly, the rich hybridity of our internationally connected students who bring astonishing perspectives to school and society. We can no longer afford to passively or actively ask students to check their identities and lived experiences at the classroom door. The damage that this neocolonial practice does to our students and our future as a nation is irredeemable. Not only are we deforming the identities and life possibilities of individual students, we are squandering the dynamic resources and perspectives that minoritized youth bring to schools. If promoted through a student-centered pedagogy, these assets could advance our nation's societal and educational futures towards equity and social justice.

Students can work with and through the question of what it means to be American in order to confront neocolonial flows. A few classroom actions might include:

1. Students writing essays about what it means to be American. How are they American, and in what ways do they feel they are not American?

2. Students analyzing different definitions of what an American is from different sources: newspaper editorials; U.S. history textbooks; primary source documents; the U.S. Constitution; or interviews with their parents, grandparents, elected officials, community members, immigration offices and officers, etc.

3. Students presenting their conclusions through constructing a collage; writing an essay; webquest; or composing a short film, poem, song, etc. that represents the different definitions of an American that they research.

4. Students reflecting on how their definition of Americanness has developed, grown, changed, and can be expected to change or not over time.

Decolonization: Contrapuntal Readings

All of the youth, in some way, were able to read and reread their educational experiences contrapuntally (Said, 1994). In other words, the youth were able to look at accepted schooling practices and structures and name how they marginalize (e.g., racist placement in lower track classrooms); essentialize (e.g., Black and Latino experiences are not sanctioned as legitimate school and classroom subject matter); and purify (e.g., primary languages are ignored or undervalued). As discussed in my analysis of the testimonios, youth were able to reverse the gaze of the neocolonizer so that they were surveilling and disciplining school leaders.

In order for educators to support youth in decolonial actions, they must first become aware of their own, most often hidden neocolonial tendencies. For example, Erika, a White preservice teacher, explains the difference between "civilized" and "uncivilized":

> Civilized. Well, you know. You have houses. I guess technology usually comes with civilization. Farming, working, I guess. When you think of a civilized nation, you think of status, and factories, and things like that, and manufacturing.... Uncivilized, I don't know, just like, I'd just like to think of Africa and the native tribes that aren't, you know, that are doing their old customs and things. And they don't really live in pretty good houses, with electricity and stuff. They have tribal stuff. (Gallagher-Geurtsen, 2005, p. 20)

In order for Erika to support her future students in decolonial work, she needs to interrogate her tendency to see groups of people in essentialist and binary ways. Then she may be able to support students. In each testimonio there is one key person who supports the youth in the process of decolonization, for example, Ana's second-grade teacher and Cynthia's grandmother. Minoritized youth may need to have an advocate to support them in order to be able to identify and then take action against neocolonial flows and smog in schools. With the help of educators and community members who are aware of the invisible flows of neocolonialism and the postcolonial flows that students negotiate and produce, youth can engage more deeply and persistently in contrapuntal readings of school and society, diminishing neocolonialism's hold on youths' futures. It may be helpful for educators to begin a conversation about neocolonial concepts like binaries, hierarchies, essentialisms, authenticity, and nationalisms in language that is accessible to youth. Teachers should offer real-life examples, and then ask their students to compare these false constructs to their multiple realities.

Youths' Urgent Messages for Teachers

As educators, we know that it is essential that students feel comfortable in their learning environments. Given that our minoritized students may have multiple "homes" or identities, many of which are not sanctioned by the school (e.g., being a native Spanish speaker, or coming from a different home country), how do we create a space where they feel at home? How can we make students feel *at home* in our schools and classrooms while concurrently helping them to feel comfort and pride in the sense of homelessness that having hybrid identities might bring (Giroux, 2009; Sirriyeh, 2010)? Much of the youths' advice to teachers is related to feeling at home in school, for example, showing care for students.

The concept of teacher care for students is a theme that runs across the testimonios—a care that is accepting of the whole student (Noddings, 1984). Ana describes Mrs. Tohsaku as "*the most loving person*" and explains that she "*was the first teacher that saw me…the first that didn't look at me like I was stupid.*" Dung describes the teacher who helped him learn effectively: "*I felt like I was her child. I felt protection and support, the way she taught me.*" Amelia expresses that in a challenging class, the care a teacher shows makes all the difference: "*There are a lot of pages to read, but my teacher is nice—so nice. She teaches us how to be responsible, to do our work, and be respectful.*" The youth seem to be calling for a move back to student-centeredness. All of the testimonios appeal to teachers to take the time to get to know, talk to, and care for their students. The teachers who displayed those flows were motivational and encouraging to youth, helping them succeed academically and emotionally. In order to care for students, educators must get to know each student well. This is perhaps the most powerful advice that all of the five youths in this book repeatedly offer to educators: *talk to and know your students*. All of the youths felt this was a gap in their educational experience thus far. When a teacher did break the pattern of persistent teacher-centeredness, it was noticeably well-received by students. The youths assume that teachers' lack of understanding about their students helps to keep the negative judgments and neocolonial associations of minoritized youth intact. They know that teachers should, as Nadya says, "*be prepared to be surprised.*" The youths exhort, in their testimonios, that they no longer want to be labeled negatively based on their nationality. However, they do want teachers to know about their non-American identities and languages that often are primary to (or are being mined to become primary to) their self-concepts.

Both Dung and Cynthia tell educators that knowing your students is indispensable to providing them with a good and just education. They both offer examples of truly negligent educational acts that could be prevented if educators were to listen to and take into consideration their students' points of view and lived realities.

> Educators need to make a conscious effort to reach out to and know their students, which can only be possible through genuine dialogical relationships. Knowing their students will enable educators to have a sound understanding of their learning styles, their cultural, linguistic, and historical repertoires, their prior knowledge, and how to help them build on that knowledge....[This] validates students' identities while strengthening their confidence and self-esteem. (Orelus, 2007, p. 43)

Orelus (2007) further explained that to make schooling meaningful to students, teachers must base their curriculum and teaching on real-life circumstances and experiences. As described in this book, students' lives are permeated by neocolonial and postcolonial flows that must be central to teaching and curriculum in order to decolonize education and the lives of youth. Willinsky echoed this call: "It is time, then, to make a greater part of this global presence part of the [school] program, to stop ignoring the presence of this worldliness in the languages, cultures, histories, and experiences that students bring to class" (Willinsky, 2008, p. x). Further, this attention to curriculum and teaching must begin in early schooling experiences.

Youth show us that the roots of neocolonialism are deep and therefore begin to surface in classrooms from the very beginning of their schooling experiences. We need to consider thinking about early childhood education as not immune to harmful neocolonial messages. Indeed, it seems that the youths in this book explain that in their early schooling experiences, they endured the imposition of neocolonial flows. From Ana's experience of being denied Spanish by her teacher to Nadya's teachers not intervening when her schoolmates brought her to tears by telling her she was not Black enough because she had a White mother, the youths experience damaging neocolonial messages. In their book *Childhood and Postcolonization*, Cannella and

Viruru (2004) showed how early childhood education is fraught with vestiges of colonialism that have become so normalized that they are difficult to see. In fact, Cannella and Viruru explained that our youngest children are taught to yield to disciplinary power that disempowers them so that they will reproduce the dominant neocolonial norms of society.

Decolonial actions that educators may want to consider in an effort to honor the advice of youth include beginning conversations about the complexity of youths' identities very early in their schooling. Teachers may want to create a student-centered curriculum that draws upon students' cultural and linguistic funds of knowledge (Moll, Amanti, Neff, & Gonzalez, 1992). Teachers should also be unafraid to explicitly identify and dismantle neocolonial messages encountered in the school and classroom. Finally, teachers could find creative ways to talk with and listen to their students about their lives. While assessing student needs, they could use these encounters as an opportunity to experience homelessness and identify postcolonial and neocolonial flows that may surface.

Implications for Schooling

My hope is that a postcolonial analysis of minoritized youths' testimonios offers new ways of thinking about and addressing the troubling achievement gaps and distorted visions of youth that plague American schools.

> Whereas several disciplinary and interdisciplinary fields, including history, literature, anthropology, geography, ethnic studies, women's studies, and cultural studies, have extensively developed lines of inquiries and critiques regarding colonialism and imperialism within the past 20 years, the field of education in general has not. (Sintos Coloma, Means, & Kim, 2009, p. 11)

Engaging the postcolonial flows of youth in education works with intersectionality (Collins, 1998), culturally relevant pedagogy, or culturally responsive teaching (Brown, 2002; Gay, 2000; Ladson-Billings, 1995), and the need for translating multicultural social justice theory into practice (Gorski, 2006; Sleeter & Grant, 2007). Defining the identities of youth as hybrid and made up of the flows that youth construct and negotiate may be a way of thinking about what happens when aspects of identity intersect.

A focus on youths' complex postcolonial flows also works in concert with culturally responsive pedagogy and, at the same time, calls it into question. While, for example, being aware of national statistics and trends for Filipino Americans may inform teachers about the status of Filipino Americans as a whole in the United States, it also serves as a device to simplify and essentialize the complex flows that Filipino Americans survive and negotiate daily in schools (Nadal, 2008). Recognizing and drawing upon the postcolonial flows of our students may be a way of not just complicating what we mean by being culturally responsive, but may broaden the concept of cultural responsiveness to the global scale, thereby recognizing the international power manifest in flows that affect youth.

Finally, there is a well-documented and significant gap between multicultural, social justice education theory and practice (Gorski, 2006; Sleeter & Grant, 2007). Educators and educational leaders may agree with social justice education theories and even practice a form of multicultural education, but may unwittingly "undercut its commitment to equity and social justice" (Gorski, 2006, p. 167). It seems that hybridity, operationalized as flows, can offer educators a way of thinking about their diverse classrooms that complicate identities as multiple, fluid, and complex (Palmer, 2007). As well, it can assist them in considering ways to engage social justice inquiry and work through study of neocolonial and postcolonial flows. Asher's (2008) study of hybrid identities of youth showed that we need to "create curricula that draw on and represent the fluidity of identity and culture, rather than relying on fixed, often stereotypical images" (p. 18). It may be that teaching the flows of youth has a future in classrooms as a kind of socially relevant curriculum (Cammarota, 2007), or one that responds to the social conditions that require hybridization as a survival tool in neocolonial societies and institutions such as American schools. Lastly, being inspired by and inspiring youths' flows may answer Banks' (2008) call for schools to respond to the multicultural citizenship of students.

Pedagogical Revolution

As a site of possibility for decolonization, education stands alone:

> Education thus remains one of the most powerful discourses within the complex of colonialism and neo-colonialism. A powerful technology of social control, it also offers one of the most potentially fruitful routes to a dis/mantling of that old author/ity. (Ashcroft et al., 1995, p. 427)

As I have discussed extensively, the Western neocolonial flows that pervade schools need to be questioned and undressed in order to reveal their fallacies and expose their persistent drive to maintain the dominance of those in power: "The displacement of the 'centred' discourses of the West entails putting in question its universalist character and its transcendental claims to speak for everyone, while being itself everywhere and nowhere" (Hall, 1995, p. 226). The "'centred' discourses of the West" or neocolonial flows are discounted by the youths' testimonios in this book. Nonetheless, neocolonizing school practices persist.

What is a teacher to do in the face of neocolonization? Decolonization of the school can be carried out in multiple ways. To disrupt the largely hidden multinodal power structure that is neocolonialism, working to disable any of the nodes and their associated neocolonial flows with active promotion of postcolonial flows should be helpful. Any time we can make apparent the postcolonial and neocolonial flows silently governing our beliefs and actions, we are working towards a more socially just education and society. For example, students in school can engage with neocolonial messages in the media (movies, Internet, communication, language, patterns in texting, etc.):

> Many of the prejudices and stereotypes that students suffer from reflect well-schooled lessons from the age of empire about the character of difference, whether difference by culture, language, or race. These prejudices are in the educational air we breathe, with trace elements found in *National Geographic* specials, and with levels that approach toxicity in Disney movies, such as *Ali Baba and the Forty Thieves*. (Willinsky, 2009, p. 96)

I agree with postcolonial school critics who argue that, "curricular knowledge should be an interdisciplinary product of heterogeneous sources" (McCarthy et al., 2005, p. 161). It should be drawn largely from the complex clashing, coalescing, and contradictory transnational and hybrid experiences of all youth in schools (McCarthy et al., 2005, p. 161). We can no longer rely on a pedagogy that distorts America's past, portraying it as a lovely and neutral flow of democracy and justice for all (Loewen, 1995; Merryfield, 2008; Willinsky, 2009). Clearly, decolonization is a dangerous practice that threatens much of what we know and do in schooling. The words of Mishra Tarc (2009) bear repeating: "[P]ostcolonial studies threaten to undo education, to unravel the passionately held-onto thought and knowledge of the modern Western-educated student and scholar" (p. 195). Therefore, it will require bravery on the part of educational leaders who should work *with* their students to engage in projects that unveil neocolonial practice, thereby utilizing students' postcolonial flows to read and write the world (Freire & Macedo, 1987).

An ahistorical approach to multicultural education is no longer tenable. Educators must consider that the history of colonial ideology has been passed down so that we carry damaging notions in our bones. In the end, it appears that getting to know who our students really are will help us to (un)know diversity. To (un)know diversity, we must position our students as our teachers. By positioning students as our teachers, we as educators are forced to come face-to-face with our preconceptions and misconceptions. As we do so, we need to magnify the private echoes of colonialism and interrogate their validity. I envision an educational landscape where neocolonial practices are no longer in the background, keeping us rooted to divisive and violent actions, but are visible, identified, and denounced in words and actions. But without pulling up these roots, they remain hidden and protected. Neocolonialism can whittle away at the complexity of identities. Neocolonial flows and smog are predatory: they kill languages and distort and destroy bodies.

As I conclude this book, I recognize that in the process of writing it, my own use of and understanding of neocolonial categorizations is unraveling, and that this process compels me to develop a listening and (un)knowing posture (Kincheloe, 2009). In the process of analyzing testimonios, I recognize that it is very difficult to say too much about what people *are*—I am mostly learning what they *are not*. Youth are not fitting into any map I know. They are unmappable. I think I may recognize and understand some of the terrain that they are negotiating and surviving, but how they feel and respond to it seems to be infinite. In attempting to map youth in decolonial ways, I have unmapped my preconceptions. My urgent message for teachers is to let youths write their own maps. I have engaged in what Kincheloe (2009) called research in a critical, ontological context that "changes not only what one knows but who one actually is" (p. 186). As I fall back on categories to make sense of the youths I interviewed (even if I can find a label to foist upon them), it no longer has much meaning to me. I am changed. I am inspired by the perspectives of the youths I interviewed for this book. I am joyful about how they have helped me to arrive at moments of homelessness, wherein I am unable to place their ideas into neat slots or analytic boxes, and am left humbly listening. I think that if educators can start seeing neocolonialism—unmasking the sanctioned daily practices of schooling—they too will have the opportunity to unsettle their own and their students' binding ideas that pervade our lives like an invisible haze. Recalling the ample examples of neocolonial schooling practices that the youths address in their testimonios is one way to usurp the violent power of those practices. As Kwame Nkrumah said, "Neo-colonialism is…the worst form of imperialism. For those who practise it, it means power without responsibility and for those who suffer from it, it means exploitation without redress" (Nkrumah, 1965, p. xi, as cited in Young, 2001, p. 44). In spite of the flows, smog, or fog that the neocolonial system produces and maintains, minoritized youth persist in their creation and performance of decolonizing postcolonial flows. It is the job of anticolonial educators in schools to recognize, study, and support students' flows in an effort to disrobe and expose neocolonialism in all its unquestioned forms. My hope is that this book contributes to a small revolution, opening a crack in the neocolonial structure of schooling that cannot be closed or mended.

Study Guide

The following questions and activities are designed to assist the reader in working with the text, to deepen understanding of key postcolonial concepts presented, and to make connections to experience, prior coursework, schools, and classrooms. The questions are organized by chapter or address the book overall.

Introduction

1. Make sense of how the author describes a neocolonial school by drawing a diagram or sketch of the "multinodal" and "rhizomatic" system of neocolonial flows. Create symbols, scenes, or characters to represent the flows that keep students in their place. Add examples of neocolonial flows from your current school or past schooling experiences. Label pictures and symbols as necessary.

2. Answer the question posed in the introductory chapter: "When one nation wants to colonize another, taking control of their land and people, what are the most powerful tools they can utilize to achieve their goals?" In pairs or as a small group, make a clear plan as to how a specific country you choose could or did attempt to recreate another in its own image for the long term. Compare your tools or strategies to those outlined in the introductory chapter. Can any of these tools or strategies be identified in the school or classroom setting?

Chapter 1

1. How would you describe testimonio work? How is it praxis? What might a guidebook for working with testimonios include, and what shouldn't it include and why? Create an outline with guiding questions for each part of a guidebook.

2. Read other scholarly accounts of testimonio work. Could testimonio work be considered a decolonizing practice? Why, or why not? Give examples from the testimonios you read.

Chapter 2

1. Reflect on your current or past school and identify who was surveilling whom? What behaviors and standards were considered sanctioned and unsanctioned? What sort of discipline or praise was enacted for which behaviors? Create a chart to keep track of the information. Explain how this system of surveillance and discipline structures the overall environment of the school.

2. In what ways does mimicry play out in Ana's testimonio? Think about schooling and how mimicry may be required of students and teachers to be successful. Describe 5–10 examples of school-sanctioned mimicry. Next, determine if and when mimicry becomes mockery. What is the turning point? What effects does mockery have on the neocolonial school structure?

Chapter 3

1. Cynthia's physical appearance does not match the neocolonial conception of an essentialized Mexican American. How does Cynthia negotiate the flows of essentialism throughout her testimonio? How does she respond to essentializing flows when she identifies them? How do essentialisms harm people in school settings? Spend a day noting essentializing flows that you notice in schools. To disinter them, it may be helpful to utilize the sentence frame, "All [category of people] are…" or "To be [characteristic] you must be/have…." Draw conclusions about how and why essentialisms become part of the hidden network of neocolonialism.

2. Where are the borders of the United States? Cynthia defines an American as anyone who "works and contributes to society in some way." Create a mock debate about the question: Who is and is not an American? A student or group can play Cynthia, and another person or group can represent a neocolonial perspective on Americanness. Research and study your perspectives. Choose a moderator and address the following questions: How does one become American? What are the defining characteristics of an American? Are there different kinds of Americans? Has or should the definition of an American change over time? What characteristics define a non-American? Considering the heterogeneous school population in the United States, what should the curriculum teach about Americanness?

Chapter 4

1. What does it mean to be "White"? What does it mean to be "Black"? How does Nadya answer these questions? How do you answer these questions? What are the benefits of these categories (i.e., Black and White) and what are the drawbacks? Is Nadya arguing for a colorblind approach to teaching students? Why or why not? Considering Nadya's testimonio as a whole, how should schools approach neocolonial categorizations made up of youths' real cultural and linguistic identities or flows?

2. Nadya's powerful anticolonial advice to teachers is: "*Be prepared to be surprised.*" How can educators be prepared to be surprised but, at the

same time, value students' cultural and linguistic identities? Cite at least five scholarly sources that support your answer to the question.

Chapter 5

1. Consider Amelia's statement, *"I always feel Filipina first."* How does her contention that her identity is primarily Filipina work with and against neo-colonial flows discussed in the introductory chapter? What should the role of the school be when considering the hybrid identities of minoritized youth?

2. Identify an English as a Second Language (ESL) classroom or locate an ESL curriculum. Drawing upon your observations of the classroom or program, what role does English learning play in the lives of students inside and outside of school? What kinds of language are used to describe the learning and teaching process? How is English portrayed? How are native languages portrayed? How does the classroom or program align with, and/or conflict with, the neocolonial flows of English as a naturally superior language at the top of a hierarchy of languages?

Chapter 6

1. In his testimonio, Dung recognizes that minoritized students are often blamed for their own academic "failures." Choose two other testimonios and record instances where students are blamed for their school "failures." What kinds of policies have schools created that have their foundation in blaming minoritized students for their own failure? How do these policies support neocolonialism in schooling?

2. Dung's advice to teachers of immigrant students could be stated as: *"It's not that the students need to understand and adapt to the school, but the teachers need to understand and adapt to the students."* Interview a teacher and ask them to share how their students must adapt to their classroom. Ask for specific examples. Next, share the above quote with the teacher and ask, "In what 10 primary ways would you have to change your curriculum and teaching if you were to understand and adapt to your students to a very high degree?" Report on the interview and close with your conclusions about how youths' postcolonial flows and decolonization could play a role in the action plan of the teacher you interviewed.

Chapter 7

1. Choose one of the following questions to answer, and cite five scholarly sources to support your ideas: How can educators teach themselves and their students to become willful world citizens, fearless of and even in-

spired by the sense of homelessness that a decolonizing pedagogy requires (Giroux, 2009; Salvio, 1998)? How can teachers and students recognize and critique their own and the school's neocolonial flows, and then become border crossers that read and write the world from multiple postcolonial perspectives, even when it may mean letting go of cherished beliefs, ideologies, and power (Freire & Macedo, 1987; Giroux, 2009)?

2. The author calls for a revolutionary pedagogy with the goal of decolonizing schooling. What other pedagogical revolutions have taken place in the history of U.S. schooling? Choose one or two to study in depth. What incited the call for revolution? What strategies were utilized to carry out the pedagogical reforms? How successful or not was the revolution, and why? Based on this, take a stand on the merit of the author's call for pedagogical revolution and its chances for success.

Overall

1. Select both a testimonio from one of the chapters and a philosophy of education (e.g., critical race theory, constructivism, poststructural feminism, etc.) and analyze the testimonio according to the chosen philosophy. Your analysis should answer the following questions: What is the purpose of schooling? Who has power and who does not? Whose perspectives are valid and reliable? What problems and possibilities does the testimonio reveal? What actions should be taken by the student, teachers, and schools as a whole based on the problems and possibilities revealed in the analysis? Compare and contrast your analysis with that of the author and/or your reading peers.

2. What does it mean to be American? Look at different definitions of what an American is from diverse sources: newspaper editorials, U.S. history textbooks, international sources, films, primary source documents, the U.S. Constitution, interviews from parents, grandparents, elected officials, community members, immigration offices and officers, etc. Next, construct a collage or a short film; write an essay, poem, song, etc. that represents the different definitions of an American that you have researched.

3. Review the sections titled "Urgent Messages for Teachers" in each testimonio chapter and make a list of practical classroom-based strategies from the youths' advice for teachers that could be distributed and utilized at a particular school.

Appendix

Interview Protocol

Thank you for being willing to talk with me about the book I am writing. The book will be for teachers about youth who have more than a European American, English-speaking background. Because our school classrooms are more and more diverse, teachers need to understand their students who have backgrounds different from their own. There are some new ideas out there about multicultural education and I want to see what you think of these ideas— if you can relate to them or not. Please feel free to share as much as you like, and remember that you will have the opportunity to review the interview transcripts and change, delete, or omit anything that is written. The more details and examples you can offer, the better I will be able to understand your experiences. I also hope that you will challenge me, disagree with me, and be as open and honest as possible. I want to put these ideas to the test and see what you think of them. I am hoping you will feel comfortable questioning them.

If I may, I will tell you a little about myself before we begin. I am 37 years old. I grew up in California in a White native English-speaking family. I have an older sister and two step-brothers. We travelled, lived, and went to public schools in Europe when we were young, so we learned how to function in different cultures, and grew to appreciate other languages. I learned Spanish and became a bilingual teacher in California. I saw the racism that my students experienced every day, and I began to be accepted in my Mexican American school community. Later, I went to graduate school and studied multicultural-multilingual teacher education and talked more and more with people of color about the daily and institutional racism they experienced. I then started teaching at Utah State University. I left the university to spend more time with my children and consult with teachers and schools.

1. Tell me a little about yourself and your background. (For example, your age, your family(ies), your cultures, your languages and dialects, places you've lived, important life experiences that make you who you are, and how you have arrived where you are now in your life, etc.)

2. So, we are both living in this country called the United States of America. But we know that people have very different ideas about what an American is. Do you think there is an "American culture"? What is an American to you? What makes someone American? How would different people answer the question: What is a real American?

3. How would you describe yourself to a friend, a family member, a stranger, etc.? Do you consider yourself to be "American"? Why, and why not?

4. Next, I want to tell you about a person. Adelia is a 20-year-old Mexican American woman living in the United States. She and her brother were raised in the U.S. but her wealthy parents live in Mexico City. She considers Mexico to be her home, but she will live in the U.S. because she knows the culture well here. Most of the friends she has are students in her college Multicultural Club because she feels like Whites just don't get what her life is like. She says her parents don't understand some of the things she does and tease her that she is becoming an American. She speaks Spanish and English. How are you similar and/or different from Adelia?

5. What parts of your background are important to you? Why? How do you use all of your rich background knowledge to your advantage?

6. I want to share the following poem with you and then ask you to share your ideas about the poem. Karen, a Latina, native Spanish speaker, who has always lived in New York City, wrote the following poem about other people's problems with the different parts of her background:

> Spanish shouldn't be spoken in America
> To be American
> You have to speak English
> No accents
> You are in America
> Don't you want to be American?
>
> To be Latina
> You have to speak like a Latina
> Speak it proudly
> Don't speak like you're not Hispanic!
> Do you want to be a disgrace to the Latin community?
> Don't you want to be Latina?
>
> I'm Latina
> Soy Americana   (I am American)
> Hablo en Inglés   (I speak English)
> I speak Spanish
> ¿Por qué no me tratas de conocer? (Why don't you try to get to know me?)
> Before you decide not to accept me.
> ¡Soy parte de dos mundos!   (I am a part of two worlds!)
> Why can't you just accept me?
>
> *By Karen Garcia*
> *Translation by Tricia Gallagher-Geurtsen*

Karen says she is a part of two worlds or has two identities. Do you feel like you are a part of two or more worlds or identities? If so, what are the worlds/identities, and how do you work with and within those worlds/identities?

Are there any parts of your background/identities that you *or other people* think conflict and how do you deal with those conflicts? If you can think of one, would you tell a story about this?

Do you see your identity as complex? If yes, what makes it complex?

7. Karen, who wrote the poem above, said that sometimes she was treated unfairly because some people thought she was not quite Latina enough or not quite American enough. Have you ever had a similar experience of "not being quite enough" of who people thought you should be? If so, would you describe it and/or tell a story about this?

8. Here is a self-portrait of Ritu, drawing herself at home. She is an Indian American, native Kanada and English speaking, second-grade girl learning Spanish. What do you think of the picture? How might you draw a self portrait of yourself in different places (for example, at home, school, work, with friends, etc.)?

Samuel is a Puerto Rican and Cuban American teenager who listens to country music with his friends at school and to reggaeton with his Cuban American grandfather. Samuel speaks Spanish, English, and Spanglish. How do you think a White, English-only speaking teacher would respond to all Samuel knows and understands? How would you explain this to a White teacher?

9. How do the different parts of your background matter in schools/in your education?

10. Think about the schools you have attended and the teachers you have had. Who did they want you to be? How do you think they would describe the person they wanted you to be?

11. Tanya is a Black American who says that sometimes she has to "play White" to get people to help her in the school office. Can you relate? If so, tell a story about this. What is it like to "play" or "perform" a certain identity? Could you get by without it? What is it like to "shift" identities? Do you know some people who don't shift identities?

12. What do you think your K–12 teacher(s) knew about you?

13. What do you think your K–12 teacher(s) need(ed) to know about you? What do you wish your teacher(s) knew/had known about you?

14. Do you think that any of your schools or teachers tried to "Americanize" you? If so, what was that like? What did they do and what did you do?

15. Do you think that your teachers ever tried to "treat everyone the same"? What was that like? Did you ever challenge teachers who seemed to be making everyone into the same kind of person?

16. When thinking about everything we have talked about so far, how did/do you do in school? How did the books you read and the classes you took relate to you or not?

17. What contributes/contributed to your success in school? What did/does not contribute to your success?

18. What advice do you have for teachers?

19. Is there anything else I should know?

20. Can I email you with follow-up questions after I have reviewed your answers?

References

Abdi, A. A., & Richardson, W. G. (2008). Decolonizing democratic education: An introduction. In A. A. Abdi & G. Richardson (Eds.), *Decolonizing democratic education: Transdisciplinary dialogues* (pp. 1–11). Rotterdam, The Netherlands: Sense.

Abdi, A. A., & Richardson, W. G. (Eds.). (2008). *Decolonizing democratic education: Transdisciplinary dialogues*. Rotterdam, The Netherlands: Sense.

Alarcón, D. C. (1992). The Aztec palimpsest: Toward a new understanding of Aztlán, cultural identity, and history. *Aztlán 19*(2), 33–68.

Anzaldúa, G. (1999). *Borderlands = La frontera: The new Mestiza* (2nd ed.). San Francisco, CA: Aunt Lute Books.

Ashcroft, B., Griffiths, G., & Tiffin, H. (Eds.). (1995). *The post-colonial studies reader*. London, UK: Routledge.

Ashcroft, B., Griffiths, G., & Tiffin, H. (2000). *Post-colonial studies: The key concepts*. London, UK: Routledge.

Asher, N. (2008). Listening to hyphenated Americans: Hybrid identities of youth from immigrant families. *Theory into Practice*, *47*(1), 12–19.

Asher, N. (2009). Decolonization and education: Locating pedagogy and self at the interstices in global times. In R. Sintos Coloma (Ed.), *Postcolonial challenges in education*, (pp. 67–77). New York, NY: Peter Lang.

Au, K. H., & Jordan, C. (1981). Teaching reading to Hawaiian children: Finding a culturally appropriate solution. In E. T. Trueba, G. P. Guthrie, & K. H. Au (Eds.), *Culture and the bilingual classroom: Studies in classroom ethnography* (pp. 139–152). Rowley, MA: Newbury House.

Bailin, S. (2009). Response: Aesthetic criticism, interpretation, and the creation of ideals. *Philosophy of Education*, 39–42. Retrieved from *Philosophy of Education* Archive, http://ojs.ed.uiuc.edu/index.php/pes/article/view/2676/1006

Banks, J. A. (2008). Diversity, group identity, and citizenship education in a global age. *Educational Researcher*, *37*(3), 129–139.

Banks, J. A., & McGee Banks, C. A. (2004). *Handbook of research on multicultural education* (2nd ed.). San Francisco, CA: John Wiley & Sons.

Barone, T. (2001a). Pragmatizing the imaginary: A response to a fictionalized case study of teaching. Further comment. *Harvard Educational Review*, *71*(4), 734–741.

Barone, T. (2001b). *Touching eternity: The enduring outcomes of teaching*. New York, NY: Teachers College Press.

Bartlett, L., & Brayboy, B. M. J. (2006). Race and schooling: Theories and ethnographies. *The Urban Review*, *37*(5), 361–374.

Basch, L., Glick Schiller, N., & Szanton Blanc, C. (2008). Transnational projects: A new perspective. Theoretical premises. In S. Khagram & P. Levitt (Eds.), *The transnational studies reader: Intersections and innovations*, 261–272. New York, NY: Routledge.

Beverley, J. (2005). *Testimonio*, subalternity, and narrative authority. In N. K. Denzin & Y. S. Lincoln (Eds.), *The SAGE handbook of qualitative research* (3rd ed., pp. 547–557). Thousand Oaks, CA: Sage.

Bhabha, H. K. (1994). *The location of culture*. London, UK: Routledge.

Blair, H., & Fredeen, S. (2009). Putting knowledge into practice: Creating spaces for Cree immersion. *Canadian Journal of Native Education, 32*(2), 62–77.

Brown, D. F. (2002). *Becoming a successful urban teacher*. Portsmouth, NH: Heinemann.

Cammarota, J. (2007). A social justice approach to achievement: Guiding Latina/o students toward educational attainment with a challenging, socially relevant curriculum. *Equity and Excellence in Education, 40*(1), 87–96.

Cannella, G. S., & Viruru, R. (2004). *Childhood and postcolonization: Power, education, and contemporary practice*. New York, NY: RoutledgeFalmer.

Clance, P. R., & Imes, S. A. (1978). The imposter phenomenon in high achieving women: Dynamics and therapeutic intervention. *Psychotherapy: Theory, Research and Practice, 15*(3), 241–247.

Collins, P. H. (1998). *Fighting words: Black women and the search for justice*. Minneapolis, MN: University of Minnesota Press.

Coulter, C. A., & Smith, M. L. (2009). The construction zone: Literary elements in narrative research. *Educational Researcher, 38*(8), 577–590.

Daza, S. L. (2009). The noninnocence of recognition: Subjects and agency in education. In R. Sintos Coloma (Ed.), *Postcolonial challenges in education*, (pp. 326–343). New York, NY: Peter Lang.

Denzin, N. K. (1992). The many faces of emotionality: Reading *persona*. In C. Ellis & M. G. Flaherty (Eds.), *Investigating subjectivity: Research on lived experience* (pp. 17–30). Newbury Park, CA: Sage.

Denzin, N. K. & Lincoln, Y. S. (2005). Introduction: The discipline and practice of qualitative research. In N. K. Denzin, & Y. S. Lincoln (Eds.), *The SAGE handbook of qualitative research* (pp. 1–32). Thousand Oaks, CA: Sage.

Dimitriadis, G. (2005). *Performing identity/performing culture: Hip hop as text, pedagogy, and lived practice*. New York, NY: Peter Lang.

Dimitriadis, G., & McCarthy, C. (2001). *Reading and teaching the postcolonial: From Baldwin to Basquiat and beyond*. New York, NY: Teachers College Press.

Du Bois, W. E. B. (1996). Of our spiritual strivings. In W. E. B. Du Bois, *The souls of Black folk* (pp. 3–12). New York, NY: Penguin.

Dutro, E., Kazemi, E., Balf, R., & Lin, Y-S. (2008). "What are you and where are you from?": Race, identity, and the vicissitudes of cultural relevance. *Urban Education, 43*(3), 269–300.

The Economist. (2001, November 1). Kenneth Hale: Kenneth Locke Hale, a master of languages, died on October 8th, aged 67. *The Economist*. Retrieved from http://www.economist.com/node/842137

El-Haj, T. R. A. (2010). "The beauty of America": Nationalism, education, and the war on terror. *Harvard Educational Review, 80*(2), 242–274.

Erikson, E. H. (1975). *Life history and the historical moment*. New York, NY: Norton.

Fanon, F. (1965). *The wretched of the earth* (C. Farrington, Trans.). New York, NY: Grove Press.

Fanon, F. (1967). *Black skin, White masks*. New York, NY: Grove Press.

Flores, J., & Yúdice, G. (2008). Living borders/buscando América: Languages of Latino self-formation. In S. Khagram & P. Levitt (Eds.), *The transnational studies reader: Intersections and innovations*, 347–352. New York, NY: Routledge.

Foucault, M. (1977). *Discipline and punish: The birth of the prison*. New York, NY: Pantheon Books.

Freire, P. (1970). *Pedagogy of the oppressed* (M. B. Ramos, Trans.). New York, NY: Seabury Press.

Freire, P., & Macedo, D. (1987). *Literacy: Reading the word and the world*. Westport, CT: Bergin & Garvey.

Gallagher-Geurtsen, T. M. (2003). *Radical hybrid literacy practices of one teacher in a classroom of learners of second languages*. (Unpublished doctoral dissertation). Teachers College, Columbia University, New York, NY.

Gallagher-Geurtsen, T. M. (2005, April). *Developing preservice teachers' multicultural competencies in a social studies methods course: A focus on hierarchies and dualisms*. Paper presented at the American Educational Research Association Annual Meeting, Division K, Section 2, Montreal, Canada.

Gallagher-Guertsen, T. M. (2009). Inspiring hybridity: A call to engage with(in) global flows of the multicultural classroom. *Multicultural Perspectives*, *11*(4), 200–203.

Gay, G. (2000). *Culturally responsive teaching: Theory, research, and practice*. New York, NY: Teachers College Press.

Gee, J. P. (1996). *Social linguistics and literacies: Ideology in discourses* (2nd ed.). London, UK: Taylor & Francis.

Ghosh, R., Abdi, A. A., & Naseem, A. (2008). Identity in colonial and postcolonial contexts: Select discussions and analyses. In A. A. Abdi & W. G. Richardson (Eds.), *Decolonizing democratic education: Trans-disciplinary dialogues* (pp. 57–66). Rotterdam, The Netherlands: Sense.

Giroux, H. A. (2009). Paulo Friere and the politics of postcolonialism. In A. Kempf (Ed.), *Breaching the colonial contract: Anti-colonialism in the U.S. and Canada* (pp. 79–89). Dordrecht, The Netherlands: Springer.

Gonzales, P., Williams, T., Jocelyn, L., Roey, S., Kastberg, D., & Brenwald, S. (2009). *Highlights from TIMSS 2007: Mathematics and science achievement of U.S. fourth- and eighth-grade students in an international context*. Washington, DC: National Center for Education Statistics (NCES), Institute of Education Sciences, U.S. Department of Education.

González, M. S., Plata, O., García, E., Torres, M., & Urrieta, L. (2003). Testimonios de inmigrantes: Students educating future teachers. *Journal of Latinos and Education*, *2*(4), 233–243.

Gorski, P. C. (2006). Complicity with conservatism: The de-politicizing of multicultural and intercultural education. *Intercultural Education*, *17*(2), 163–177.

Gould, S. J. (1996). *The mismeasure of man* (Rev. ed.). New York, NY: W.W. Norton.

Greene, M. (2001). Foreword. In G. Dimitriadis & C. McCarthy, *Reading and teaching the postcolonial: From Baldwin to Basquiat and beyond* (pp. vii–viii). New York, NY: Teachers College Press.

Hall, S. (1992). The West and the rest: Discourse and power. In. S. Hall & B. Gieben (Eds.), *Formations of modernity* (pp. 275–331). Cambridge, UK: Polity Press.

Hall, S. (1995). New ethnicities. In B. Ashcroft, G. Griffiths, & H. Tiffin (Eds.), *The post-colonial studies reader* (pp. 223–227). New York, NY: Routledge.

Hargreaves, A., & Shirley, D. (2008). Beyond standardization: Powerful new principles for improvement. *Phi Delta Kappan, 90*(2), 135–143.

Hickling-Hudson, A. (2009). *Southern theory* and its dynamics for postcolonial education. In R. Sintos Coloma (Ed.), *Postcolonial challenges in education* (pp. 365–375). New York, NY: Peter Lang.

hooks, b. (1990). *Yearning: Race, gender, and cultural politics.* Boston, MA: South End Press.

Jara, R., & Vidal, H. (Eds.). (1986). *Testimonio y literatura.* Minneapolis, MN: University of Minnesota, Institute for the Study of Ideologies and Literature.

Jurkovic, G. J. (1997). *Lost childhoods: The plight of the parentified child.* New York, NY: Brunner/Mazel.

Kanu, Y. (2009). Introduction. In Y. Kanu (Ed.), *Curriculum as cultural practice: Postcolonial imaginations* (pp. 3–29). Toronto, Canada: University of Toronto Press.

Kanu, Y. (Ed.). (2009) *Curriculum as cultural practice: Postcolonial imaginations.* Toronto, Canada: University of Toronto Press.

KewalRamani, A., Gilbertson, L., Fox, M. A., & Provasnik, S. (2007). *Status and trends in the education of racial and ethnic minorities* (NCES 2007-039). Washington, DC: National Center for Education Statistics (NCES), Institute of Education Sciences, U.S. Department of Education.

Khagram, S., & Levitt, P. (2007). *The transnational studies reader: Intersections and innovations.* New York, NY: Routledge.

Kincheloe, J. L. (2009). Critical ontology and indigenous ways of being: Forging a postcolonial curriculum. In Y. Kanu (Ed.), *Curriculum as cultural practice: Postcolonial imaginations* (pp. 181–202). Toronto, Canada: University of Toronto Press.

King, J. (1991). Dysconscious racism: Ideology, identity, and the miseducation of teachers. *Journal of Negro Education, 60*(2), 133–146.

Ladson-Billings, G. (1994). *The dreamkeepers: Successful teachers of African American children.* San Francisco, CA: Jossey-Bass.

Ladson-Billings, G. (1995). Toward a theory of culturally relevant pedagogy. *American Educational Research Journal, 32*(3), 465–491.

Linton, R. (1936). *The study of man: An introduction.* New York, NY: Appleton-Century-Crofts.

Loewen, J. W. (1995). Lies my teacher told me: Everything your American history textbook got wrong. New York, NY: Touchstone.

Marshall, C., & Rossman, G. B. (2011). *Designing qualitative research* (5th ed.). Thousand Oaks, CA: Sage.

McCarthy, C., Giardina, M. D., Harewood, S. J., & Park, J-K. (2005). Contesting culture: Identity and curriculum dilemmas in the age of globalization, postcolonialism, and multiplicity. In C. McCarthy, W. Crichlow, G. Dimitriadis, & N. Dolby (Eds.). *Race, identity, and representation in education* (2nd ed., pp. 153–165). New York, NY: Routledge.

Merryfield, M. M. (2000). Why aren't teachers being prepared to teach for diversity, equity, and global interconnectedness? A study of lived experiences in the making of multicultural and global educators. *Teaching and Teacher Education, 16*(4), 429–443.

Merryfield, M. M. (2008). Decolonizing social studies and global education. In A. A. Abdi & W. G. Richardson (Eds.), *Decolonizing democratic education: Trans-disciplinary dialogues* (pp. 87–96). Rotterdam, The Netherlands: Sense.

Minh-ha, T. T. (1995). No master territories. In B. Ashcroft, G. Griffiths, & H. Tiffin (Eds.), *The post-colonial studies reader* (pp. 215–218). New York, NY: Routledge.

Mishra Tarc, A. (2009). Postcolonial studies as re-education: Learning from J. M. Coetzee's *Disgrace*. In R. Sintos Coloma (Ed.), *Postcolonial challenges in education* (pp. 195–214). New York, NY: Peter Lang.

Moll, L. C., Amanti, C., Neff, D., & Gonzalez, N. (1992). Funds of knowledge for teaching: Using a qualitative approach to connect homes and classrooms. *Theory Into Practice, 31*(2), 132–141.

Moraga, C. (1993). *The Last Generation*. Cambridge, MA: South End Press.

Nadal, K. L. (2008). A culturally competent classroom for Filipino Americans. *Multicultural Perspectives, 10*(3), 155–161.

Nettle, D., & Romaine, S. (2000). *Vanishing voices: The extinction of the world's languages.* New York, NY: Oxford University Press.

Noddings, N. (1984). *Caring: A feminine approach to ethics and moral education.* Berkeley, CA: University of California Press.

O'Hearn, C. C. (1998). Introduction. In C. C. O'Hearn (Ed.), *Half and half: Writers on growing up biracial and bicultural* (pp. vii–xiv). New York, NY: Pantheon Books.

Olson, M. R. (1995). Conceptualizing narrative authority: Implications for teacher education. *Teaching and Teacher Education, 11*(2), 119–135.

Orelus, P. W. (2007). *Education under occupation: The heavy price of living in a neocolonized and globalized world.* Rotterdam, The Netherlands: Sense.

Ovando, C. J., Collier, V. P., & Combs, M. C. (2003). *Bilingual and ESL classrooms: Teaching in multicultural contexts* (3rd ed.). Boston, MA: McGraw-Hill.

Palmer, J. D. (2007). Who is the authentic Korean American? Korean-born Korean American high school students' negotiations of ascribed and achieved identities. *Journal of Language, Identity, and Education, 6*(4), 277–298.

Park, L. S. (2008). Continuing significance of the model minority myth: The second generation. *Social Justice, 35*(2), 134–144.

Pérez, E. (1999). *The decolonial imaginary: Writing Chicanas into history.* Bloomington, IN: Indiana University Press.

Pérez Huber, L. (2009). Disrupting apartheid of knowledge: *Testimonio* as methodology in Latina/o critical race research in education. *International Journal of Qualitative Studies in Education, 22*(6), 639–654.

Pérez-Torres, R. (2000). Refiguring Aztlán. In A. Singh & P. Schmidt (Eds.), *Postcolonial theory and the United States: Race, ethnicity, and literature* (pp. 103–121). Jackson, MS: University Press of Mississippi.

Pew Research Center for the People & the Press. (2007, January 9). *How young people view their lives, futures and politics: A portrait of "generation next."* Washington, DC: Author. Retrieved from http://people-press.org/reports/pdf/300.pdf

Rodriguez, C. (2007). E pluribus unum: The democratic case for bilingualism. *Democracy Journal, 4*, 35–47.

Said, E. W. (1979). *Orientalism.* New York, NY: Vintage Books.

Said, E. W. (1994). *Culture and imperialism*. New York, NY: Vintage Books.

Salvio, P. M. (1998). On using the literacy portfolio to prepare teachers for "willful world traveling." In W. F. Pinar (Ed.), *Curriculum: Toward new identities* (pp. 41–74). New York, NY: Garland.

Singh, A., & Schmidt, P. (2000). On the borders between U.S. studies and postcolonial theory. In A. Singh & P. Schmidt (Eds.), *Postcolonial theory and the United States: Race, ethnicity, and literature* (pp. 3–69). Jackson, MS: University Press of Mississippi.

Sintos Coloma, R. (2008). Border crossing subjectivities and research: Through the prism of feminists of color. *Race Ethnicity and Education, 11*(1), 11–27.

Sintos Coloma, R., Means, A., & Kim, A. (2009). Palimpsest histories and catachrestic interventions. In R. Sintos Coloma (Ed.), *Postcolonial challenges in education* (pp. 3–22). New York, NY: Peter Lang.

Sirriyeh, A. (2010). Home journeys: Im/mobilities in young refugee and asylum-seeking women's negotiations of home. *Childhood, 17*(2), 213–227.

Sleeter, C. E., & Grant, C. A. (2007). *Making choices for multicultural education: Five approaches to race, class, and gender* (5th ed.). Hoboken, NJ: John Wiley & Sons.

Smith, L. T. (1999). *Decolonizing methodologies: Research and indigenous people*. London, UK: Zed Books.

Solórzano, D. G., & Yosso, T. J. (2002). Critical race methodology: Counter-storytelling as an analytical framework for education research. *Qualitative Inquiry, 8*(1), 23–44.

Spiro, P. J. (2008). *Beyond citizenship: American identity after globalization*. New York, NY: Oxford University Press.

Spivak, G. C. (1988). Subaltern studies: Deconstructing historiography. In R. Guha & G. C. Spivak (Eds.), *Selected subaltern studies* (pp. 3–32). New York, NY: Oxford University Press.

Spring, J. (2004). *Deculturalization and the struggle for equality: A brief history of the education of dominated cultures in the United States* (4th ed.). New York, NY: McGraw-Hill.

Spring, J. (2008). Research on globalization and education. *Review of Educational Research, 78*(2), 330–363.

Subedi, B., & Daza, S. L. (2008). The possibilities of postcolonial praxis in education. *Race Ethnicity and Education, 11*(1), 1–10.

Thomas, W. P, & Collier, V. P. (1997). *School effectiveness for language minority students*. Washington, DC: National Clearinghouse for Bilingual Education.

Thomas, W. P., & Collier, V. P. (2002). *A national study of school effectiveness for language minority students' long-term academic achievement*. Santa Cruz, CA: Center for Research on Education, Diversity and Excellence.

U.S. Census Bureau. (2009a). *United States census population estimates for 2009*. Retrieved from http://factfinder.census.gov/servlet/QTTable?_bm=y&-context=qt&-qr_name=PEP_2009_EST_DP1&-qr_name=PEP_2009_EST_DP1PR&-ds_name=PEP_2009_EST&-CONTEXT=qt&-tree_id=809&-redoLog=true&-_caller=geoselect&-geo_id=01000US&-search_results=ALL&-format=&-_lang=en

U.S. Census Bureau. (2009b). *U.S. Population Projections for 2009*. Retrieved from http://www.census.gov/population/www/projections/2009comparisonfiles.html

U.S. Citizenship and Immigration Services (USCIS). (1952). *Immigration and nationality act. Act 312. Requirements as to understanding the English language, history, principles and form of government of the United States.* Retrieved from http://www.uscis.gov/portal/site/uscis/menuitem.f6da51a2342135be7e9d7a10e0dc91a0/?vgnextoid=fa7e539dc4bed010 VgnVCM 1000000ecd190aRCRD&vgnextchannel=fa7e539dc 4bed010VgnVCM1000000 ecd190aRCRD&CH=act

U.S. Department of Education. (2001). *No child left behind act* (Public Law (PL) 107–110). Retrieved from http://www2.ed.gov/policy/elsec/leg/esea02/index.html

Valenzuela, A. (1999). *Subtractive schooling: U.S.-Mexican youth and the politics of caring.* Albany, NY: State University of New York Press.

Villenas, S. A. (2009). Diaspora and the anthropology of Latino education: Challenges, affinities, and intersections. In R. Sintos Coloma (Ed.), *Postcolonial challenges in education* (pp. 55–63). New York, NY: Peter Lang.

Vo-Jutabha, E. D., Dinh, K. T., McHale, J. P., & Valsiner, J. (2009). A qualitative analysis of Vietnamese adolescent identity exploration within and outside an ethnic enclave. *Journal of Youth and Adolescence, 38*(5), 672–690.

Warikoo, N. K. (2007). Racial authenticity among second generation youth in multiethnic New York and London. *Poetics, 35*(6), 388–408.

White, D. G. (1999). *Too heavy a load: Black women in defense of themselves, 1894–1994.* New York, NY: W. W. Norton.

Willinsky, J. (1998). *Learning to divide the world: Education at empire's end.* Minneapolis, MN: University of Minnesota Press.

Willinsky, J. (2008). Preface. In A. A. Abdi & G. Richardson (Eds.), *Decolonizing democratic education: Trans-disciplinary dialogues* (pp. vii–x). Rotterdam, The Netherlands: Sense.

Willinsky, J. (2009). High school postcolonial: As the students ran ahead with the theory. In Y. Kanu (Ed.), *Curriculum as cultural practice: Postcolonial imaginations* (pp. 95–115). Toronto, Canada: University of Toronto Press.

Wing, J. Y. (2007). Beyond Black and White: The model minority myth and the invisibility of Asian American students. *The Urban Review, 39*(4), 455–487.

Young, R. J. C. (1995). *Colonial desire: Hybridity in theory, culture and race.* New York, NY: Routledge.

Young, R. J. C. (2001). *Postcolonialism: An historical introduction.* Oxford, UK: Blackwell.

Young, R. J. C. (2003). *Postcolonialism: A very short introduction.* New York, NY: Oxford University Press.

Index

About the Author

Tricia Gallagher-Geurtsen is a former elementary bilingual teacher who received her doctoral degree in Curriculum and Teaching and Multilingual Education from Columbia University's Teachers College. Tricia was a bilingual public elementary school teacher and a migrant education teacher in California. She is the recipient of the 2003 American Educational Research Association's Outstanding Dissertation Award for Curriculum Studies, and the 2003–2004 Mortar Board National Senior Honor Society Top Professor Award at Utah State University. Tricia writes, presents, and coaches teachers nationally about ways to meet the needs of multilingual and multicultural learners in American schools.

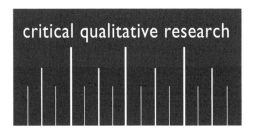

Shirley R. Steinberg & Gaile S. Cannella, *General Editors*

The Critical Qualitative Research series examines societal structures that oppress and exclude so that transformative actions can be generated. This transformed research is activist in orientation. Because the perspective accepts the notion that nothing is apolitical, research projects themselves are critically examined for power orientations, even as they are used to address curricular, educational, or societal issues.

This methodological work challenges modernist orientations and universalist impositions, asking critical questions like: Who/what is heard? Who/what is silenced? Who is privileged? Who is disqualified? How are forms of inclusion and exclusion being created? How are power relations constructed and managed? How do different forms of privilege and oppression intersect to affect educational, societal, and life possibilities for various individuals and groups?

We are particularly interested in manuscripts that offer critical examinations of curriculum, policy, public communities, and the ways in which language, discourse practices, and power relations prevent more just transformations.

For additional information about this series or for the submission of manuscripts, please contact:
Shirley R. Steinberg and Gaile S. Cannella
msgramsci@aol.com | Gaile.Cannella@unt.edu

To order other books in this series, please contact our Customer Service Department:
(800) 770-LANG (within the U.S.)
(212) 647-7706 (outside the U.S.)
(212) 647-7707 FAX

Or browse online by series:
www.peterlang.com